# National Moulding Book

## Containing The Latest Styles Of
# Mouldings

Interior House Finish, Stair And Porch Railings,
As Well As Full Size Cuts Of Frames In Use In Different Localities.

Numbers Commencing At 5000.

Cuts Giving Exact Size Of Each Moulding, With Figures
Representing The Ripping Width Of Lumber.

Adopted April 15, 1896, By
The Wholesale Sash, Door & Blind Manufacturers' Association And By
The Eastern Sash, Door & Blind Manufacturers' Association

Chicago:
Published By Rand, McNally & Company,
Printers, Surveyors, And Electrotypers.
## 1899

**Toolemera Press**
**History Preserved**
toolemerapress.com

*National Moulding Book: Containing The Latest Styles Of Mouldings; Interior House Finish, Stair And Porch Railings, As Well As Full Size Cuts Of Frames In Use In Different Localities.*

*Adopted April 15, 1896, By The Wholesale Sash, Door & Blind Manufacturers' Association And By The Eastern Sash, Door & Blind Manufacturers' Association.*

*(originally) Published By Rand, McNally & Company 1899*

No part of this book may be reproduced, stored in an electronic retrieval system, or transmitted in any form or by an means, electronic, mechanical, photocopy, photographic or otherwise without the written permission of the publisher.

Excerpts of one page or less for the purposes of review and comment are permissible.

Copyright © 2020 Gary Roberts DBA Toolemera Press

International Standard Book Number
ISBN: 978-1-0878-6443-3
(Trade Paper)

Published by
Gary Roberts DBA, The Toolemera Press
Wilmington, North Carolina USA 28401
www.toolemerapress.com

The Late Victorian era ended just as the industry was organizing the Wholesale Sash, Door And Blind Manufacturers' Association of the Northwest (specifically, manufacturers of white pine lumber from Minnesota, Wisconsin, and Michigan) around 1887. A year or two later, the first standard molding catalog, called the Universal Molding Catalog, appeared.

## Transitional Period (1890-1920)

The Transitional period witnessed the greatest amount of change in moldings. Commercial and residential design shifted from Victorian to Arts and Crafts and then finally to the Period Revival style of the 1920s. Molding styles marched in step, with the Universal Molding Catalogs of 1891, 1901, 1914, and 1920 reflected these trends.

The formation of the Wholesale Sash, Door and Blind Manufacturers' Association helped usher in this new era. This early industry association standardized millwork and developed grading rules for quality. These measures helped to create confidence in builders and architects who sought consistent quality and craftsmanship from manufacturers.

*Historic Millwork: A Guide To Restoring And Re-Creating Doors, Windows, And Moldings Of The Late Nineteenth Through Mid-Twentieth Centuries. By Brent Hull. 2003; pg 92, John Wiley, Publisher. ISBN: 0471416223*

www.toolemerapress.com

Gary Roberts, publisher of the Toolemera Press imprint, preserves in print classic books on early crafts, trades and industries. All titles are produced from the originals in his personal collection.

# NATIONAL MOULDING BOOK

CONTAINING THE LATEST STYLES OF

# MOULDINGS

Interior House Finish, Stair and Porch Railings,

AS WELL AS FULL SIZE CUTS OF FRAMES IN USE
IN DIFFERENT LOCALITIES,

## NUMBERS COMMENCING AT 5000,

CUTS GIVING EXACT SIZE OF EACH MOULDING, WITH FIGURES REPRESENTING
THE RIPPING WIDTH OF LUMBER.

---

ADOPTED APRIL 15, 1896, BY

The Wholesale Sash, Door & Blind Manufacturers' Association of the Northwest
AND BY
The Eastern Sash, Door & Blind Manufacturers' Association.

---

CHICAGO:
PUBLISHED BY RAND, McNALLY & COMPANY,
PRINTERS, ENGRAVERS, AND ELECTROTYPERS.
1899.

Copyright, 1896, by Rand, McNally & Co.

# INDEX.

| | PAGE. |
|---|---|
| Aprons, | 28 |
| Astragals, | 17, 18, 19 |
| Back Band, | 30 |
| Balusters, | 135 |
| Band, | 21, 23, 24 |
| Base, | 21, 22, 25, 26, 73, 74, 75, 77 |
| Battens, | 19 |
| Bay Window Frames, | 84, 85 |
| Bead Stops, | 15, 16, 17 |
| Bed, | 11, 12, 37 |
| Belt Course, | 77, 78 |
| Box Window Frames, | 86, 87, 88, 89, 97, 98, 99, 100, 101, 102, 116, 117 |
| Casings, | 41 to 67 |
| Ceiling, | 31 |
| Chair Rail, | 36 |
| Corner Beads, | 39 |
| Cornices, | 38, 39 |
| Coves, | 13 |
| Crown, | 1 to 9 |
| Door Frame, | 111 |
| Door Jambs, | 76, 110 |
| Drip Cap, | 35, 36 |
| Eastlake Stairs, | 136 |
| Electrical, | 121, 122, 123, 124 |
| Extension Window Jambs, | 75, 76 |
| Filling Strips, | 34 |
| Frame Moulding, | 78 |
| Frames, | 115, 118, 119, 120 |
| Half Rounds, | 14 |
| Hearth Borders, | 40 |
| Hook Strips, | 39, 40 |
| Hot Bed Sash, | 125, 126 |
| Hot House Fixtures, | 127, 128 |
| Imposts, | 37, 110, 111 |
| Inside Finish, | 67, 68, 69, 70, 71, 72 |
| Lattice, | 30 |
| Nosings, | 8, 10, 11, 20 |
| O G Stops, | 15, 16 |
| Outside Door Frames, | 90, 91 |
| Panel, | 22, 23 |
| Partition Frame, | 34 |
| Pew Back Rail, | 27 |

## INDEX—Continued.

|  | PAGE. |
|---|---|
| P G Stops, | 16, 17 |
| Pittsburg Frame, | 113, 114 |
| Plank Window Frames, | 82, 83, 106, 107, 109 |
| Porch Rails, | 134, 135 |
| Prices of Mouldings, | 137, 138, 139 |
| Quarter Rounds, | 14 |
| Rabbeted Panel, | 25, 26 |
| Rebated Door Jamb, | 40 |
| Rebated Shelf Cleats, | 39 |
| Return Beads, | 12, 13 |
| Reveal Window Frames, | 80, 81 |
| Room, | 81 |
| Single Sill Frame, | 79 |
| Skeleton Check Frame, | 95, 96, 103 |
| Sprung Cove, | 10 |
| Stair Rails, | 129 to 134 |
| Sub-Sill Frame, | 79 |
| Sunk Panel, | 30 |
| Threshold, | 27, 28 |
| Transom Bars, | 36, 112 |
| Wainscoting Caps, | 27, 28, 29 |
| Water Table, | 35 |
| Window Frames, | 92, 93, 94, 104, 105, 108 |
| Window Stools, | 31, 32, 33, 34 |

# CROWN MOULDINGS.

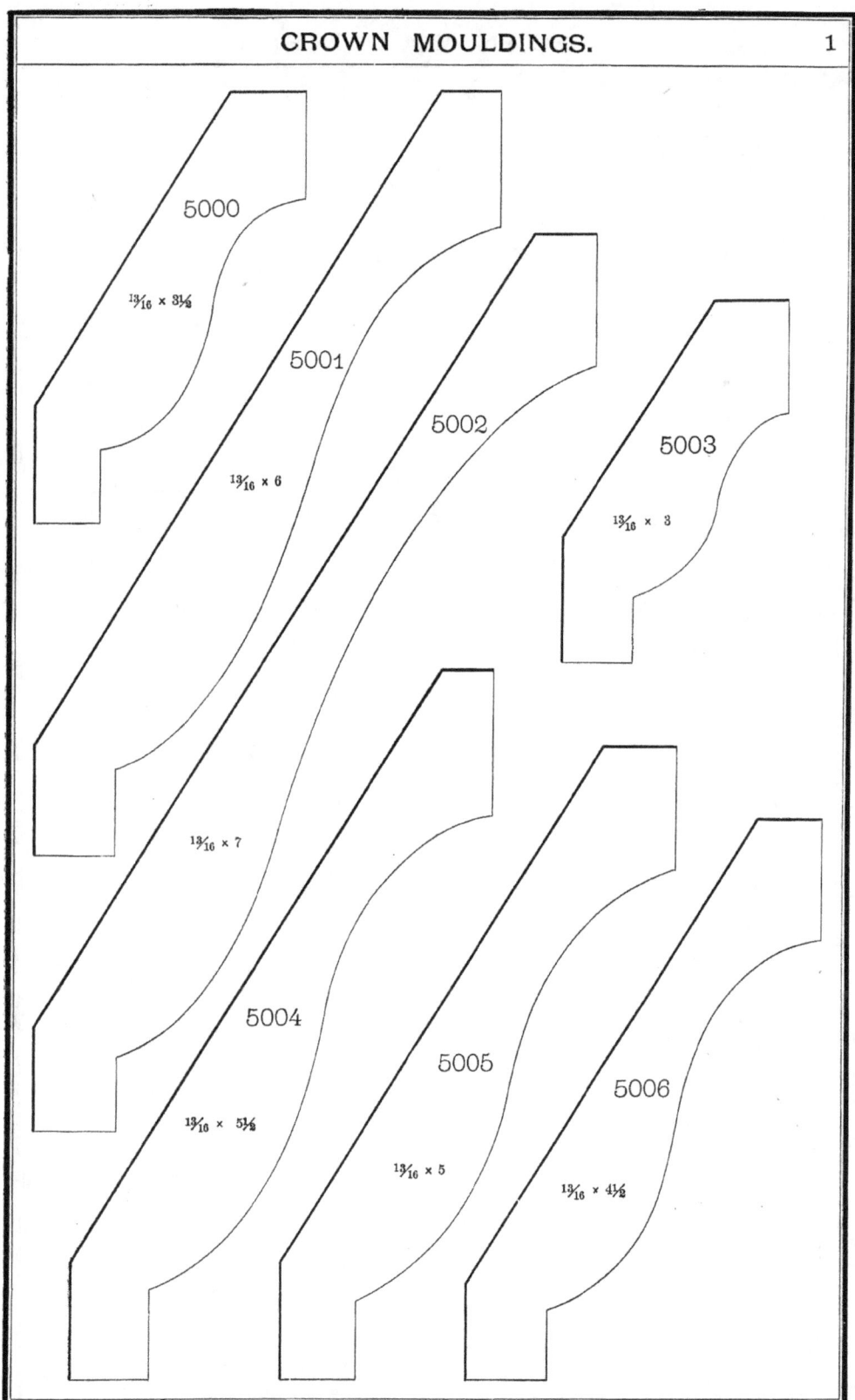

Mouldings made exact size of cuts. Figures represent the ripping width of Lumber.

# CROWN MOULDINGS.

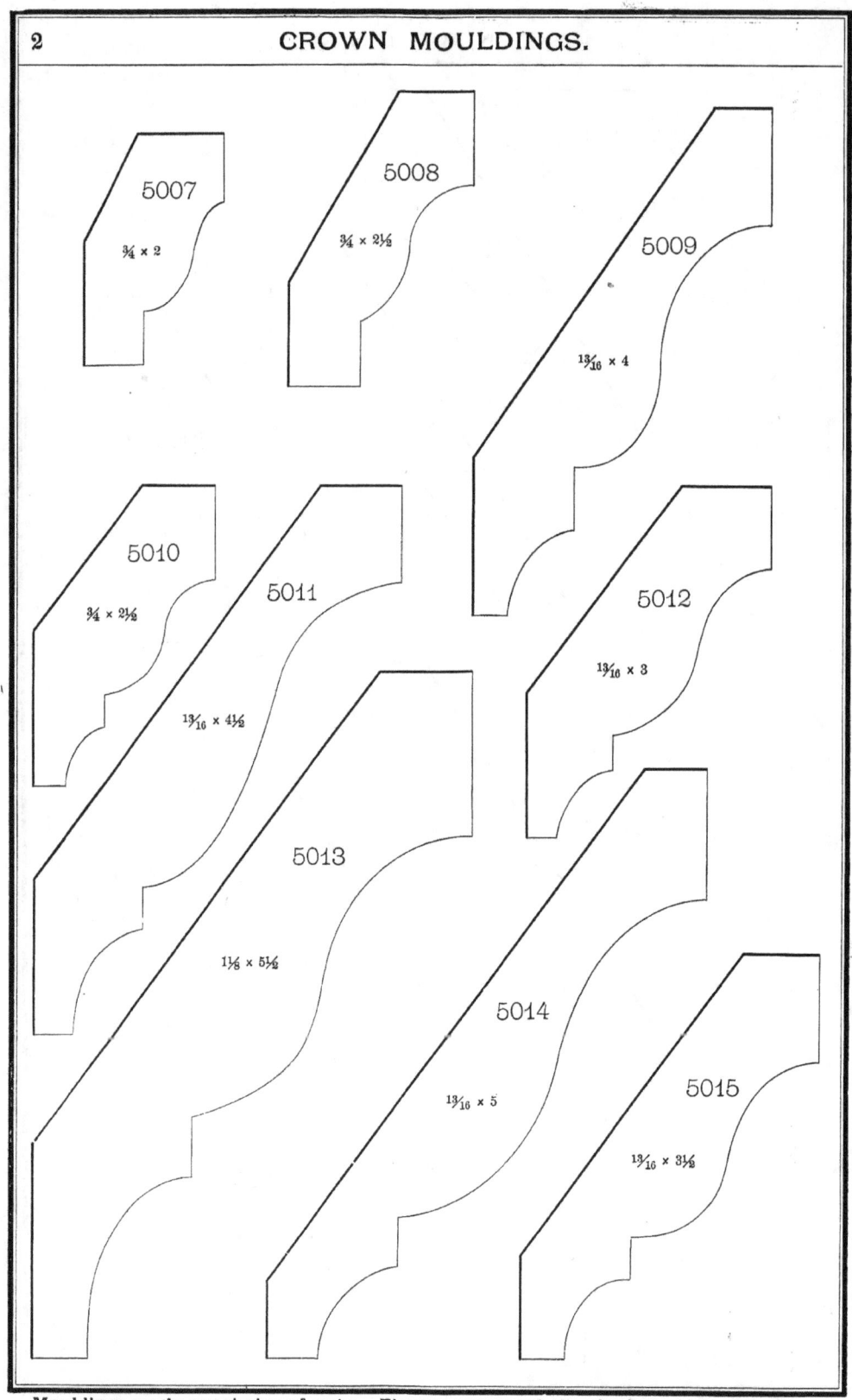

Mouldings made exact size of cuts. Figures represent the ripping width of Lumber.

# CROWN MOULDINGS.

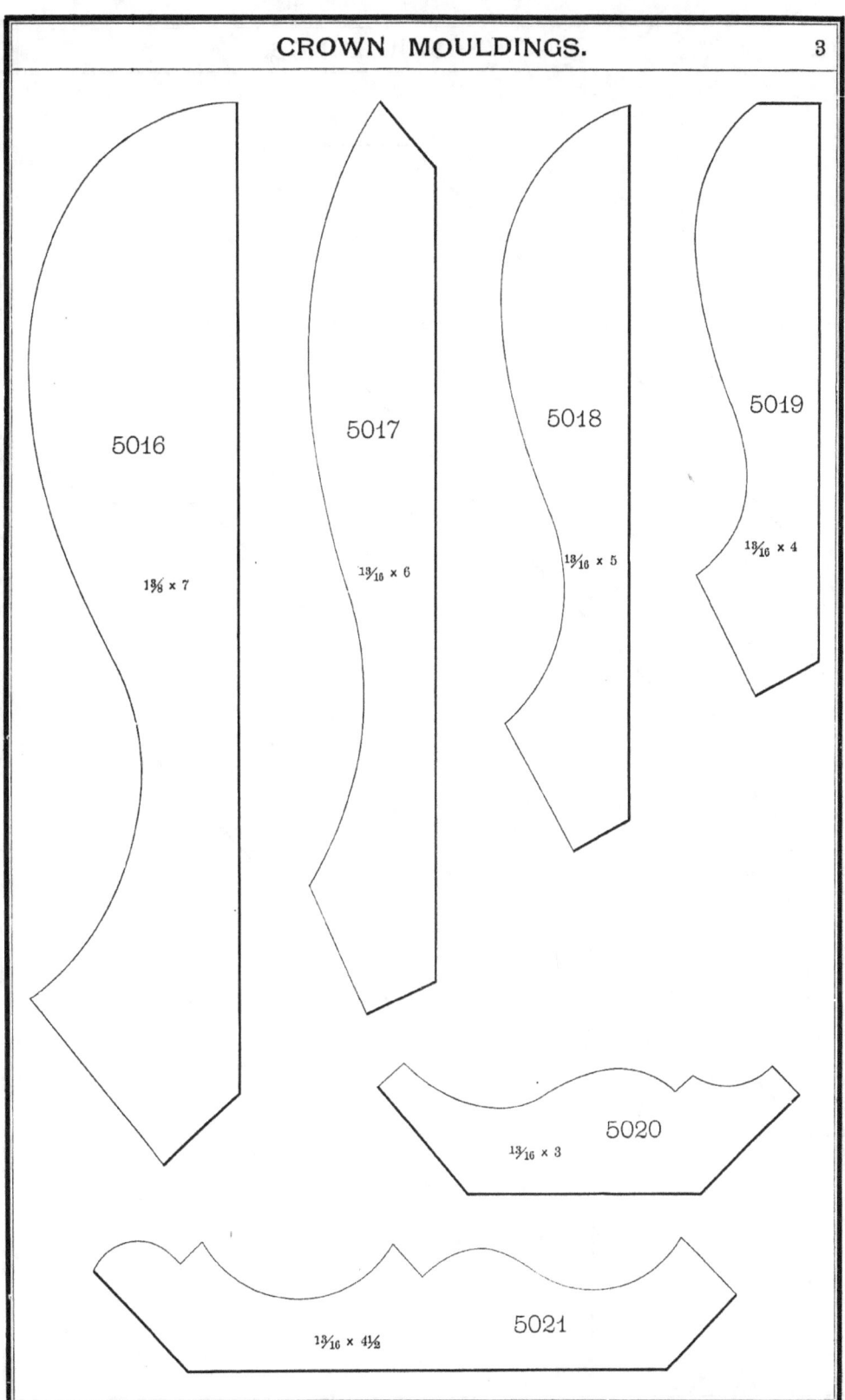

Mouldings made exact size of cuts. Figures represent the ripping width of Lumber.

# CROWN MOULDINGS.

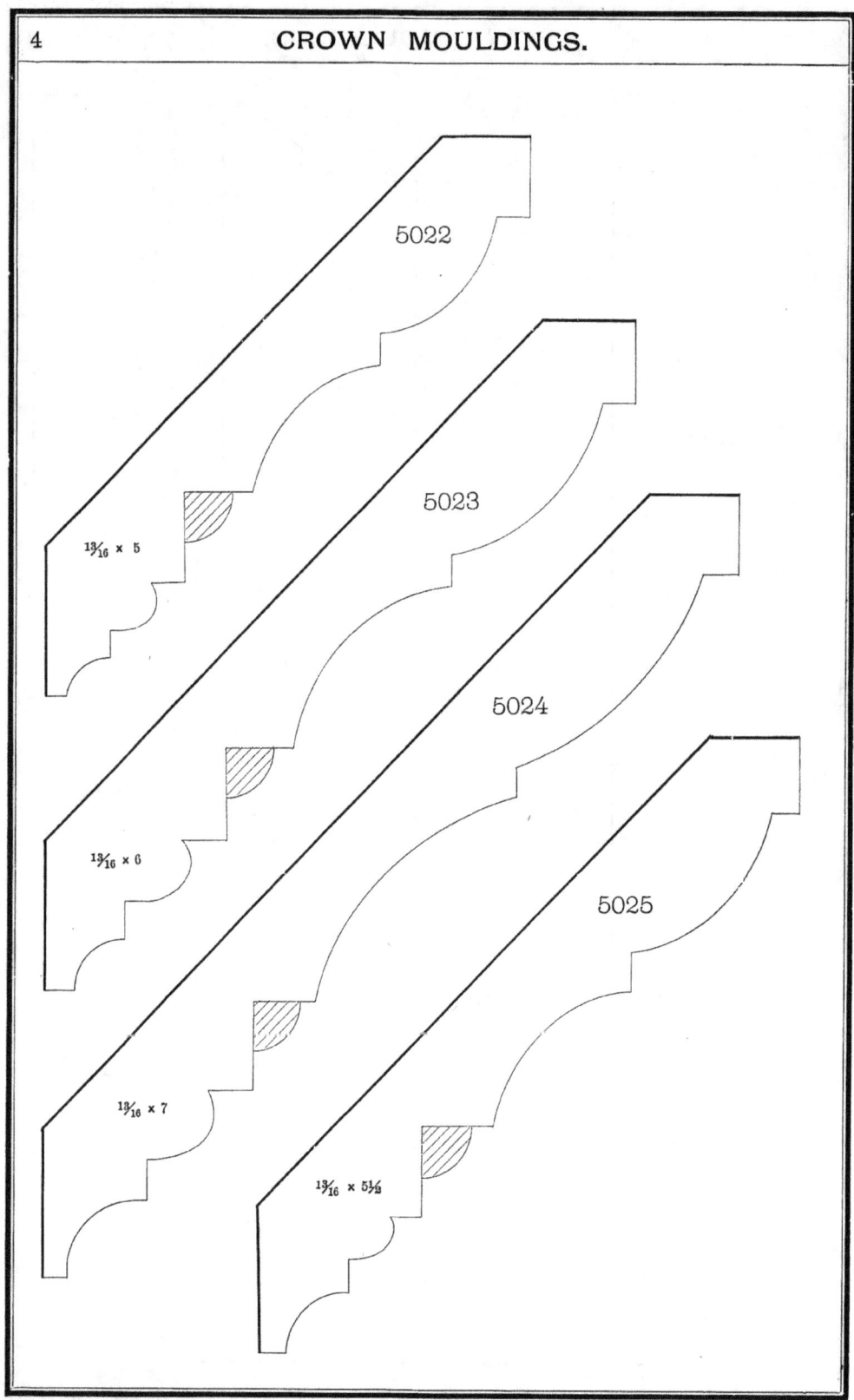

Mouldings made exact size of cuts. Figures represent the ripping width of Lumber.
When ordering the above Crown Moulding Patterns, state if dentil member is wanted.

# CROWN MOULDINGS.

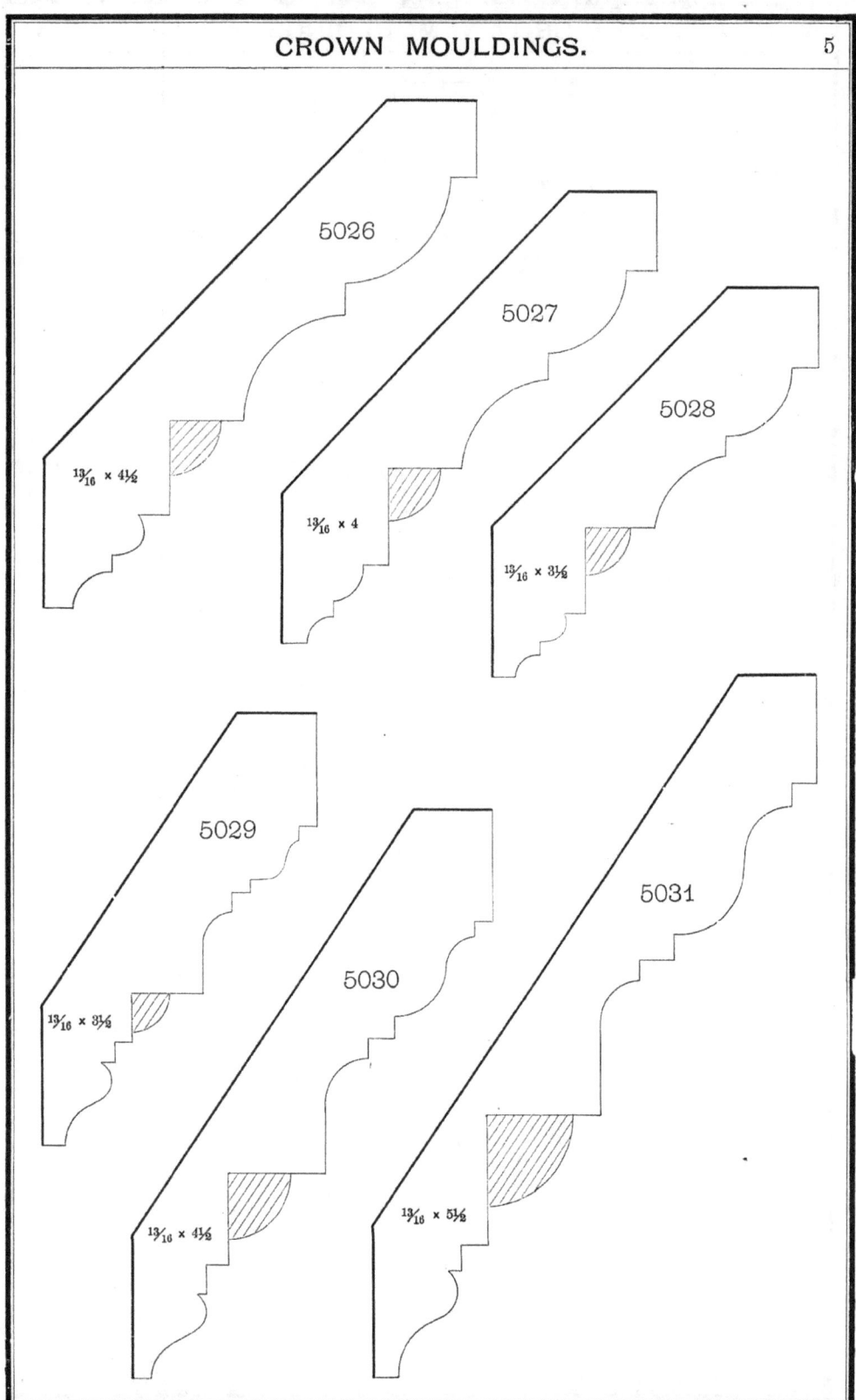

Mouldings made exact size of cuts. Figures represent the ripping width of Lumber.
When ordering the above Crown Moulding Patterns, state if dentil member is wanted.

# CROWN MOULDINGS.

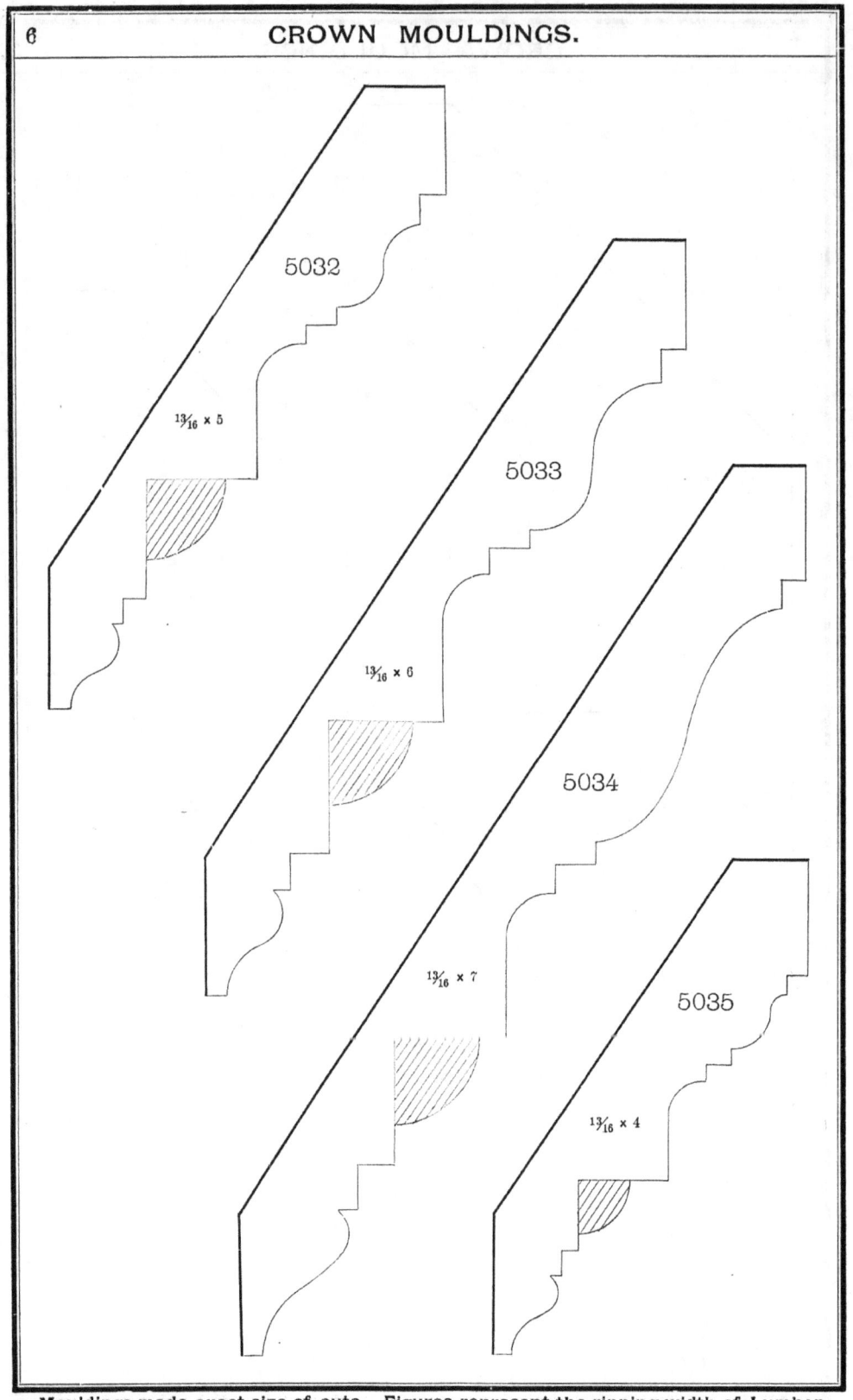

Mouldings made exact size of cuts. Figures represent the ripping width of Lumber. When ordering the above Crown Moulding Patterns, state if dentil member is wanted.

# CROWN MOULDINGS.

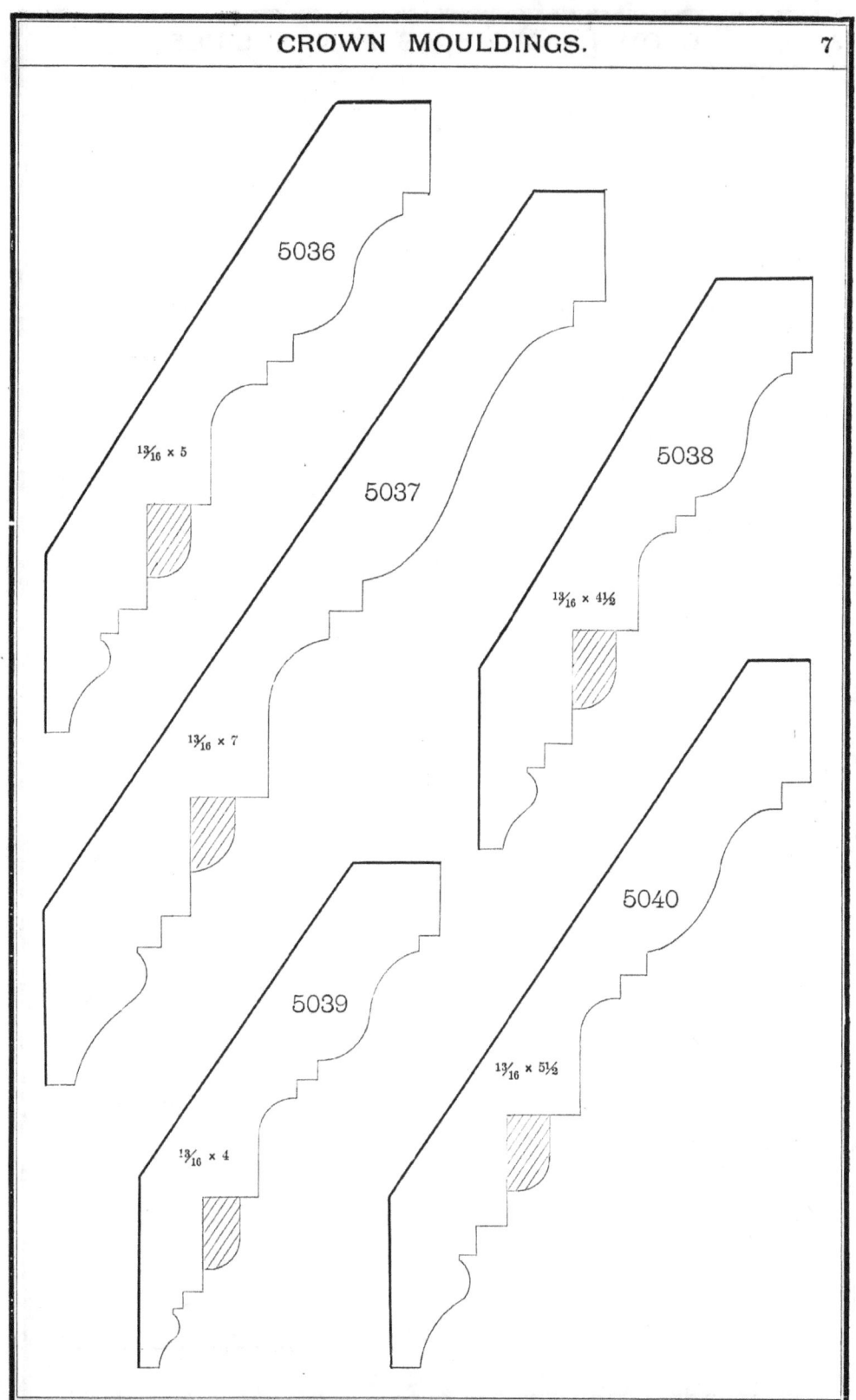

Mouldings made exact size of cuts. Figures represent the ripping width of Lumber.
When ordering the above Crown Moulding Patterns, state if dentil member is wanted.

# CROWN MOULDINGS AND NOSINGS.

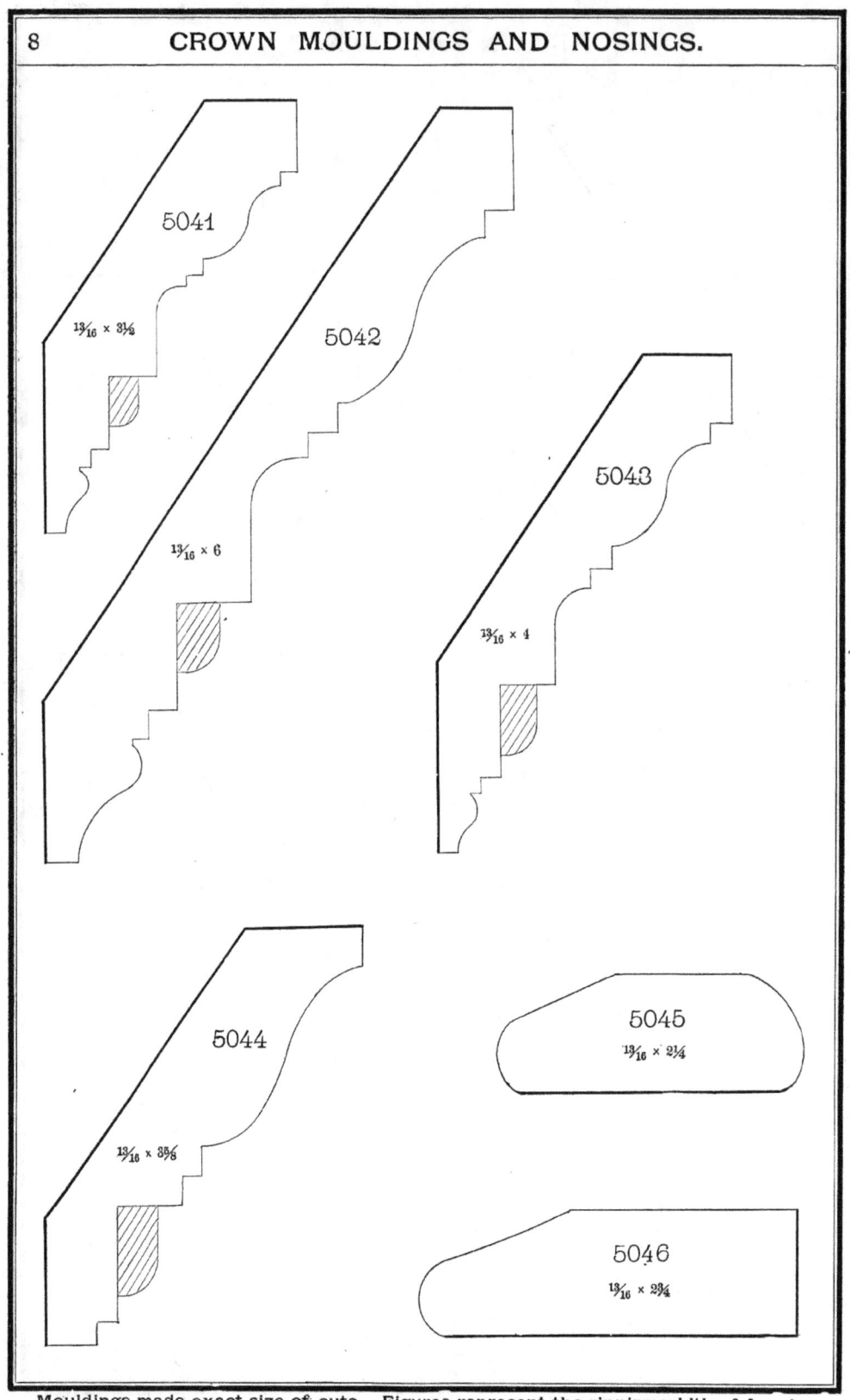

Mouldings made exact size of cuts. Figures represent the ripping width of Lumber. When ordering the above Crown Moulding Patterns, state if dentil member is wanted.

# CROWN MOULDINGS.

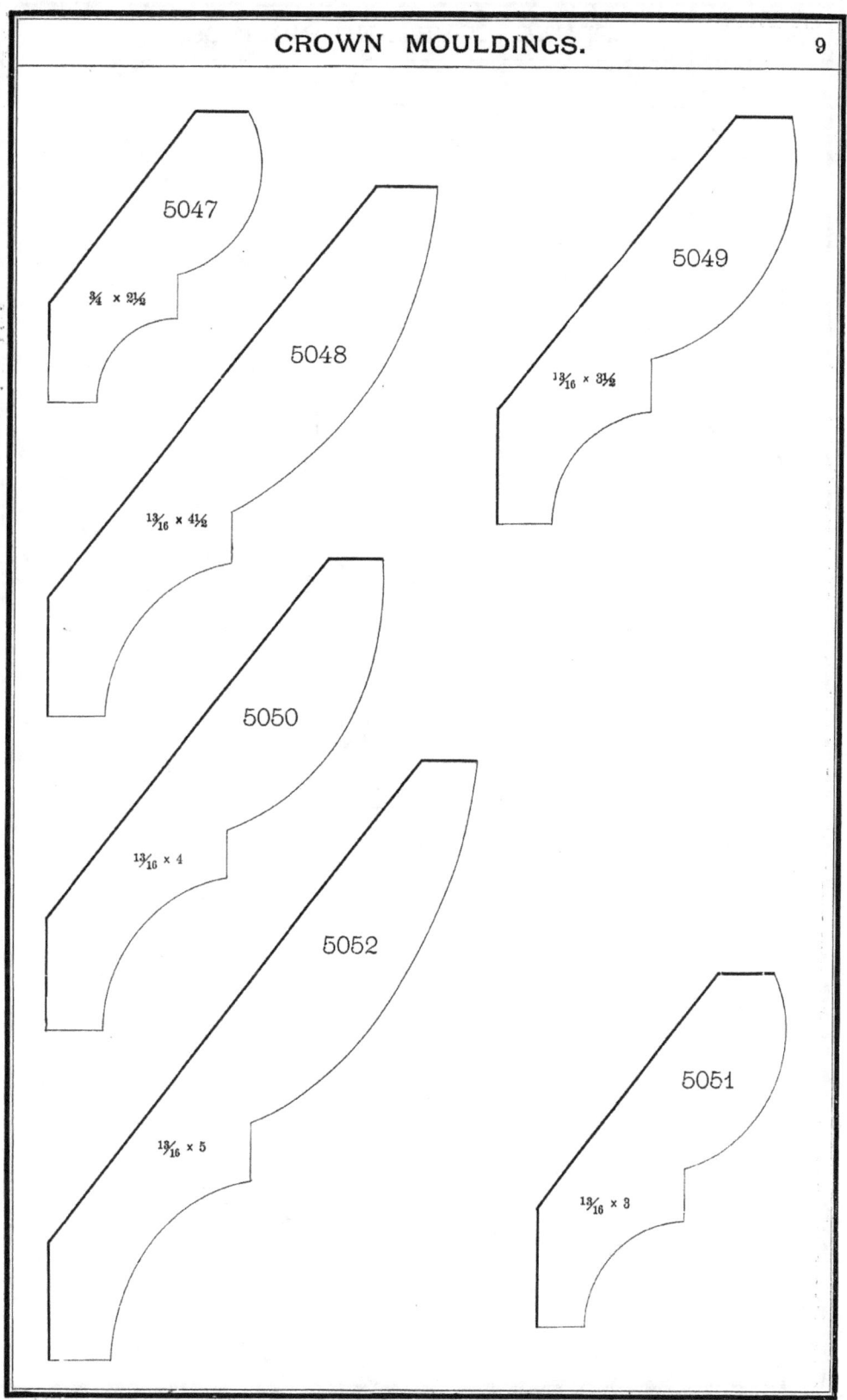

Mouldings made exact size of cuts. Figures represent the ripping width of Lumber.

## SPRUNG COVE AND NOSINGS.

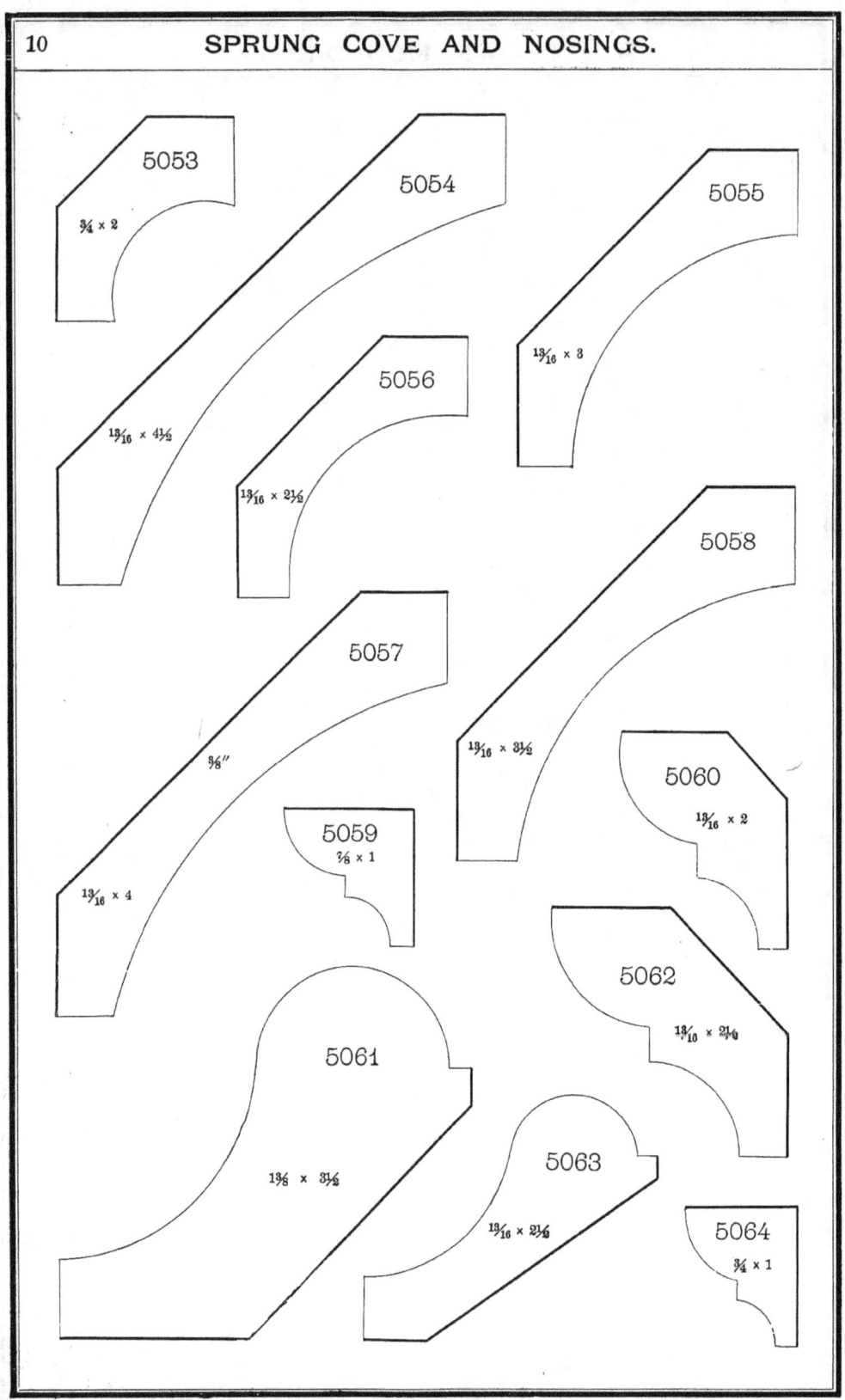

# NOSINGS AND BED MOULDINGS.

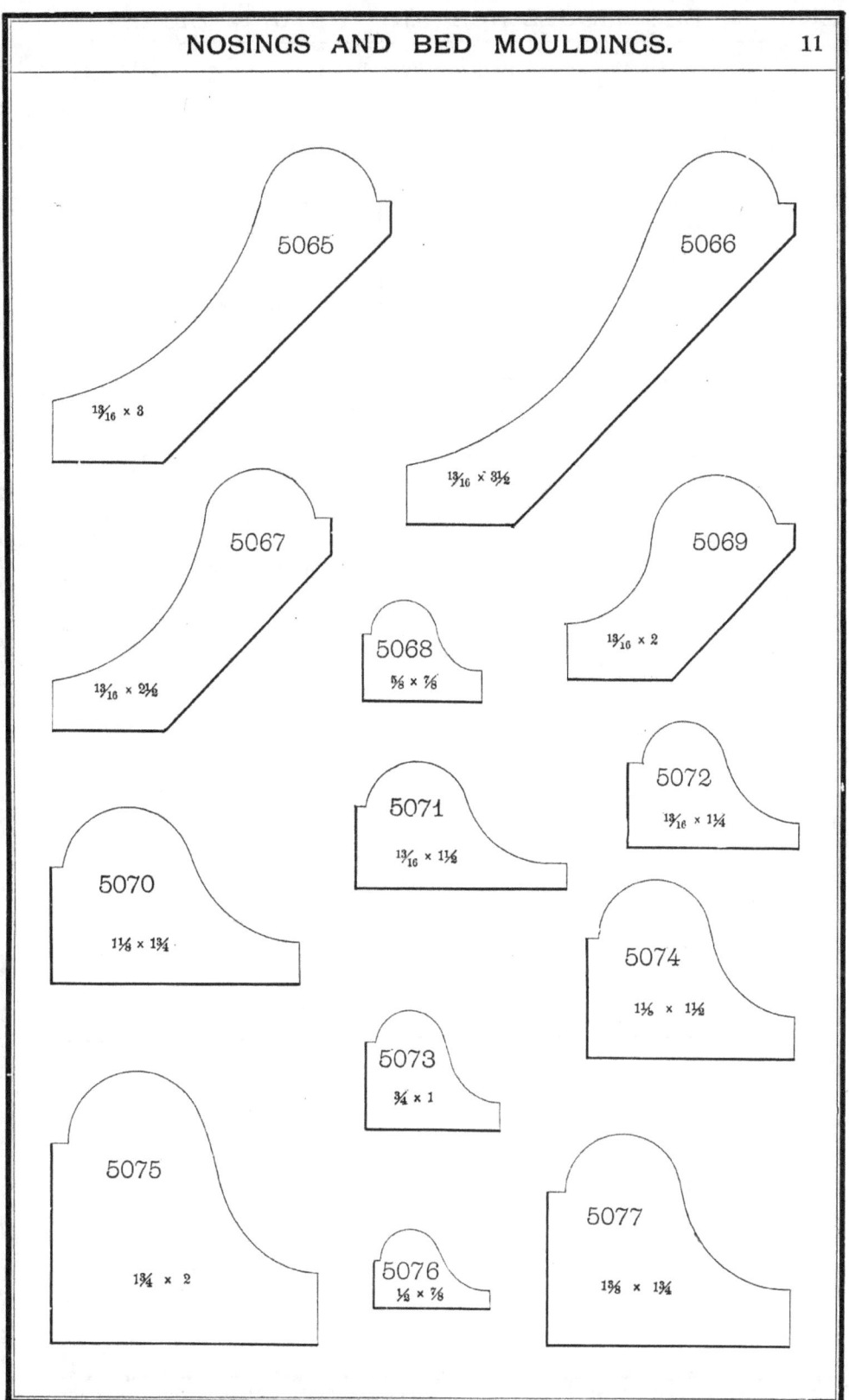

Mouldings made exact size of cuts. Figures represent the ripping width of Lumber.

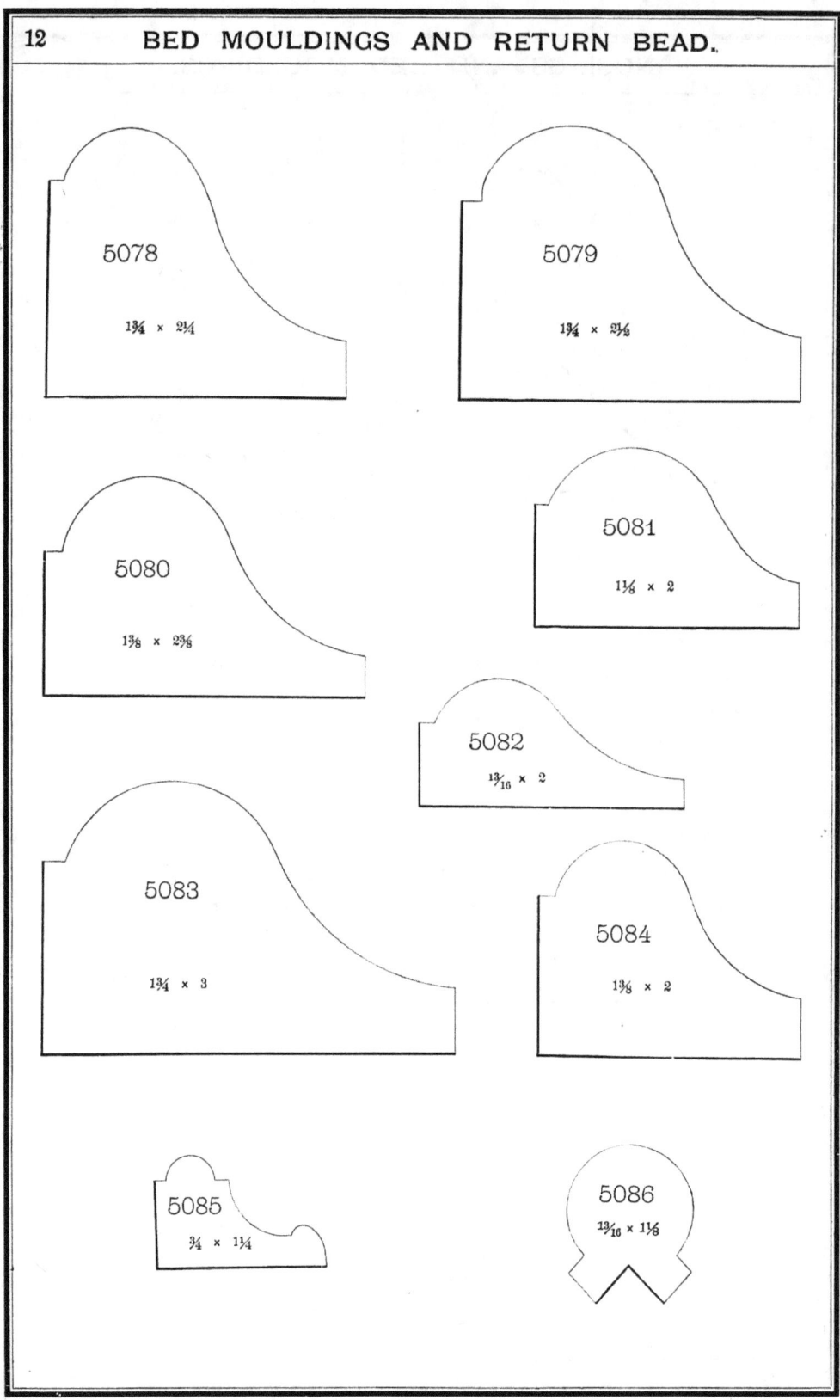

# RETURN BEADS AND COVES.

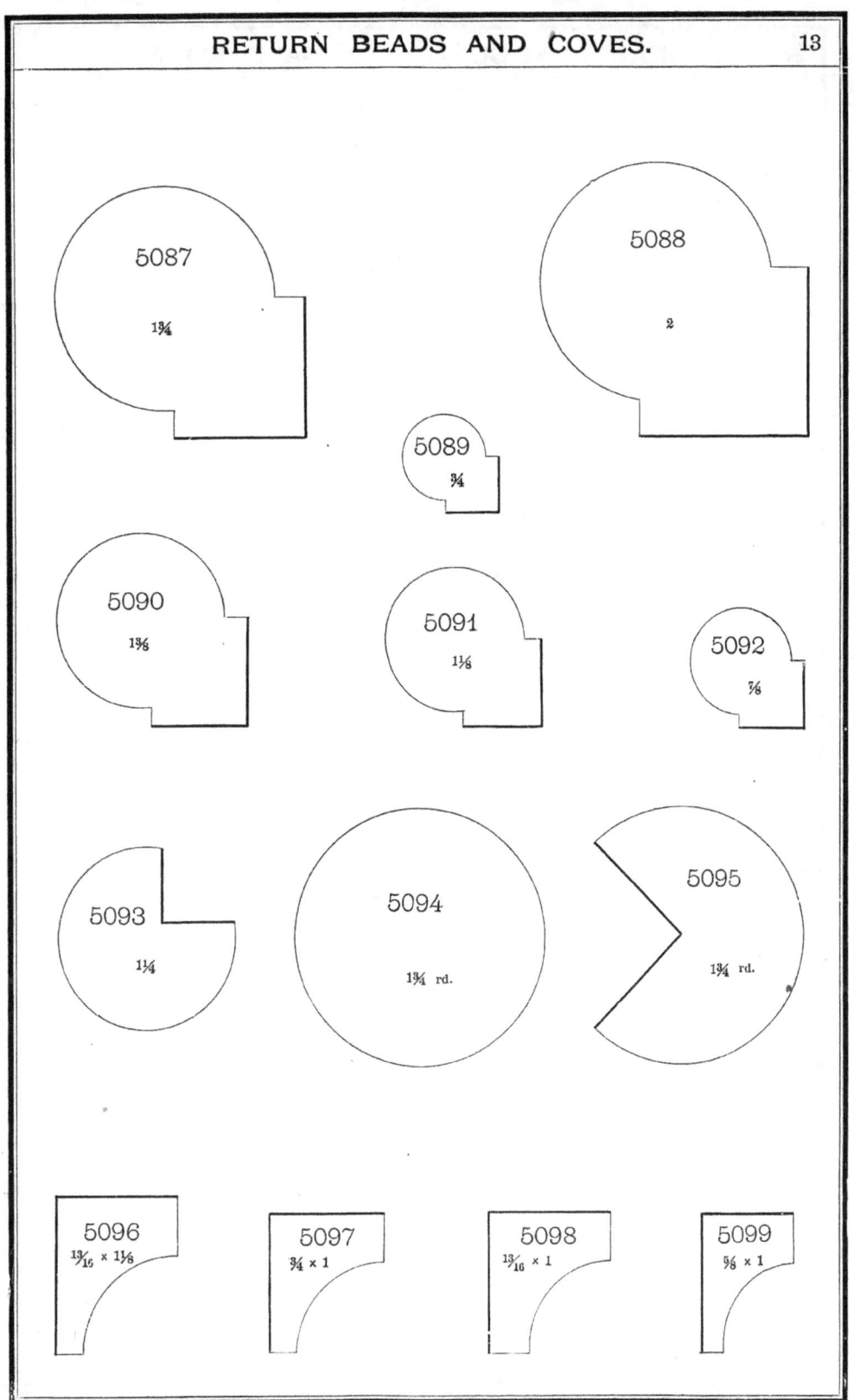

Mouldings made exact size of cuts. Figures represent the ripping width of Lumber.

# QUARTER ROUND AND HALF ROUND.

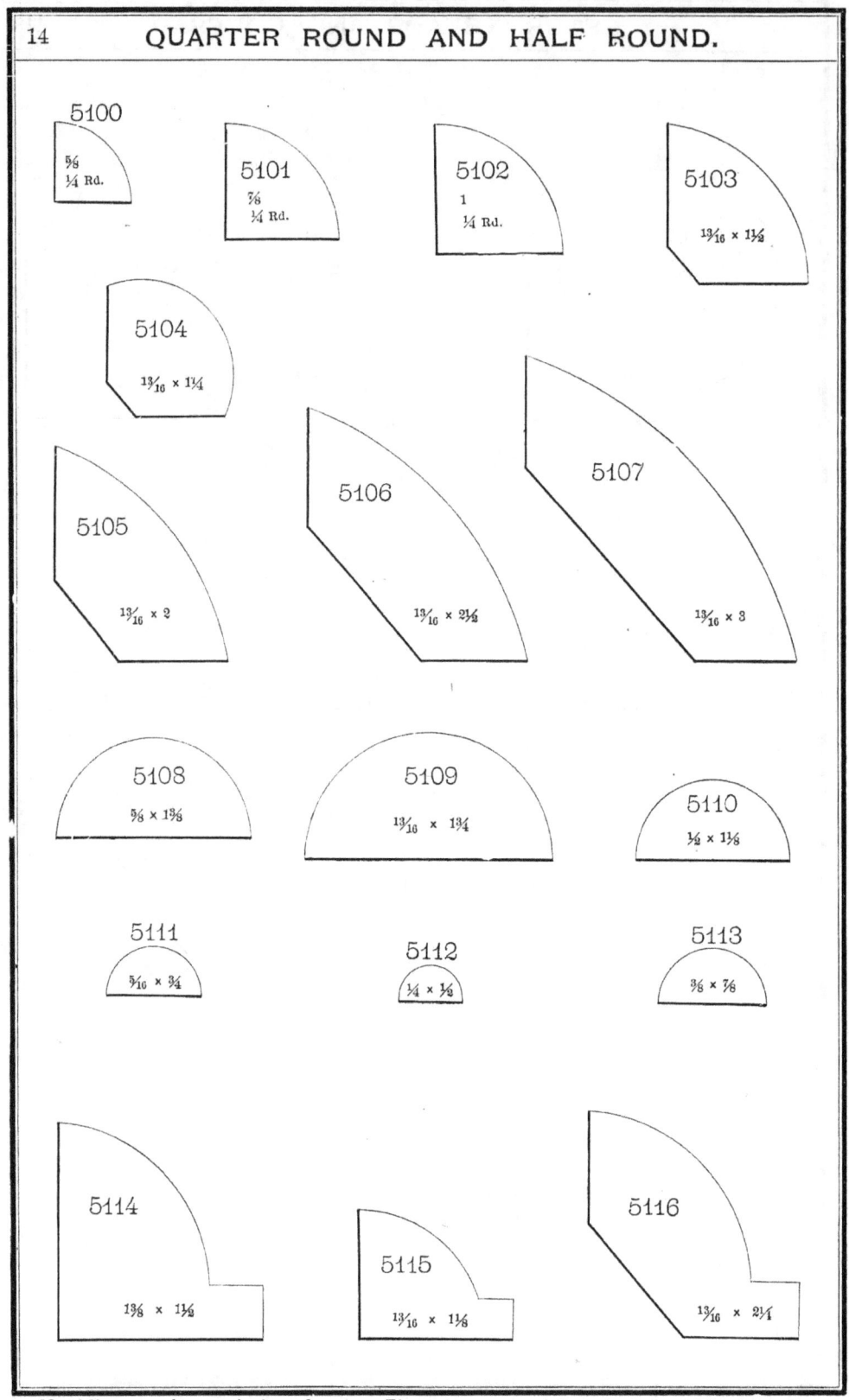

Mouldings made exact size of cuts.   Figures represent the ripping width of Lumber.

# O G AND BEAD STOPS. 15

| 5117 $7/16 \times 1\frac{1}{4}$ | 5126 $7/16 \times 1\frac{1}{4}$ |
| --- | --- |
| 5118 $7/16 \times 1\frac{1}{2}$ | 5127 $7/16 \times 1\frac{1}{2}$ |
| 5119 $7/16 \times 1\frac{3}{4}$ | 5128 $7/16 \times 1\frac{3}{4}$ |
| 5120 $7/16 \times 2$ | 5129 $7/16 \times 2$ |
| 5121 $7/16 \times 2\frac{1}{4}$ | 5130 $7/16 \times 2\frac{1}{4}$ |
| 5122 $7/16 \times 2\frac{1}{2}$ | 5131 $7/16 \times 2\frac{1}{2}$ |
| 5123 $7/16 \times 1\frac{1}{4}$ | 5132 $7/16 \times 1\frac{1}{2}$ |
| 5124 $7/16 \times 1\frac{3}{4}$ | 5133 $7/16 \times 2$ |
| 5125 $7/16 \times 2\frac{1}{4}$ | 5134 $7/16 \times 2\frac{1}{2}$ |

Mouldings made exact size of cuts. Figures represent the ripping width of Lumber.

# O. G., P. G. AND BEAD STOPS.

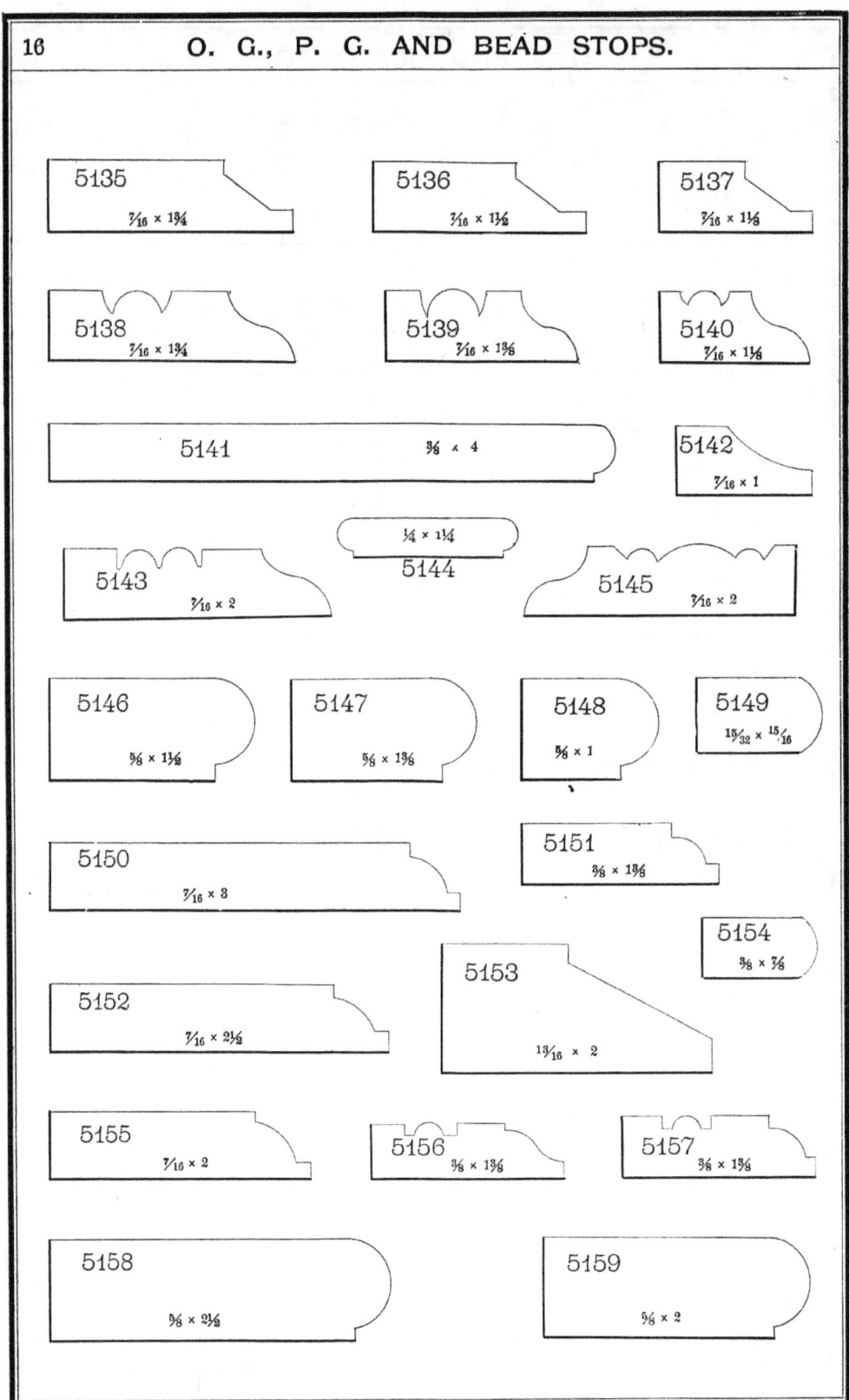

Mouldings made exact size of cuts. Figures represent the ripping width of Lumber.

# P. G. AND BEAD STOPS.    ASTRAGALS.

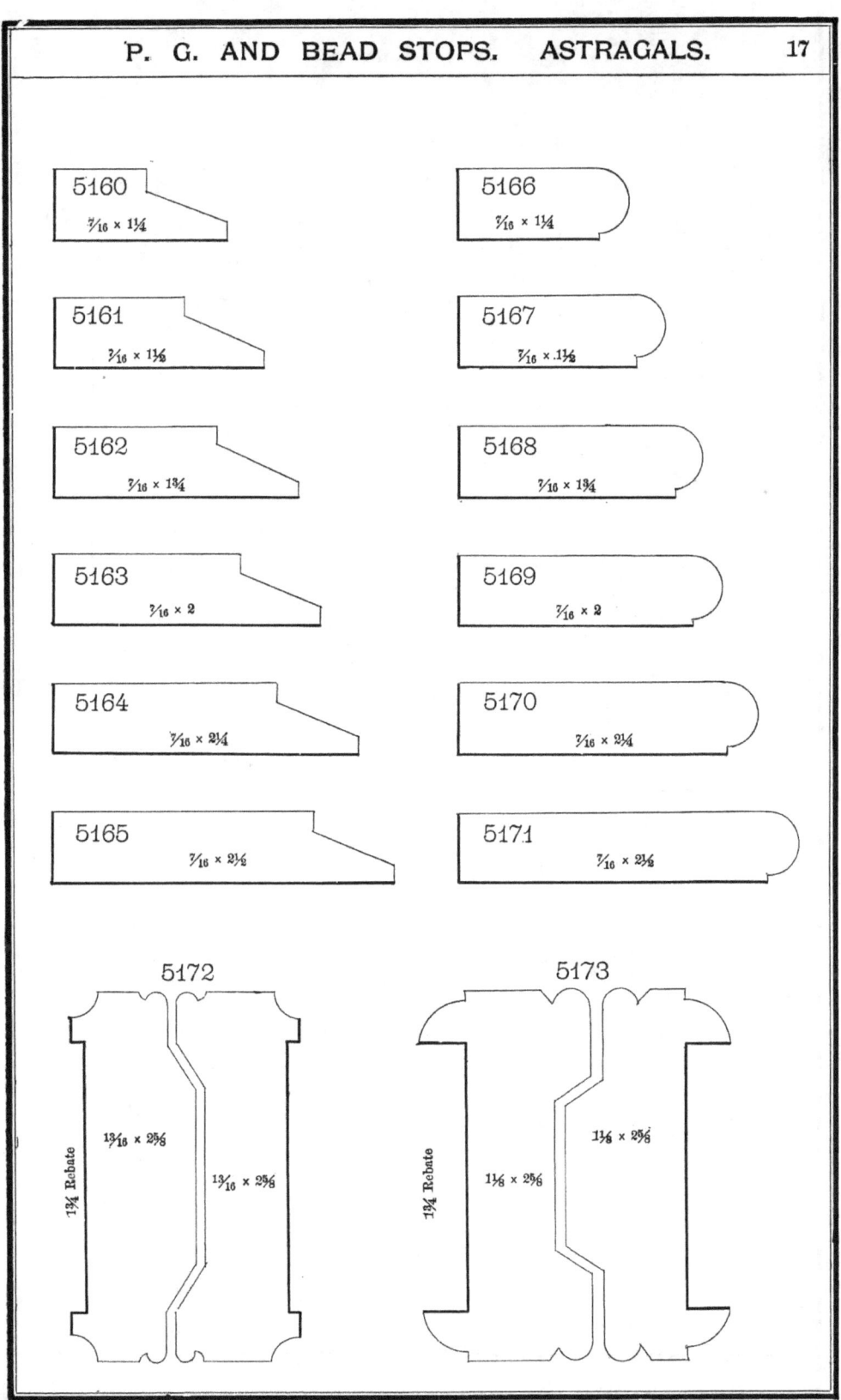

Mouldings made exact size of cuts.  Figures represent the ripping width of Lumber.

## ASTRAGALS.

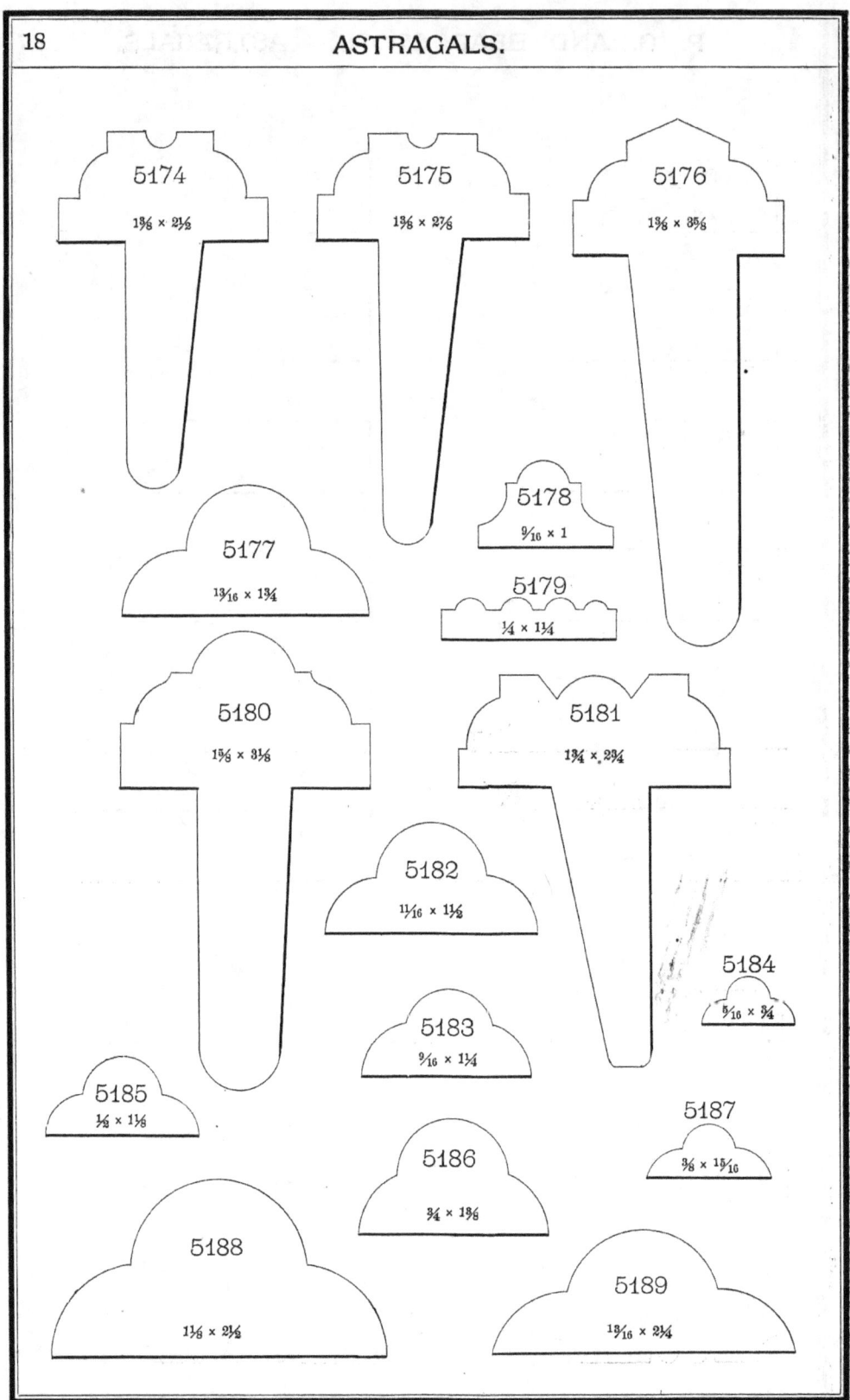

Mouldings made exact size of cuts. Figures represent the ripping width of Lumber.

## ASTRAGALS AND BATTENS.

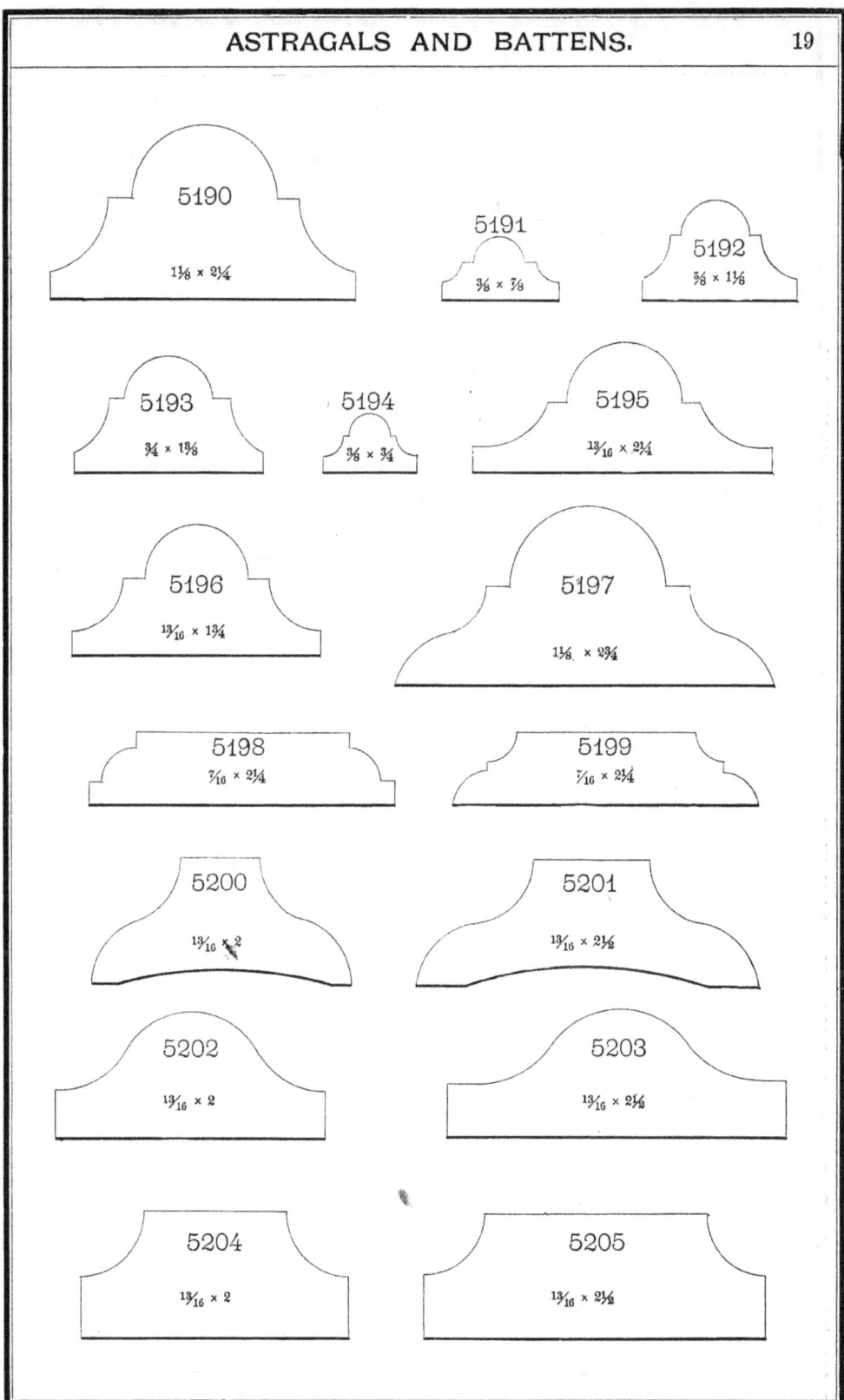

Mouldings made exact size of cuts. Figures represent the ripping width of Lumber.

## NOSINGS.

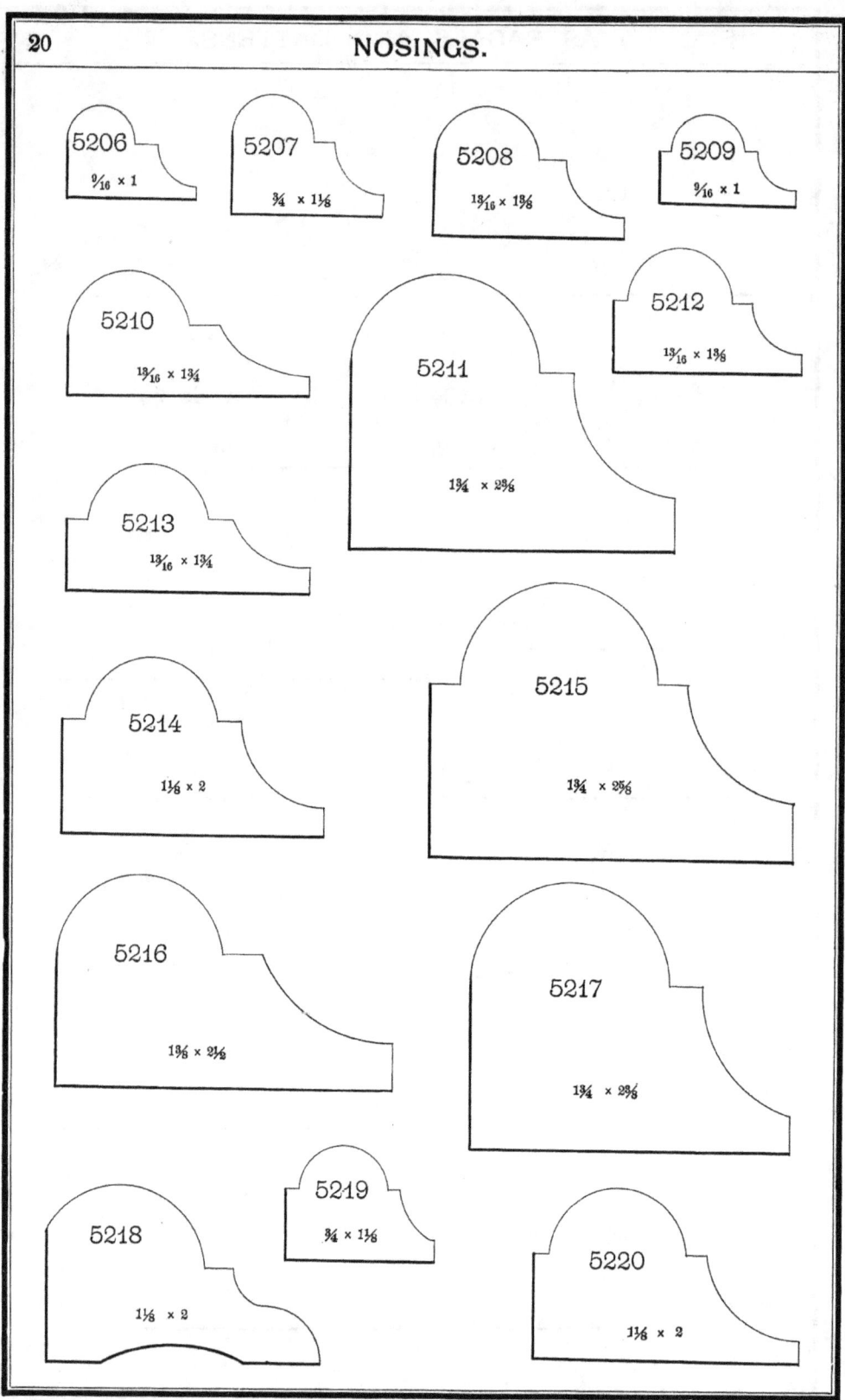

Mouldings made exact size of cuts.   Figures represent the ripping width of Lumber.

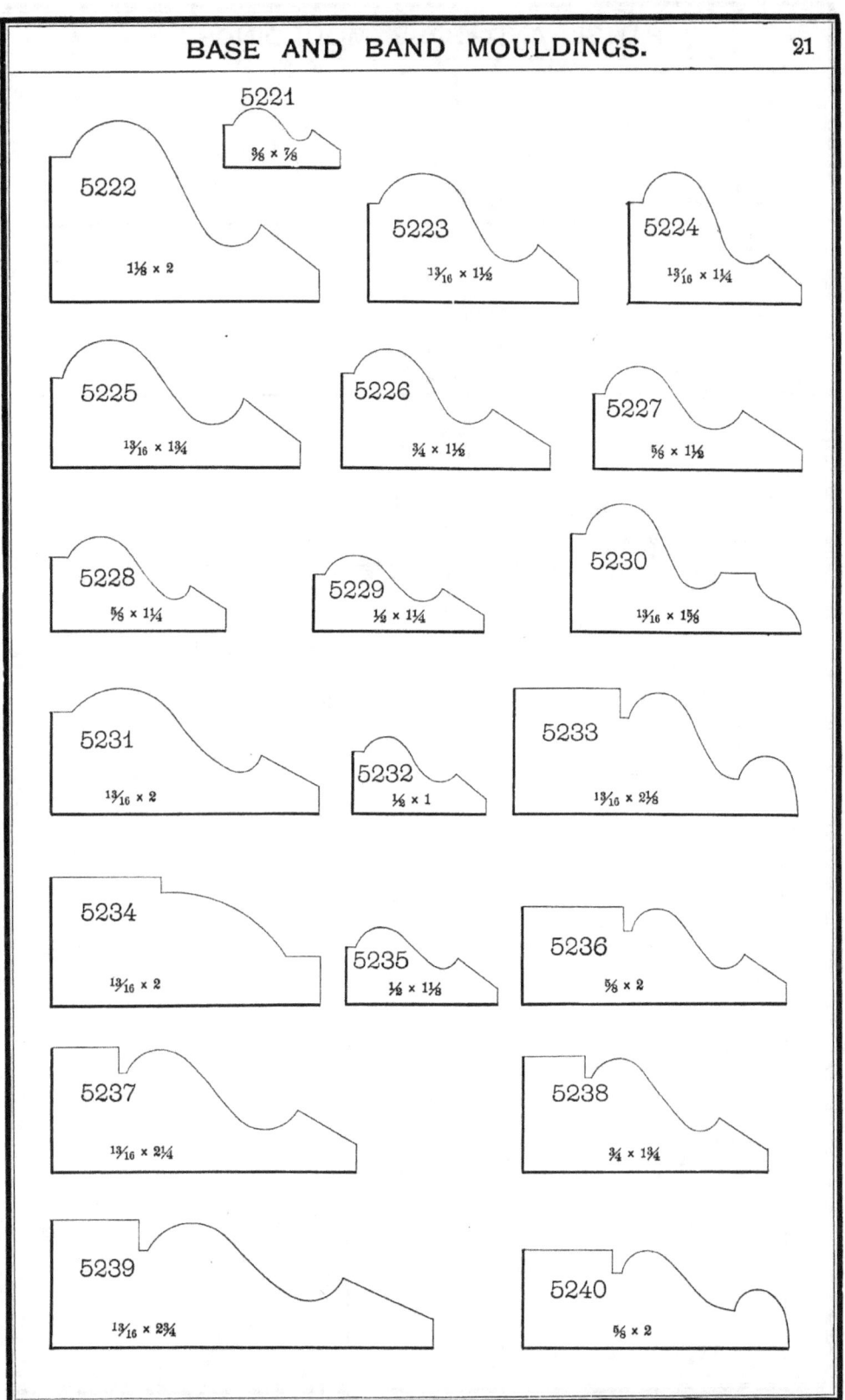

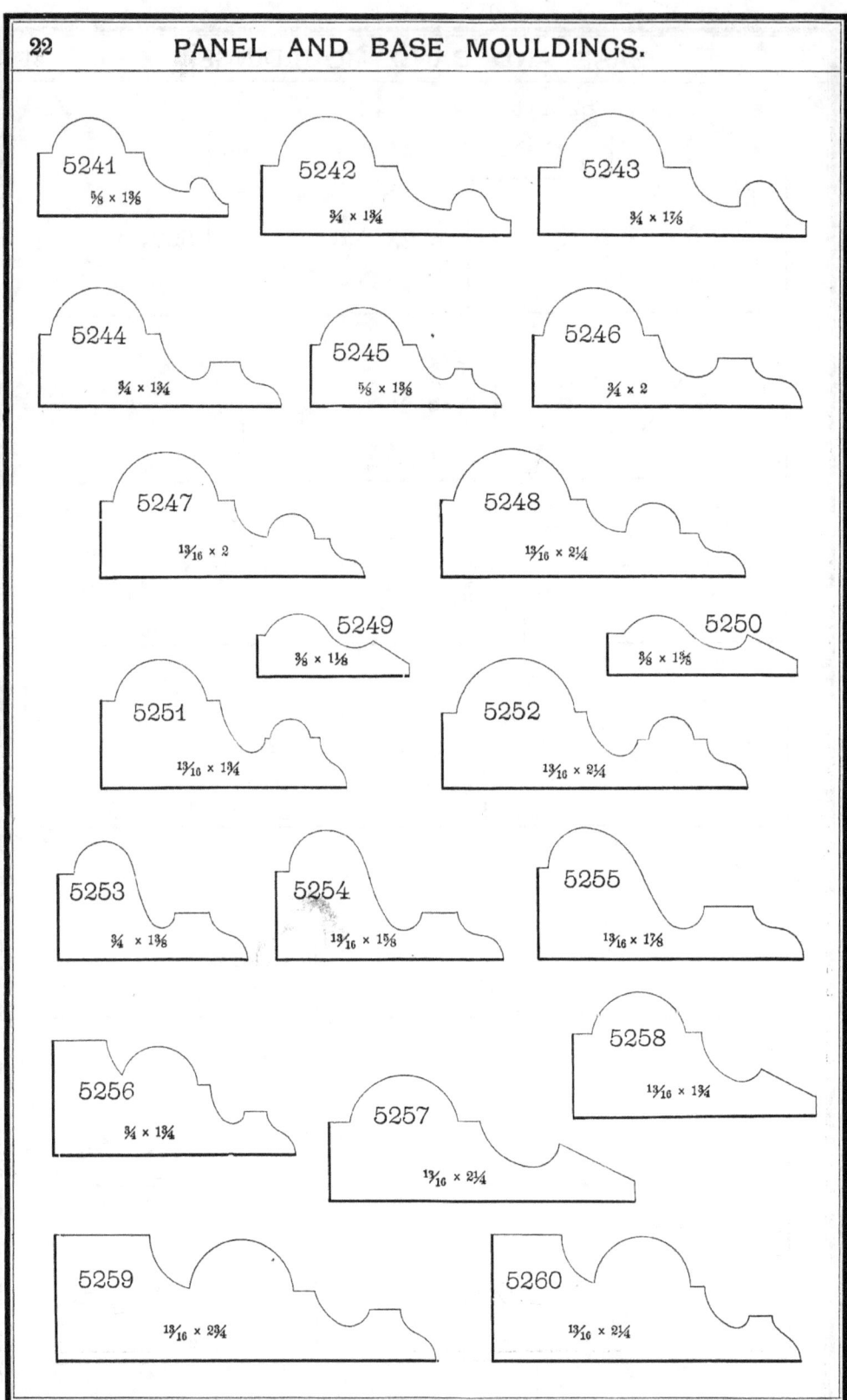

# PANEL AND BAND MOULDINGS.

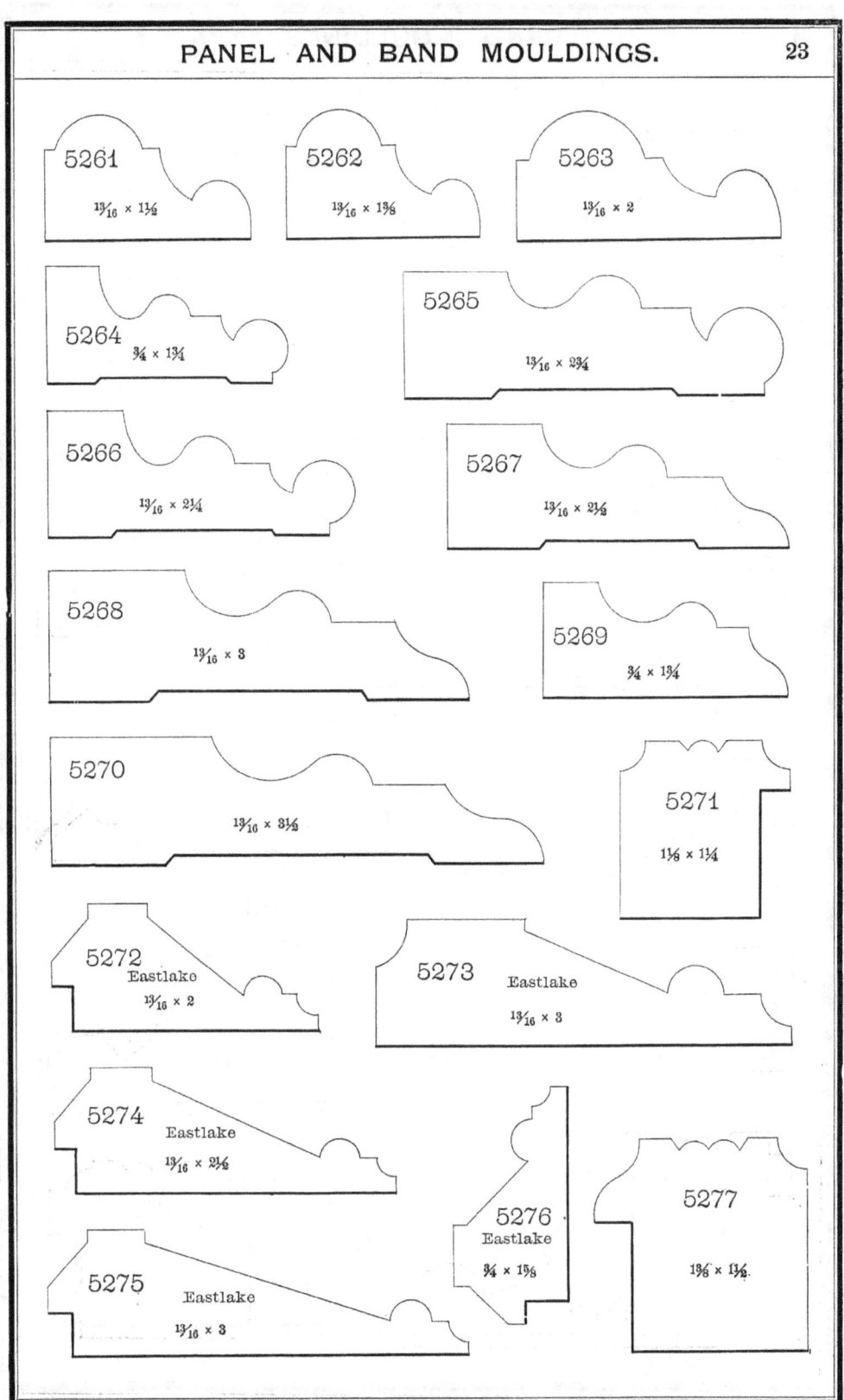

Mouldings made exact size of cuts.   Figures represent the ripping width of Lumber.

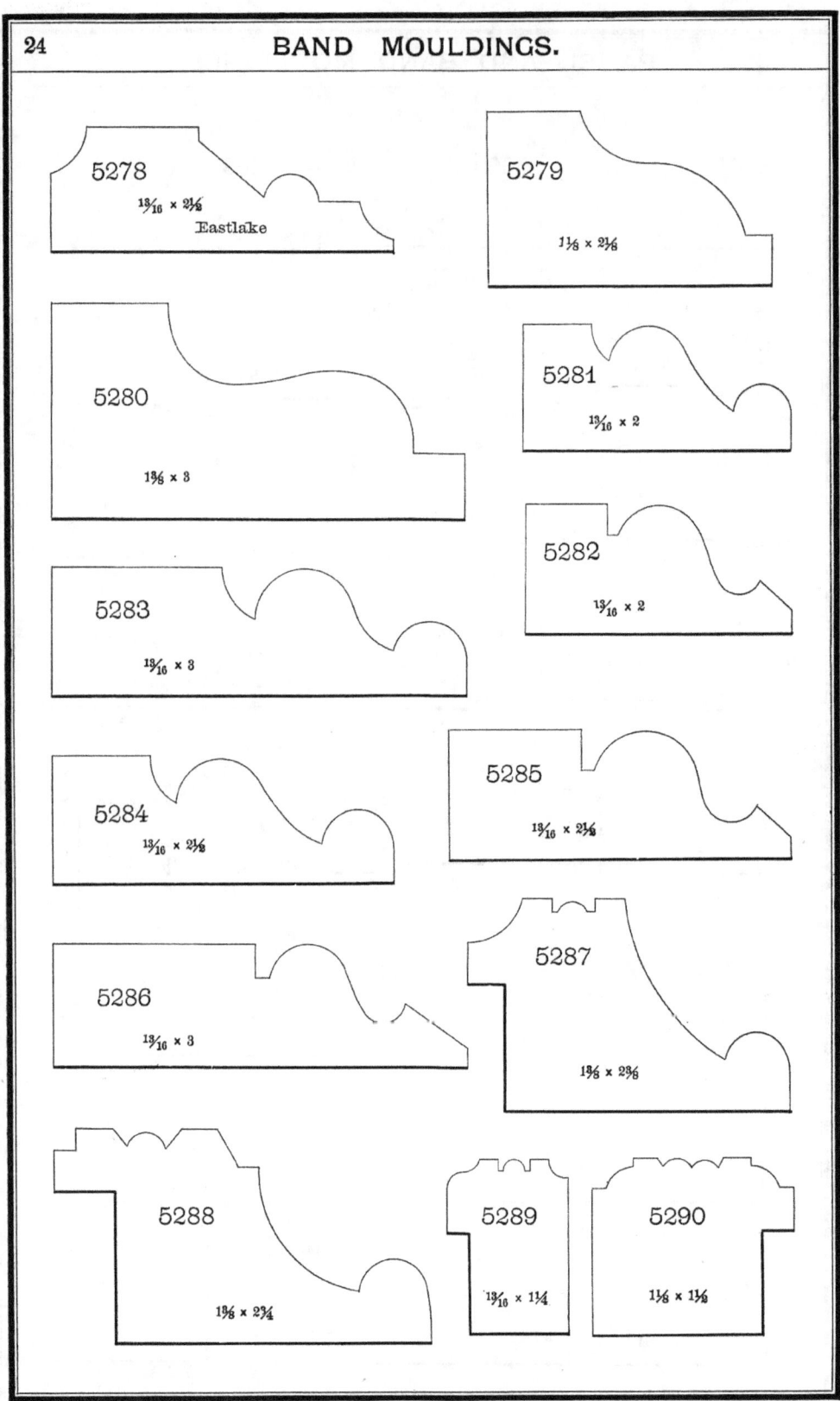

## RABBETED PANEL AND BASE MOULDINGS.

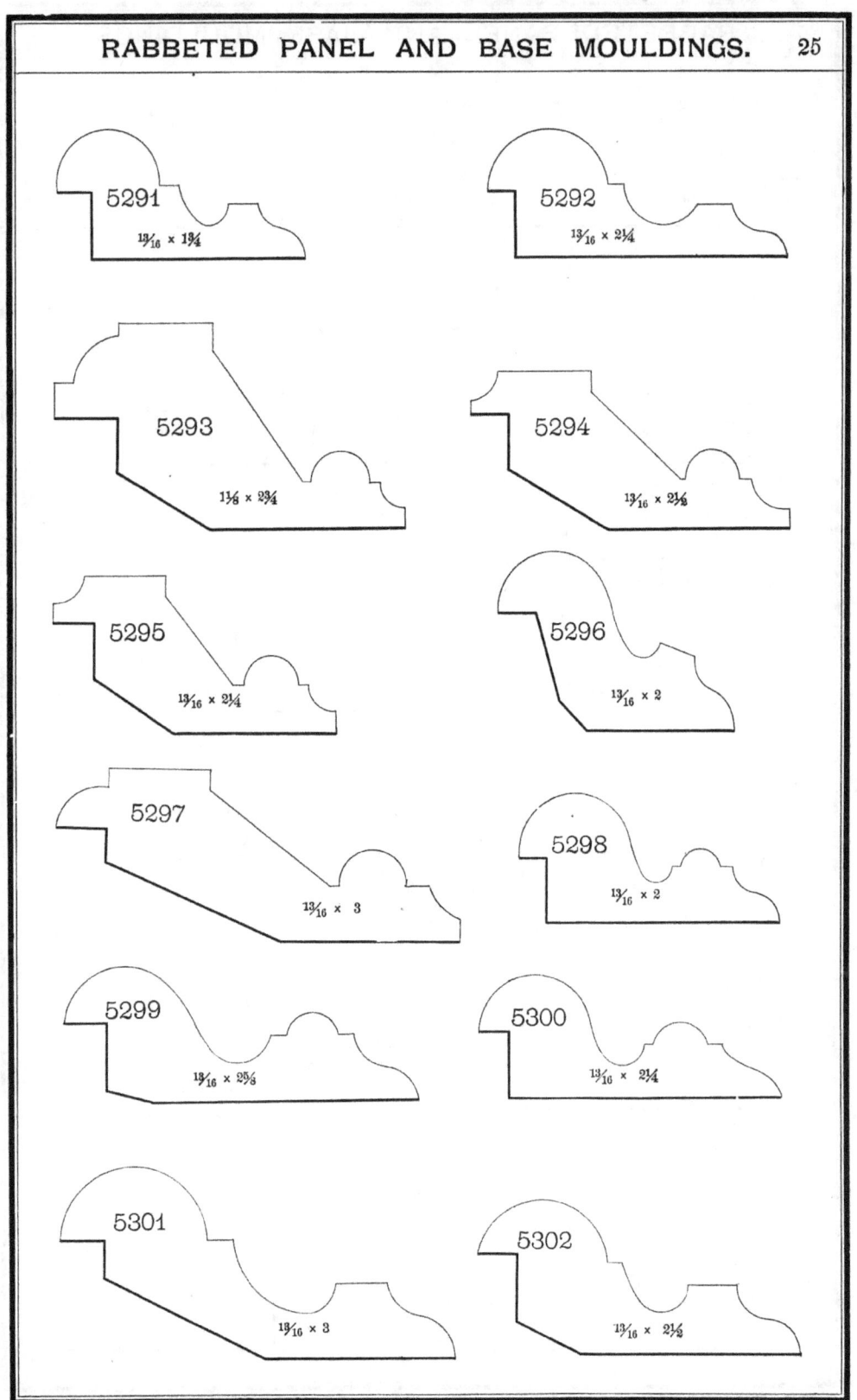

Mouldings made exact size of cuts. Figures represent the ripping width of Lumber.

## RABBETED PANEL AND BASE MOULDINGS.

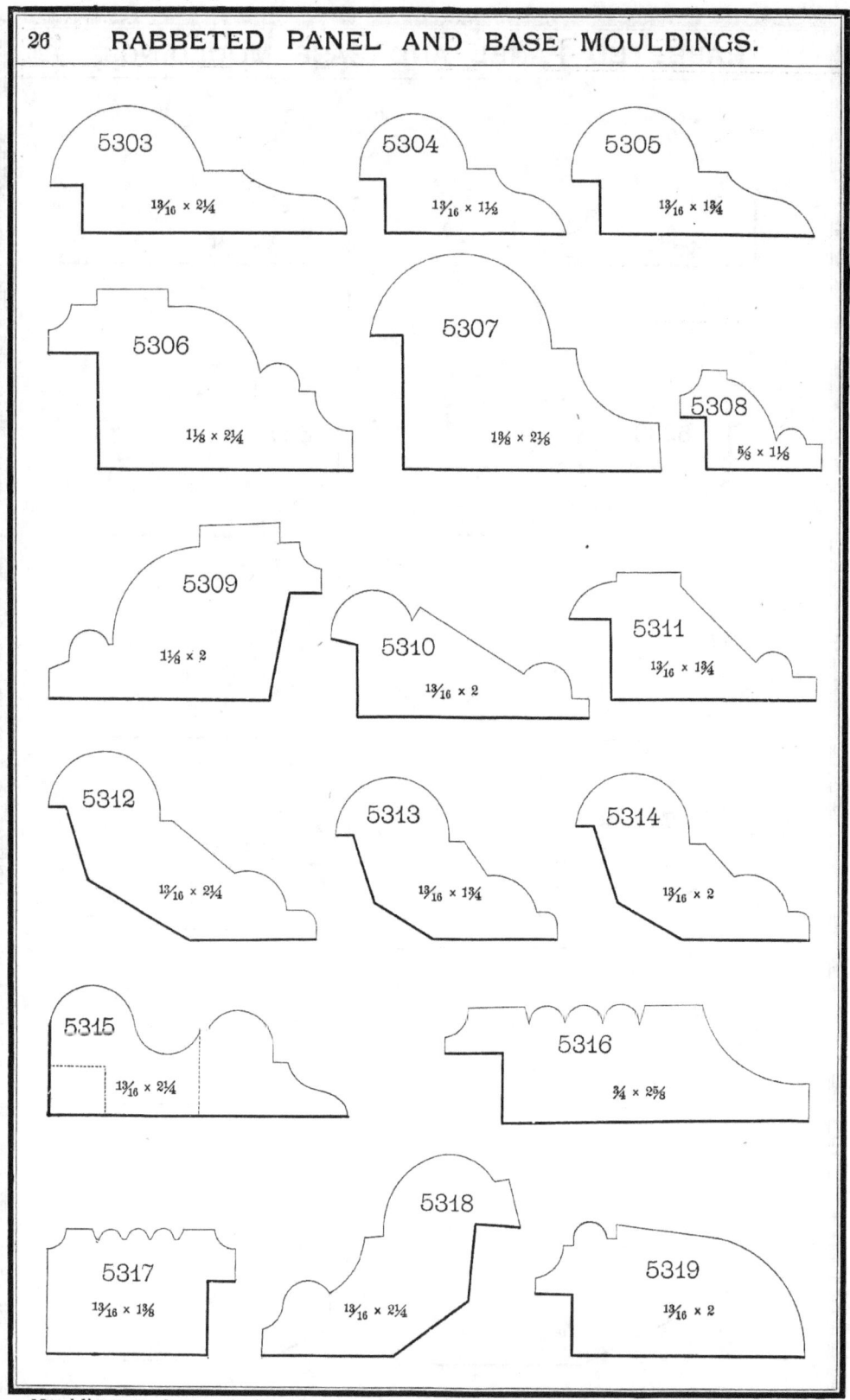

Mouldings made exact size of cuts. Figures represent the ripping width of Lumber.

## PEW BACK RAIL, WAINSCOTING CAPS AND THRESHOLDS.

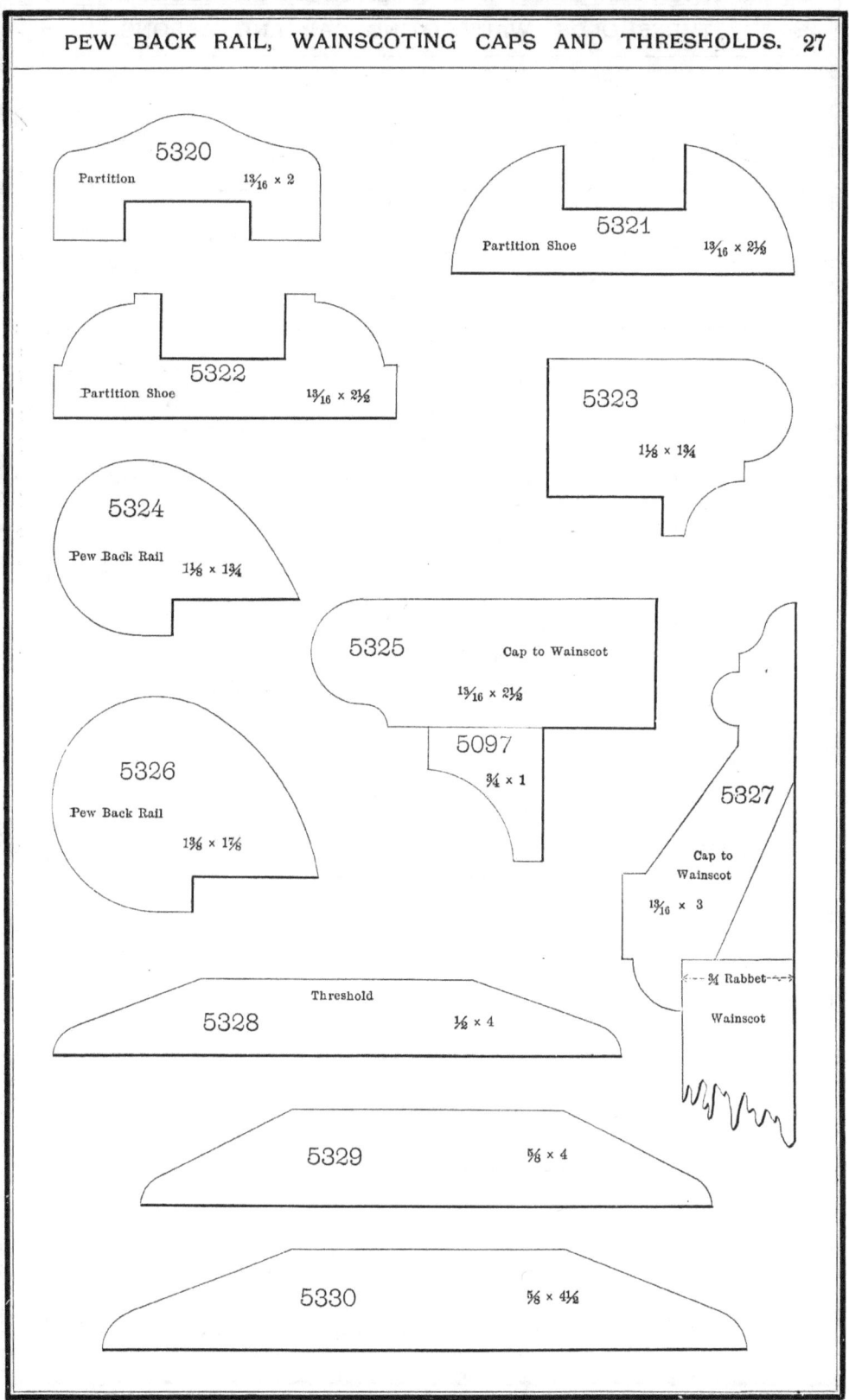

Mouldings made exact size of cuts. Figures represent the ripping width of Lumber.

## THRESHOLDS, WAINSCOTING CAP AND APRONS.

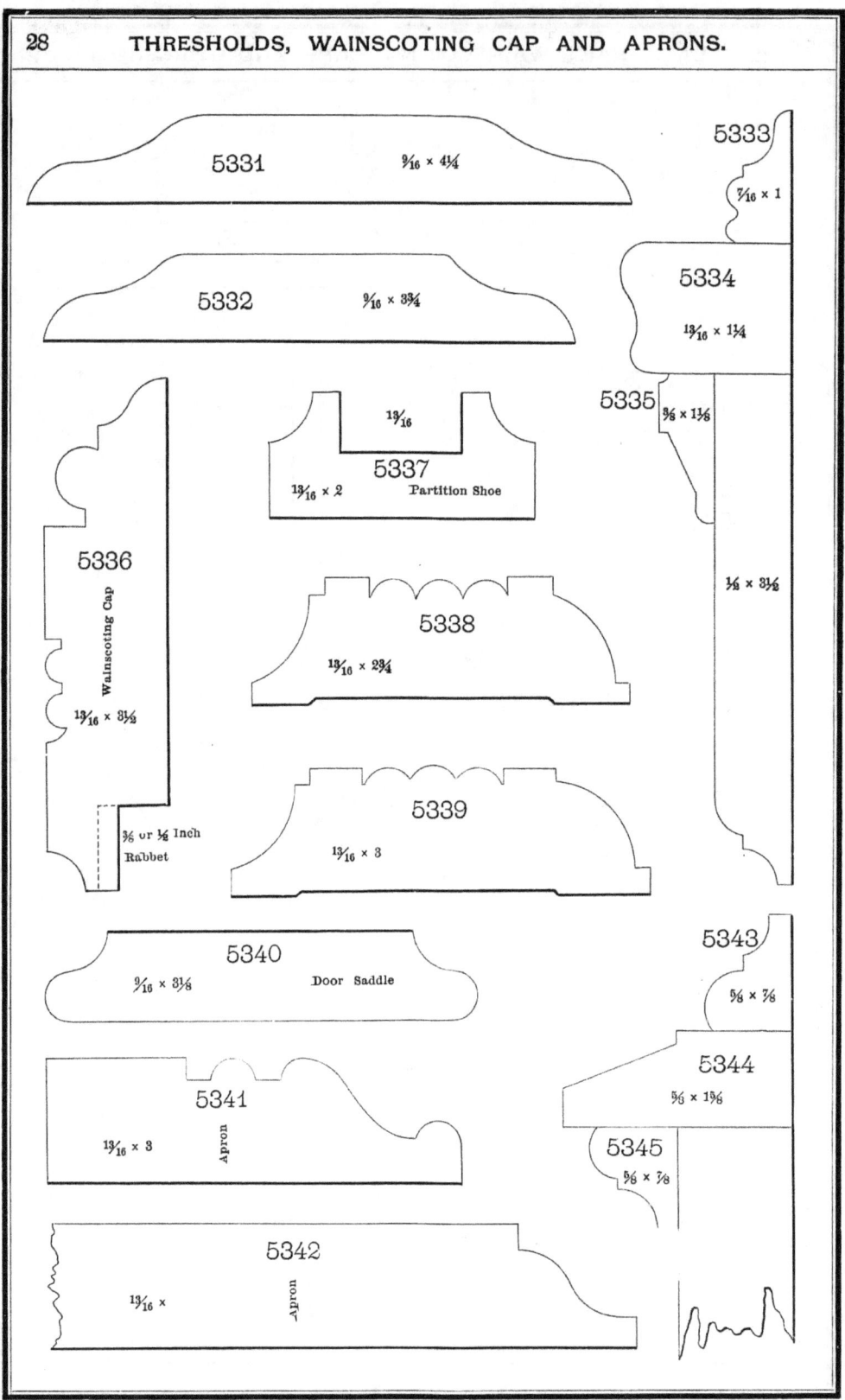

Mouldings made exact size of cuts. Figures represent the ripping width of Lumber.

# WAINSCOTING CAP MOULDINGS.

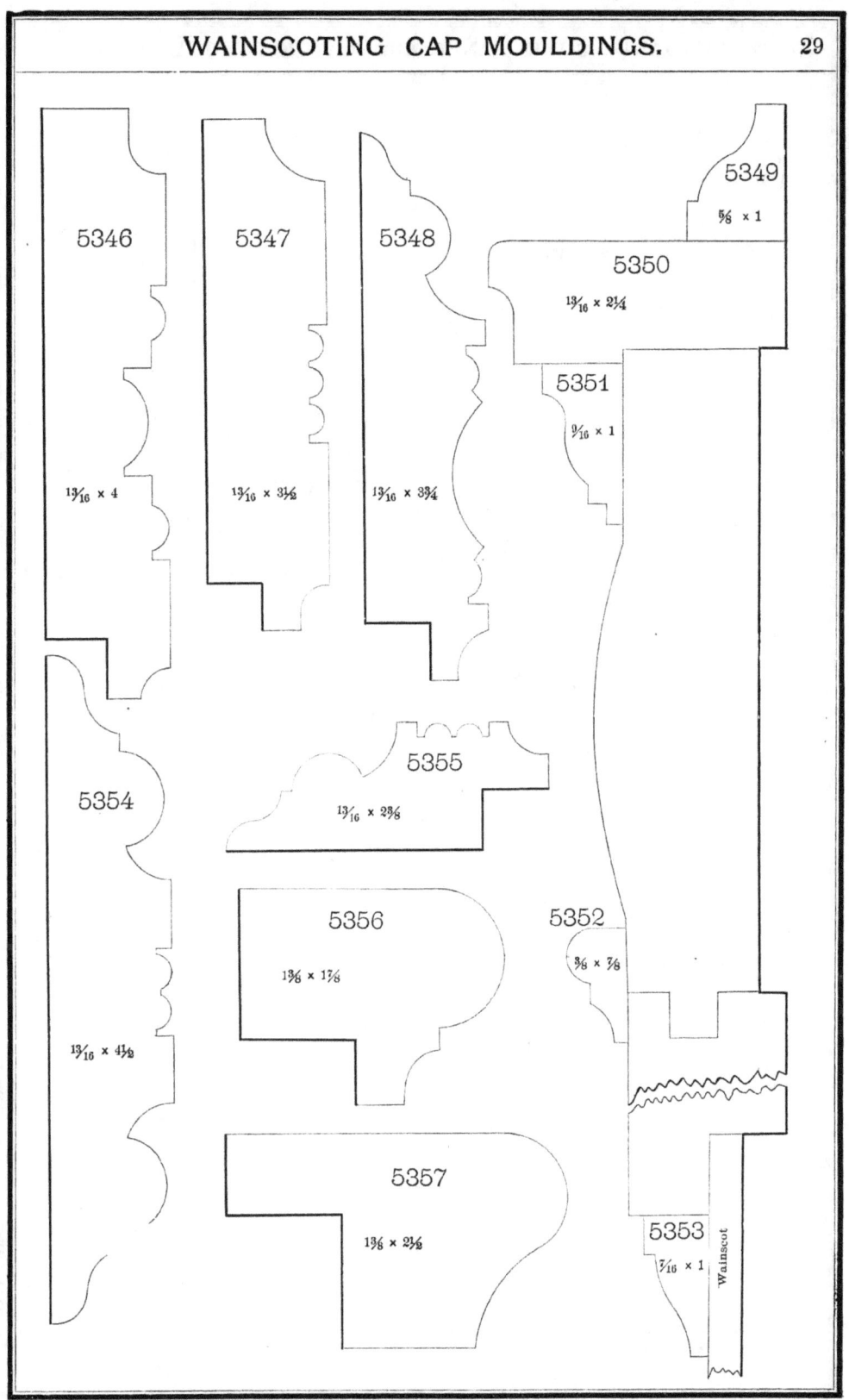

Mouldings made exact size of cuts. Figures represent the ripping width of Lumber.

## 30 BACK BAND, SUNK PANEL AND LATTICE MOULDINGS.

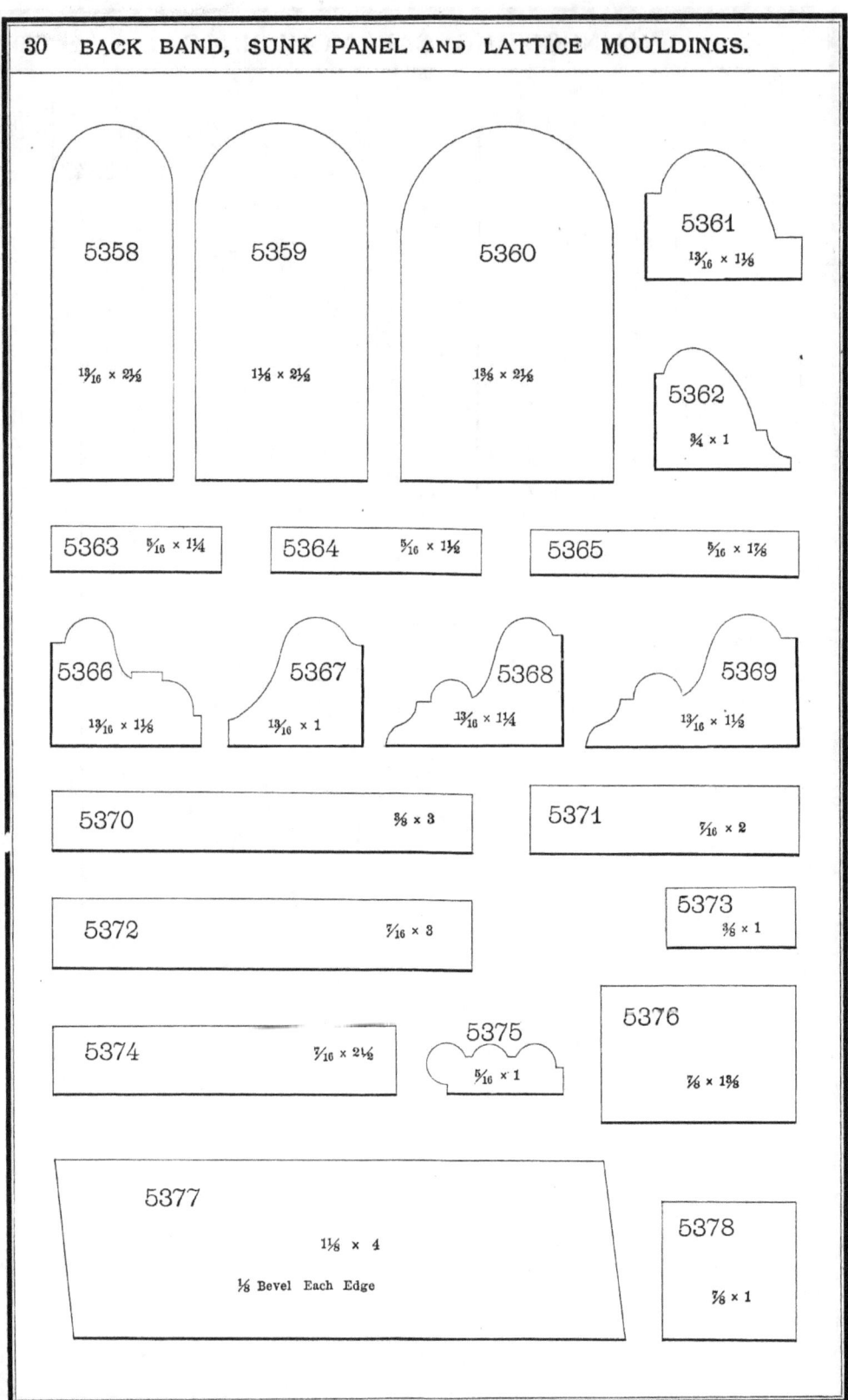

Mouldings made exact size of cuts. Figures represent the ripping width of Lumber.

## ROOM MOULDINGS, CEILING AND WINDOW STOOLS.

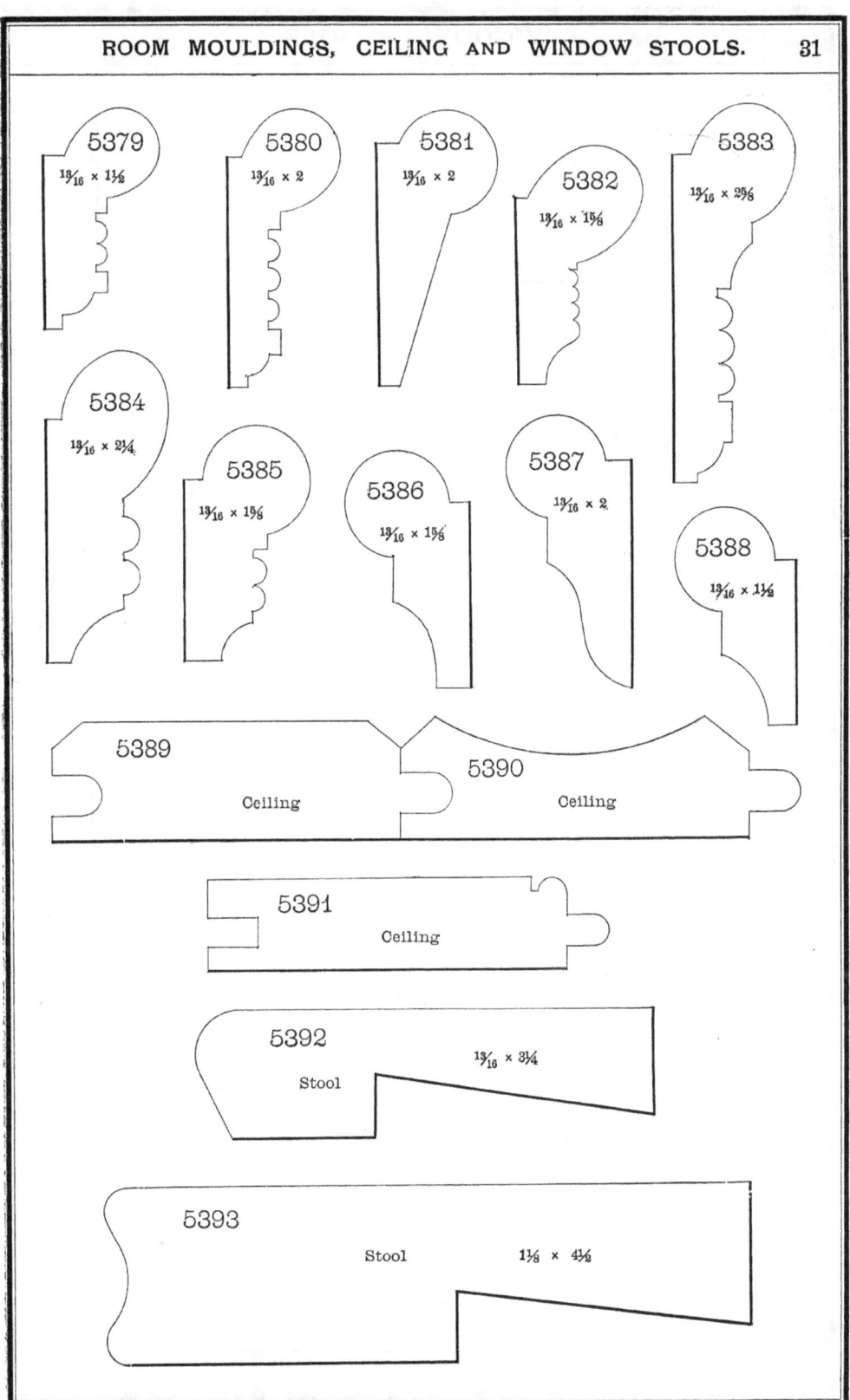

Mouldings made exact size of cuts. Figures represent the ripping width of Lumber.

# WINDOW STOOLS.

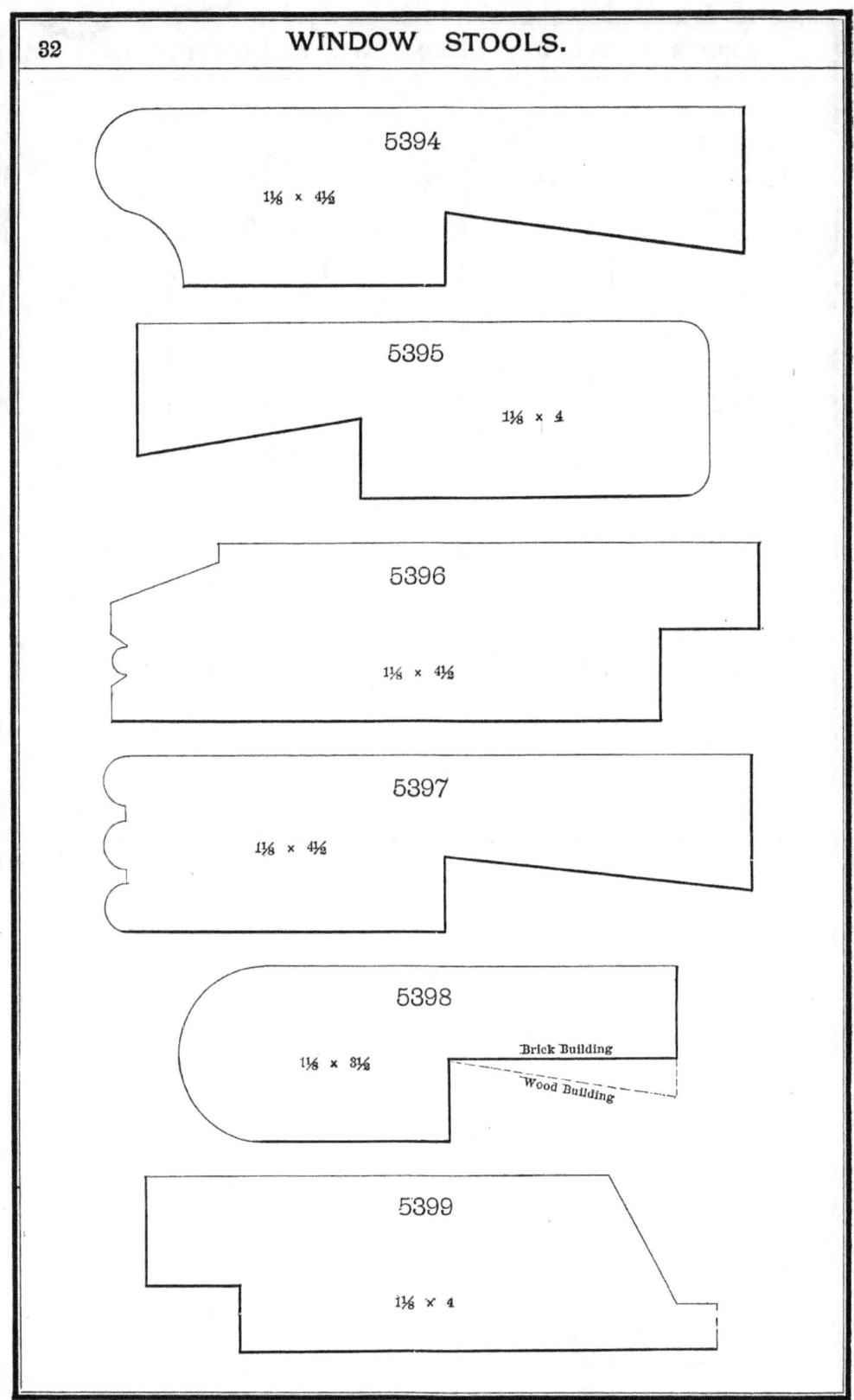

Mouldings made exact size of cuts. Figures represent the ripping width of Lumber.

# WINDOW STOOLS.

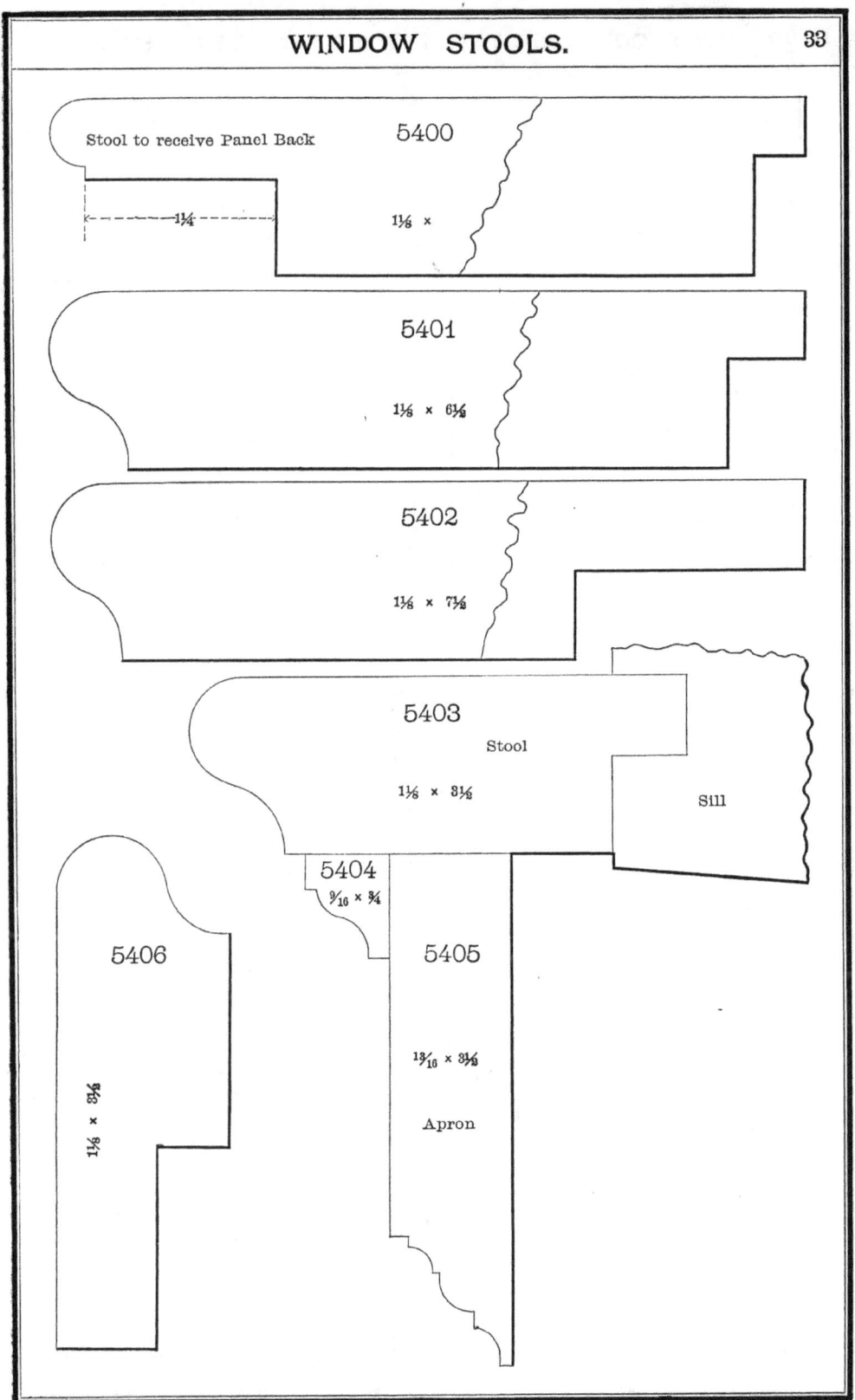

Mouldings made exact size of cuts. Figures represent the ripping width of Lumber.

## 34 WINDOW STOOL, PARTITION FRAMES AND FILLING STRIPS.

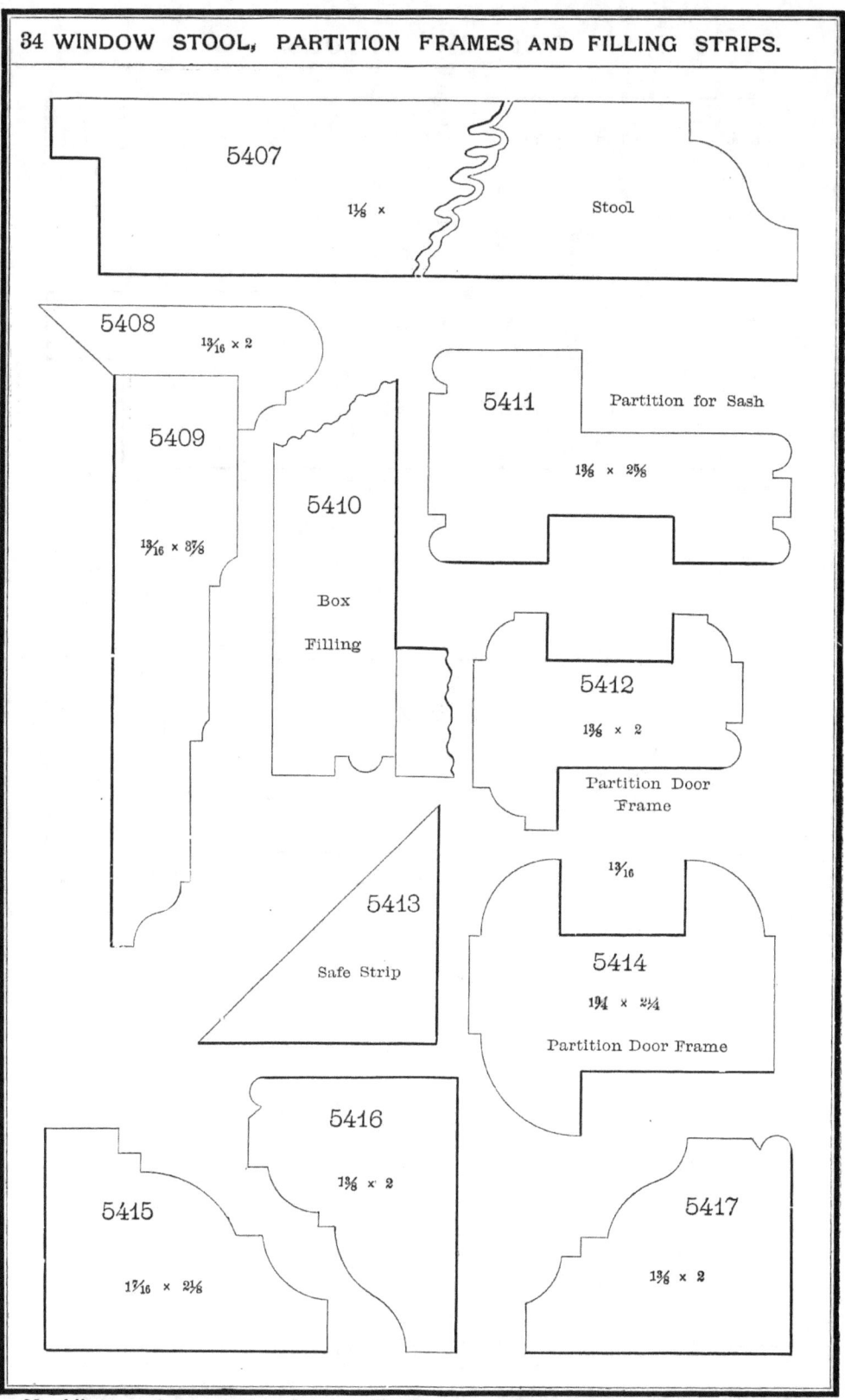

Mouldings made exact size of cuts. Figures represent the ripping width of Lumber.

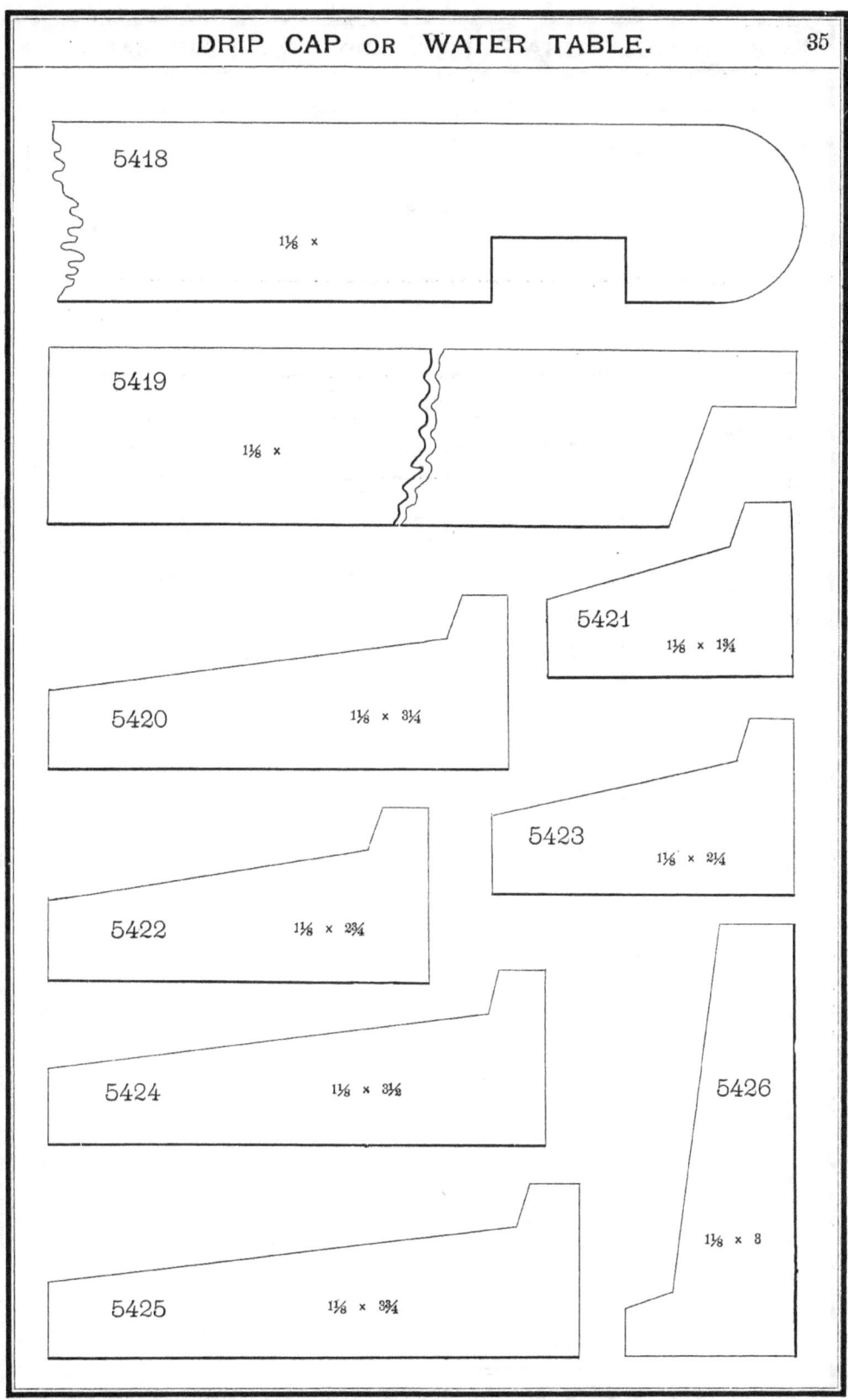

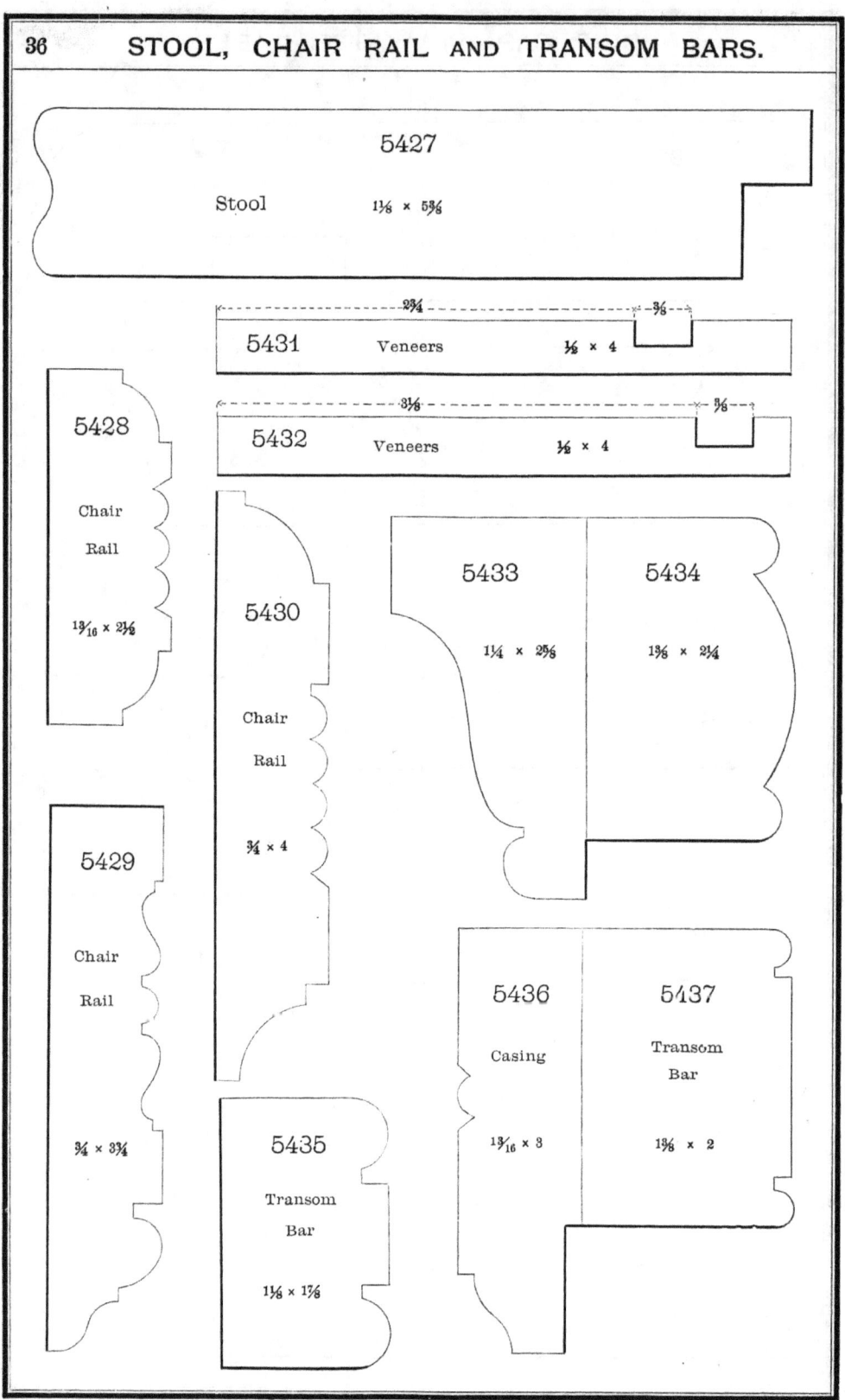

# BED MOLDS AND IMPOSTS.

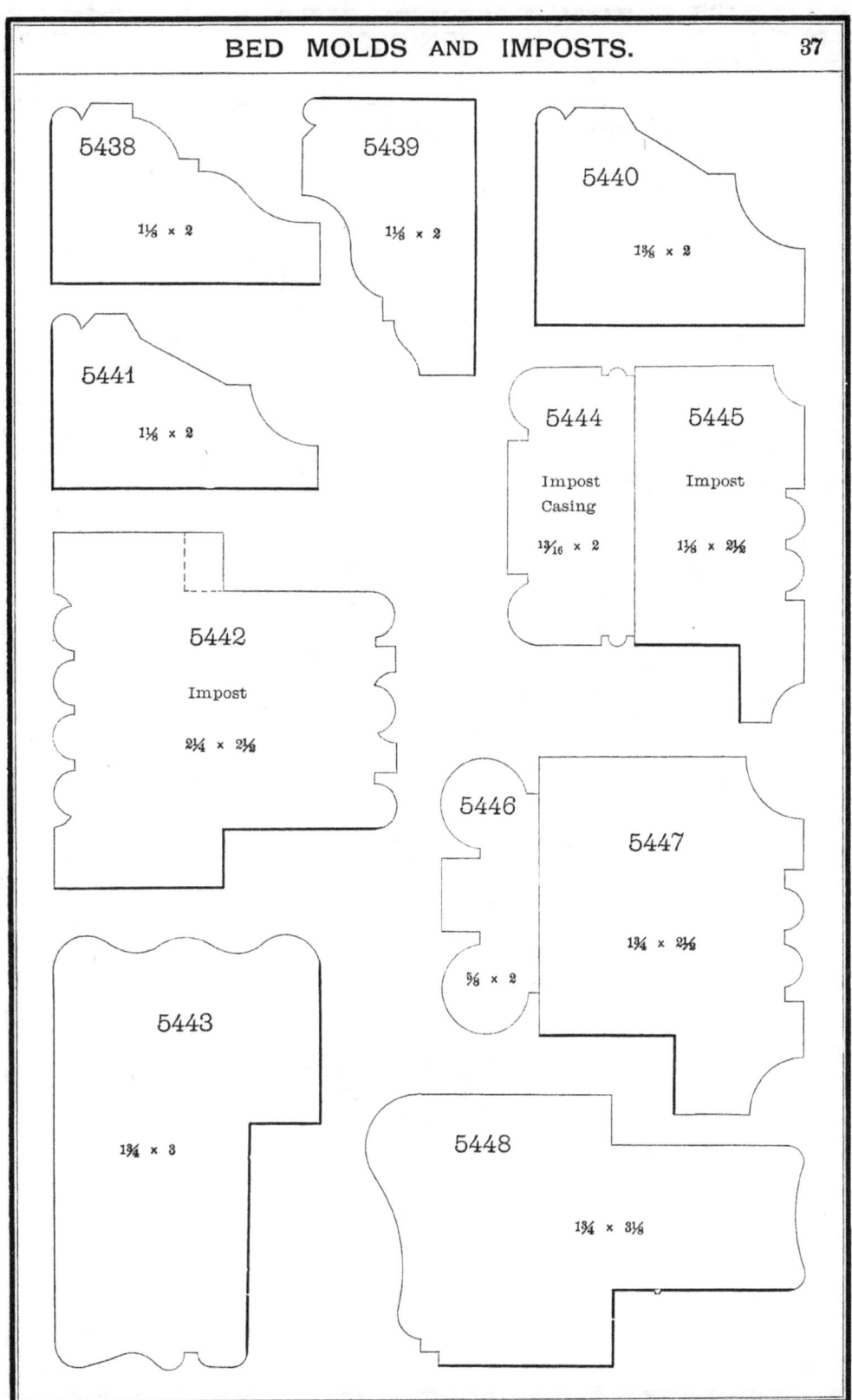

Mouldings made exact size of cuts. Figures represent the ripping width of Lumber.

## CORNICES.

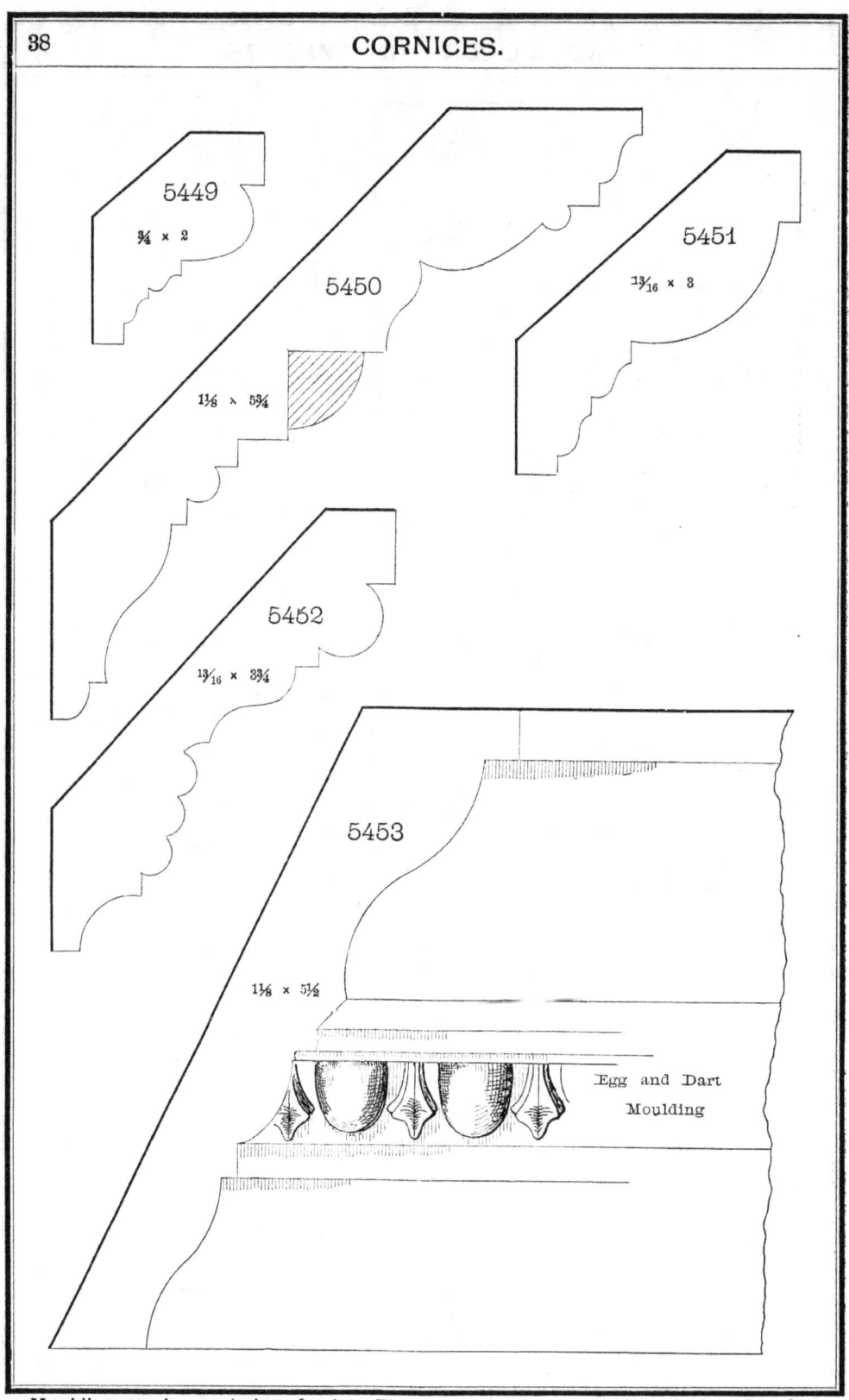

Mouldings made exact size of cuts. Figures represent the ripping width of Lumber.
When ordering the above 5450 Pattern, state if dentil member is wanted.

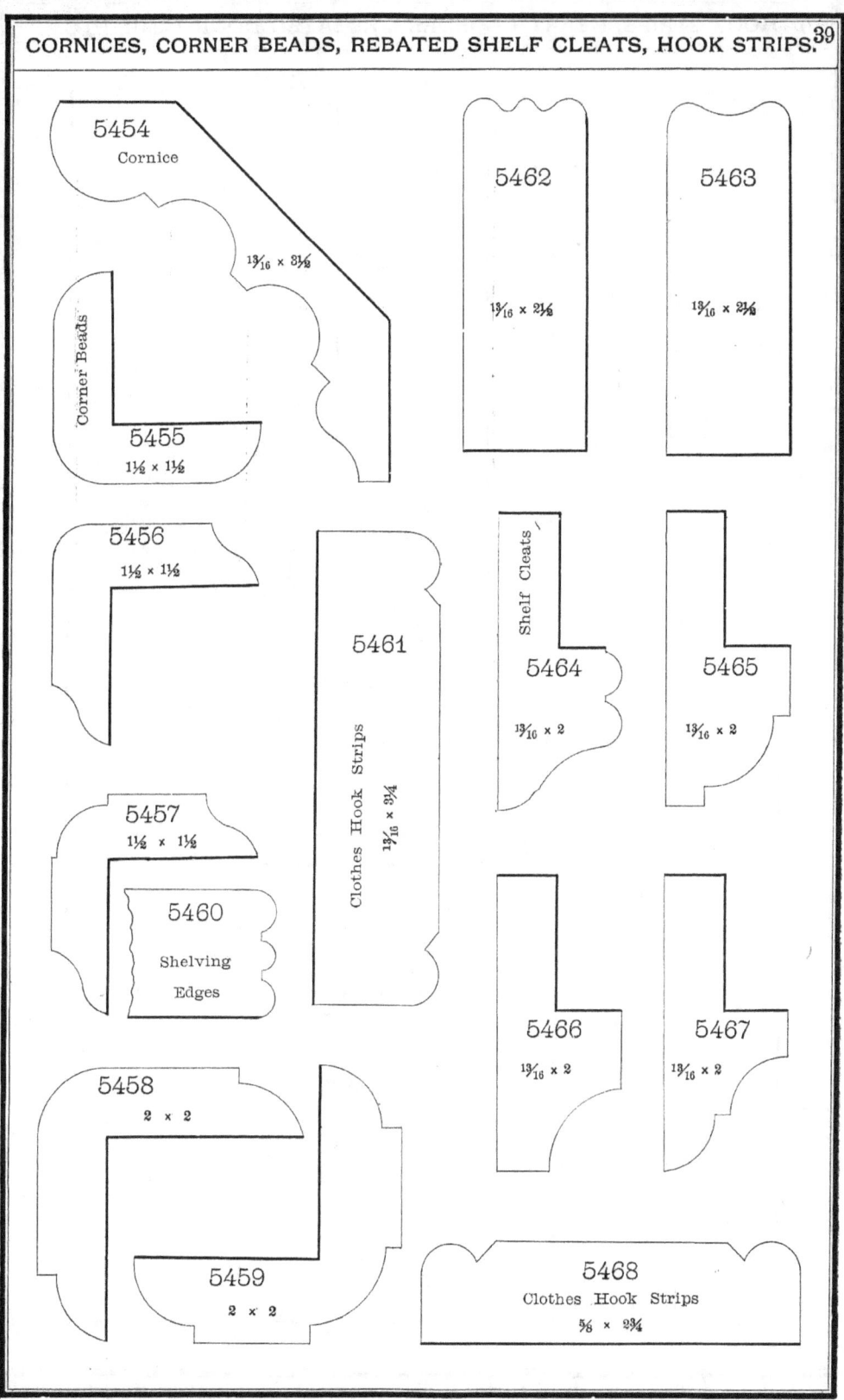

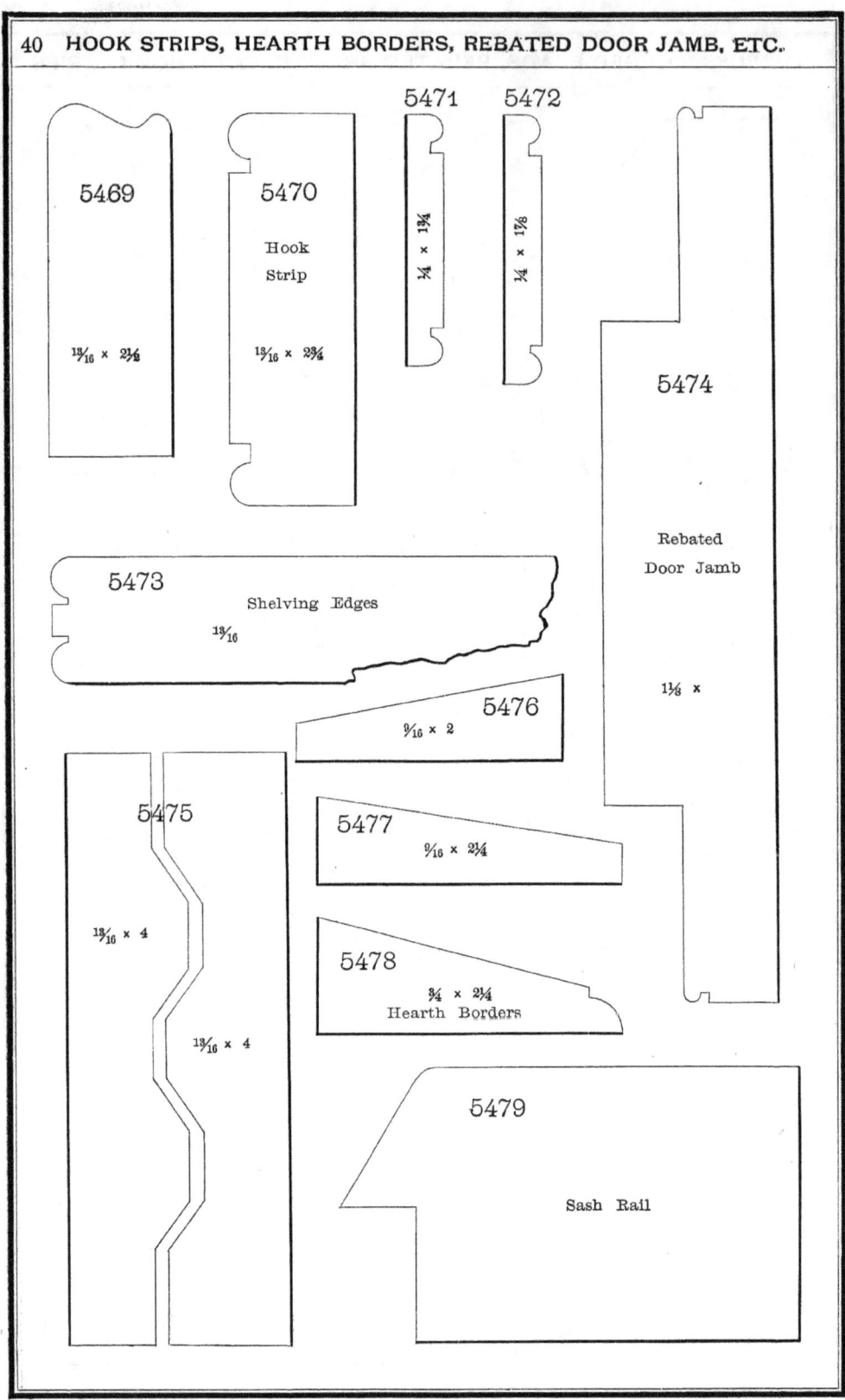

# CASINGS.

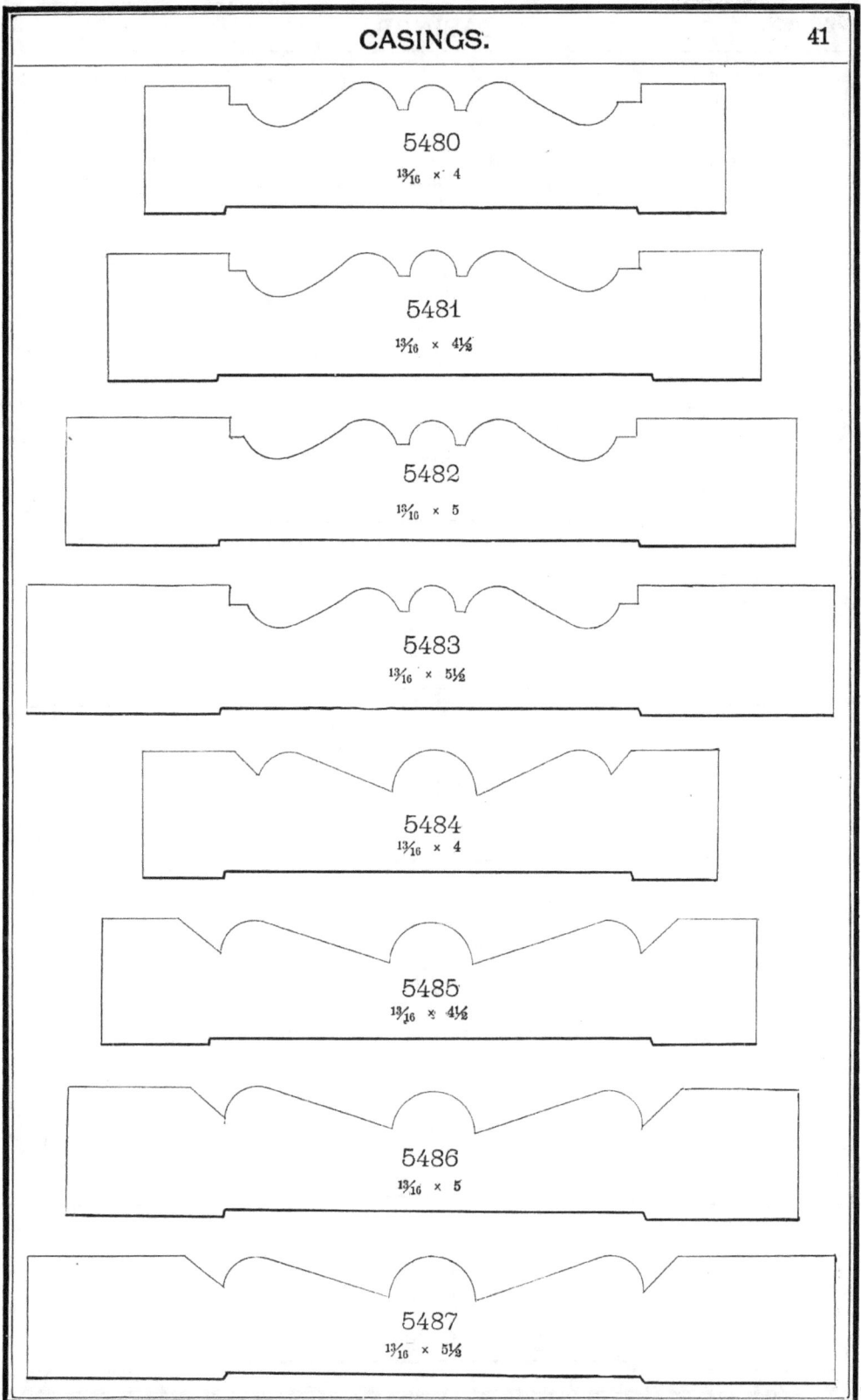

5480
13/16 × 4

5481
13/16 × 4½

5482
13/16 × 5

5483
13/16 × 5½

5484
13/16 × 4

5485
13/16 × 4½

5486
13/16 × 5

5487
13/16 × 5½

Mouldings made exact size of cuts.   Figures represent the ripping width of Lumber.

## CASINGS.

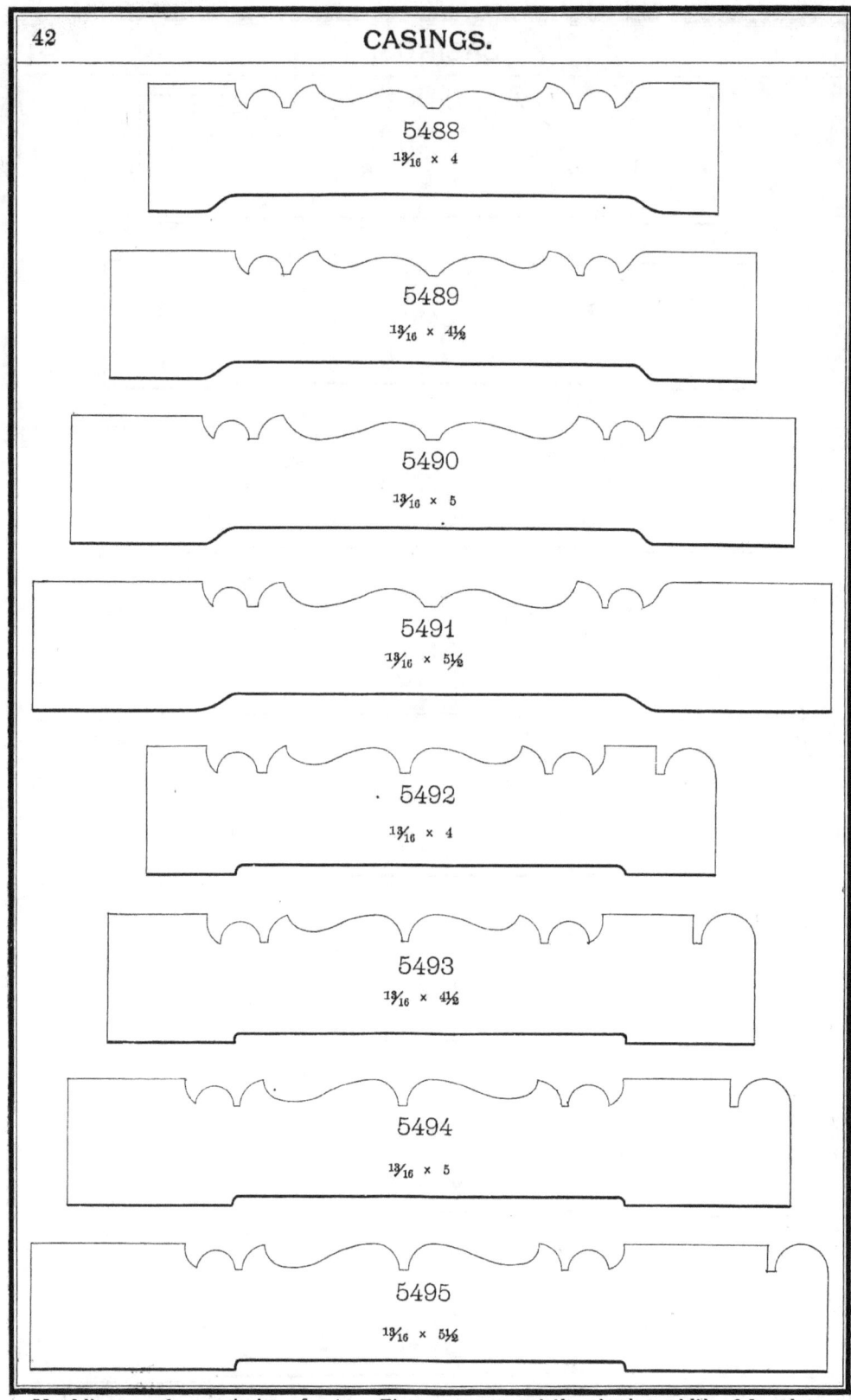

Mouldings made exact size of cuts. Figures represent the ripping width of Lumber.

# CASINGS. 43

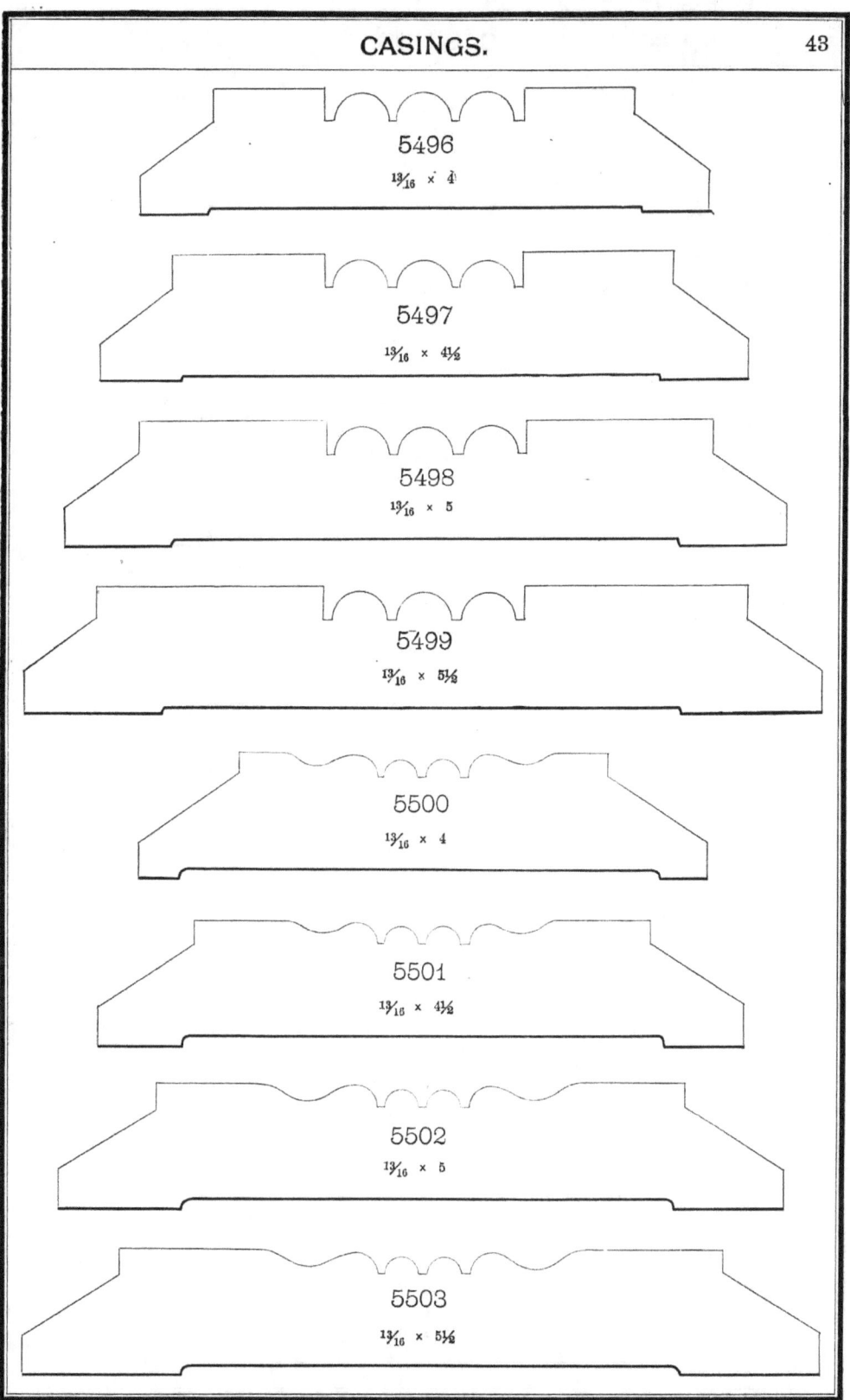

Mouldings made exact size of cuts.   Figures represent the ripping width of Lumber.

## CASINGS.

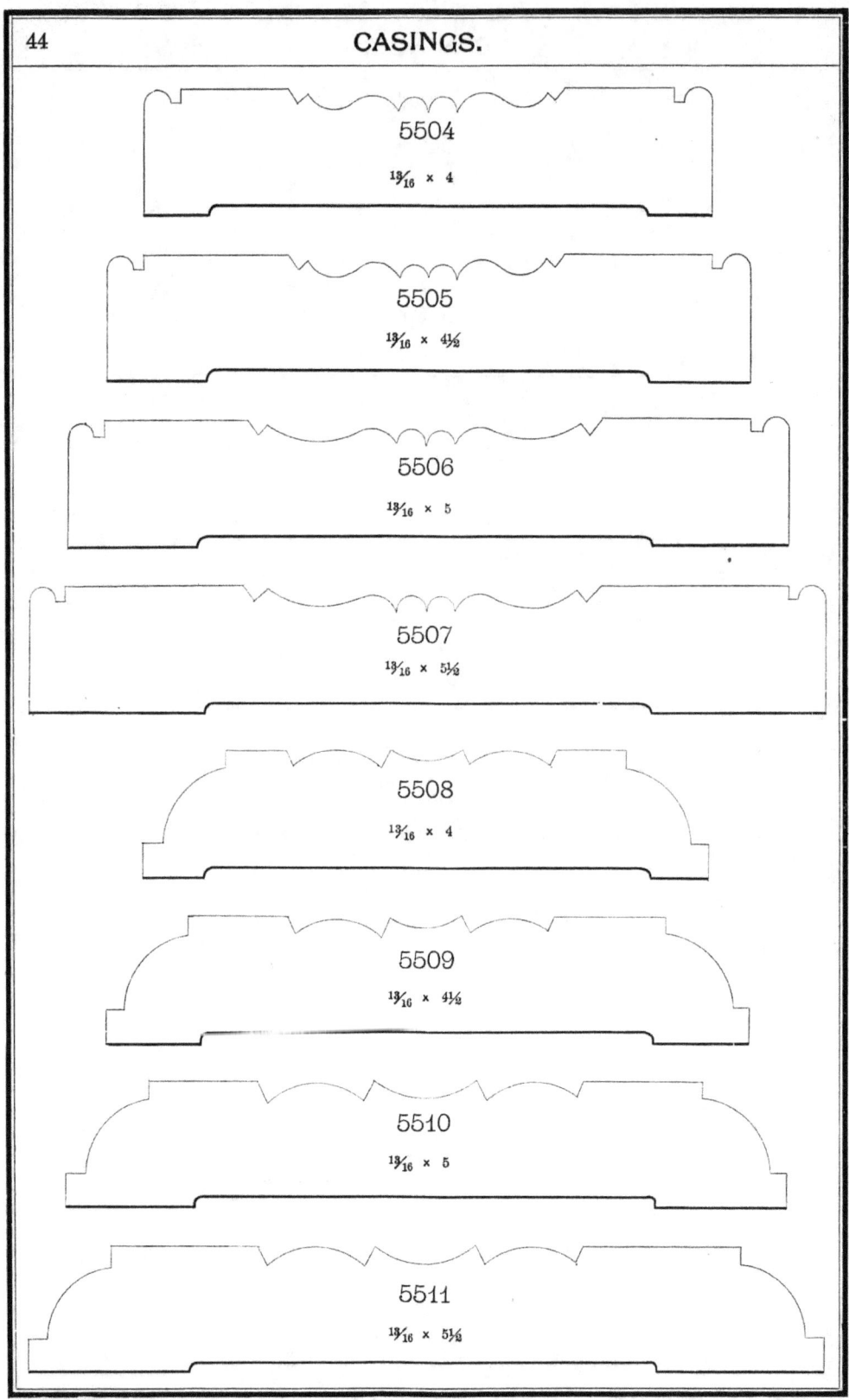

Mouldings made exact size of cuts.   Figures represent the ripping width of Lumber.

# CASINGS.

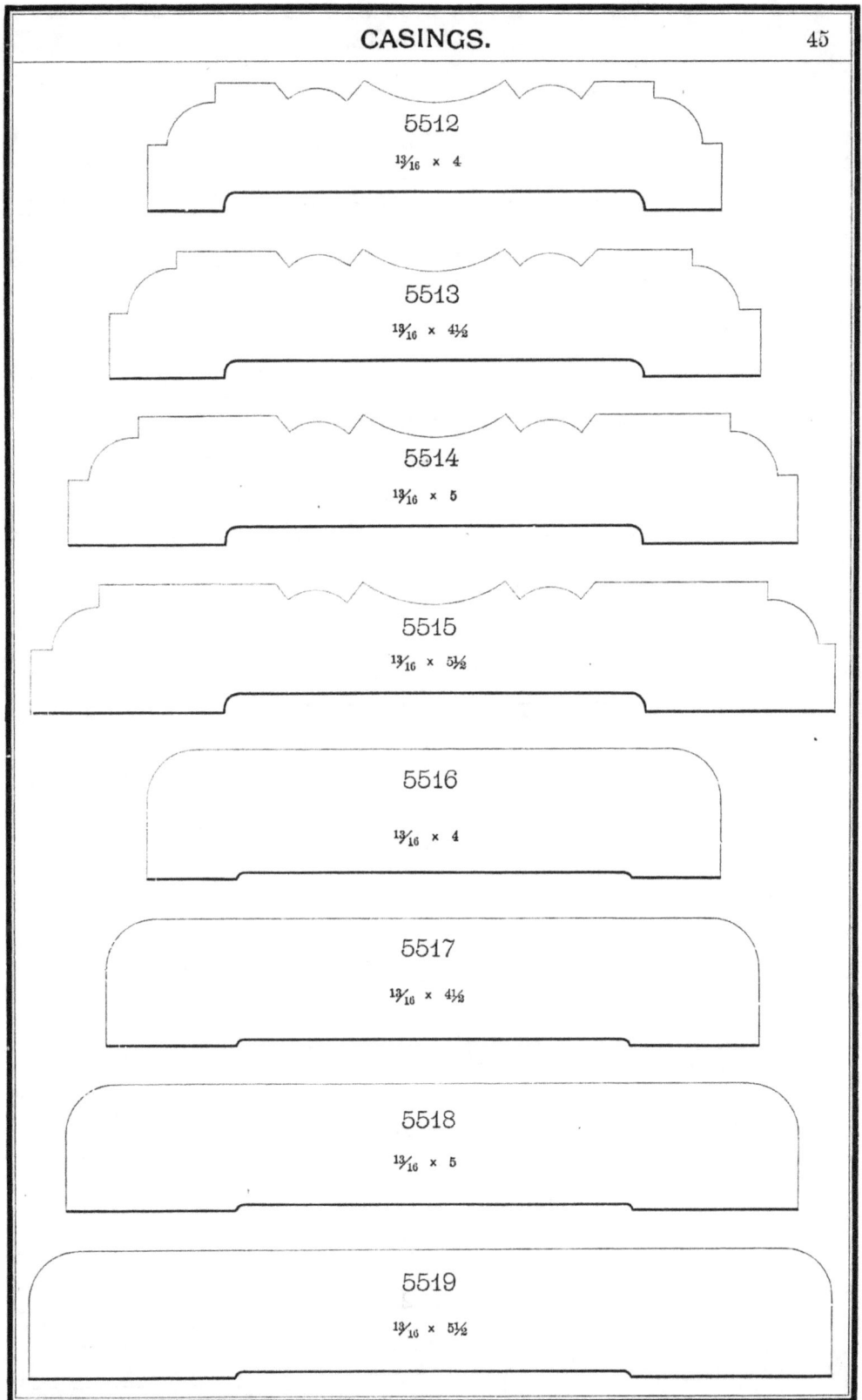

## CASINGS.

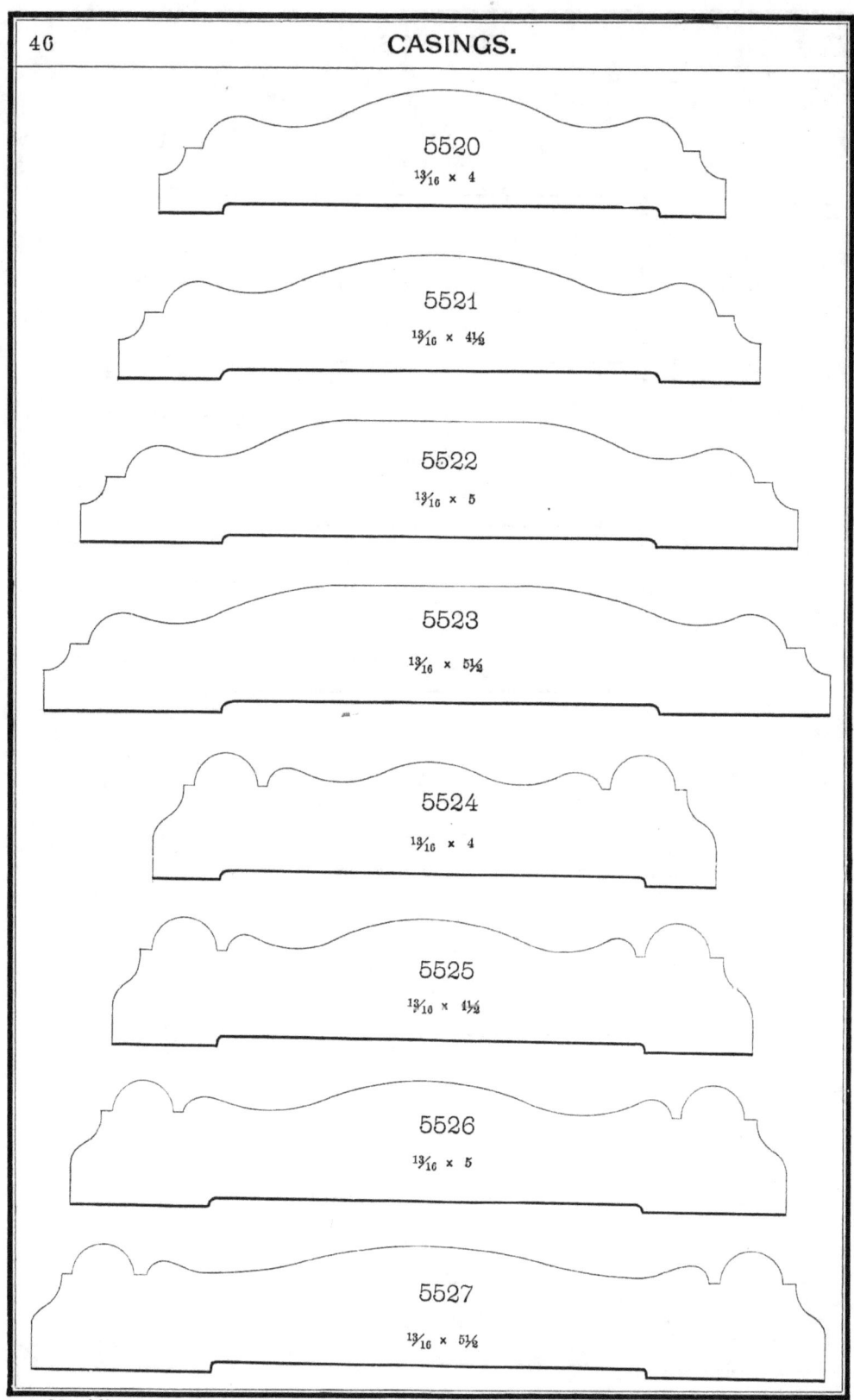

Mouldings made exact size of cuts.   Figures represent the ripping width of Lumber.

## CASINGS.

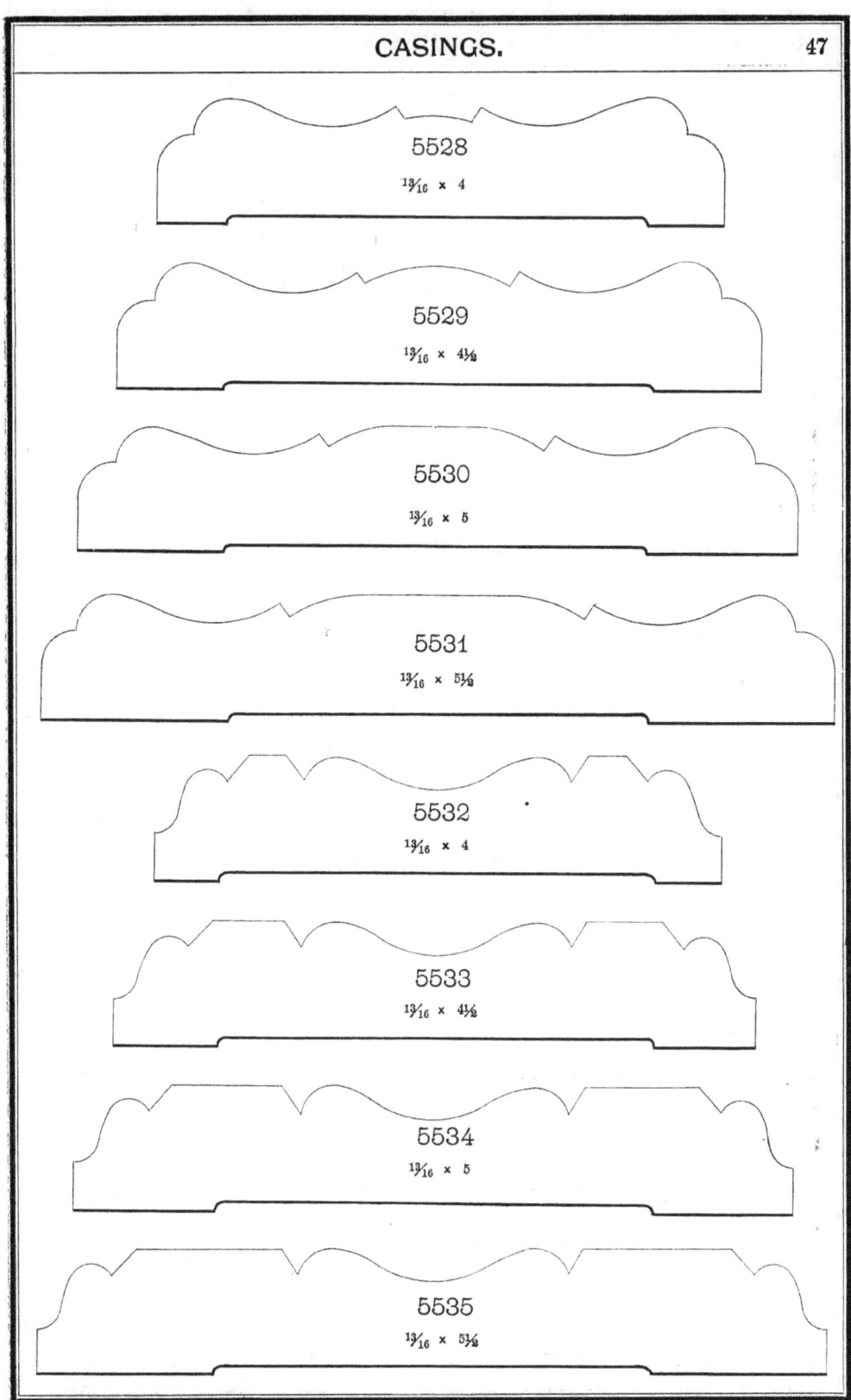

5528  
13/16 x 4

5529  
13/16 x 4½

5530  
13/16 x 5

5531  
13/16 x 5½

5532  
13/16 x 4

5533  
13/16 x 4½

5534  
13/16 x 5

5535  
13/16 x 5½

Mouldings made exact size of cuts.   Figures represent the ripping width of Lumber.

## CASINGS.

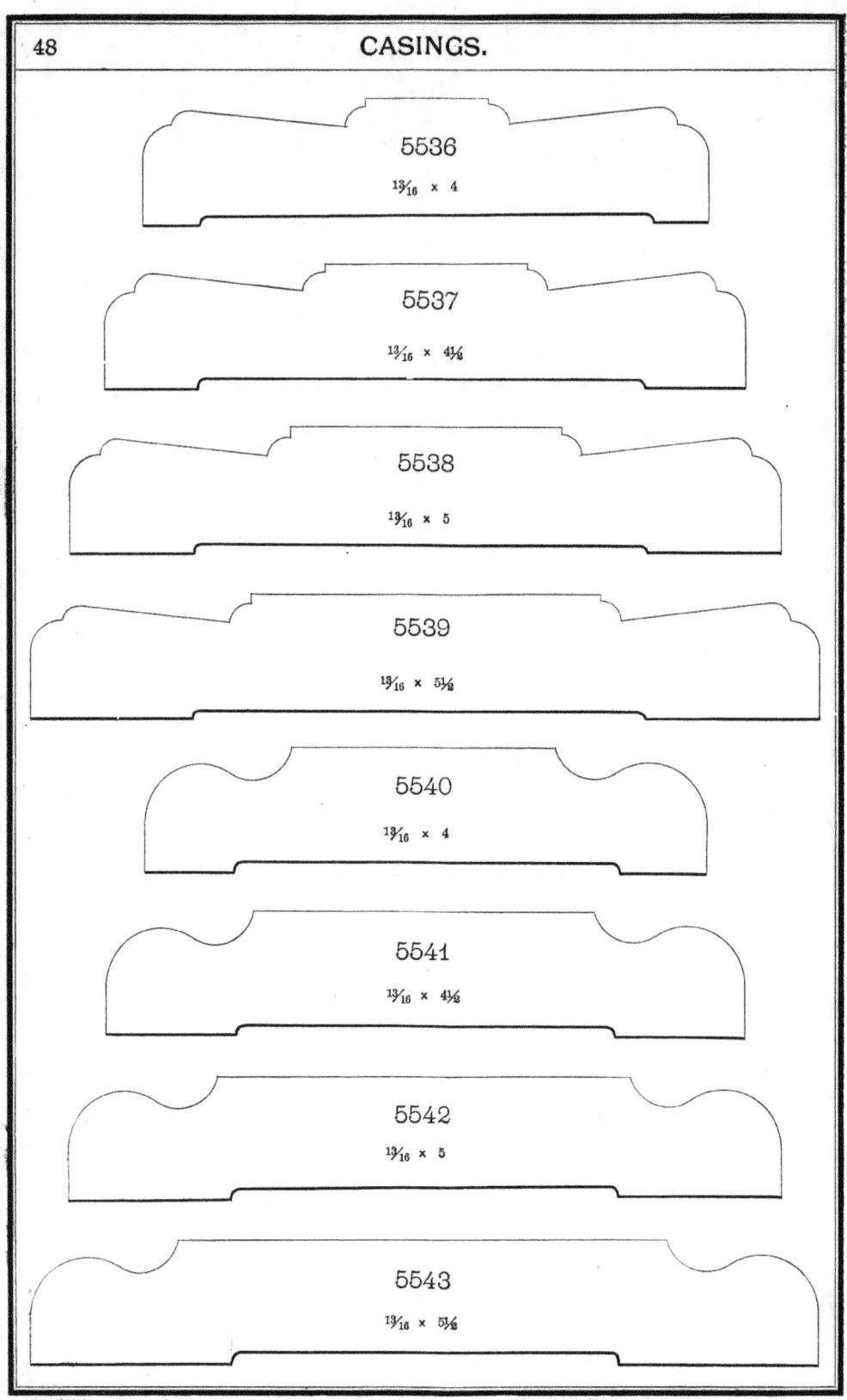

Mouldings made exact size of cuts. Figures represent the ripping width of Lumber.

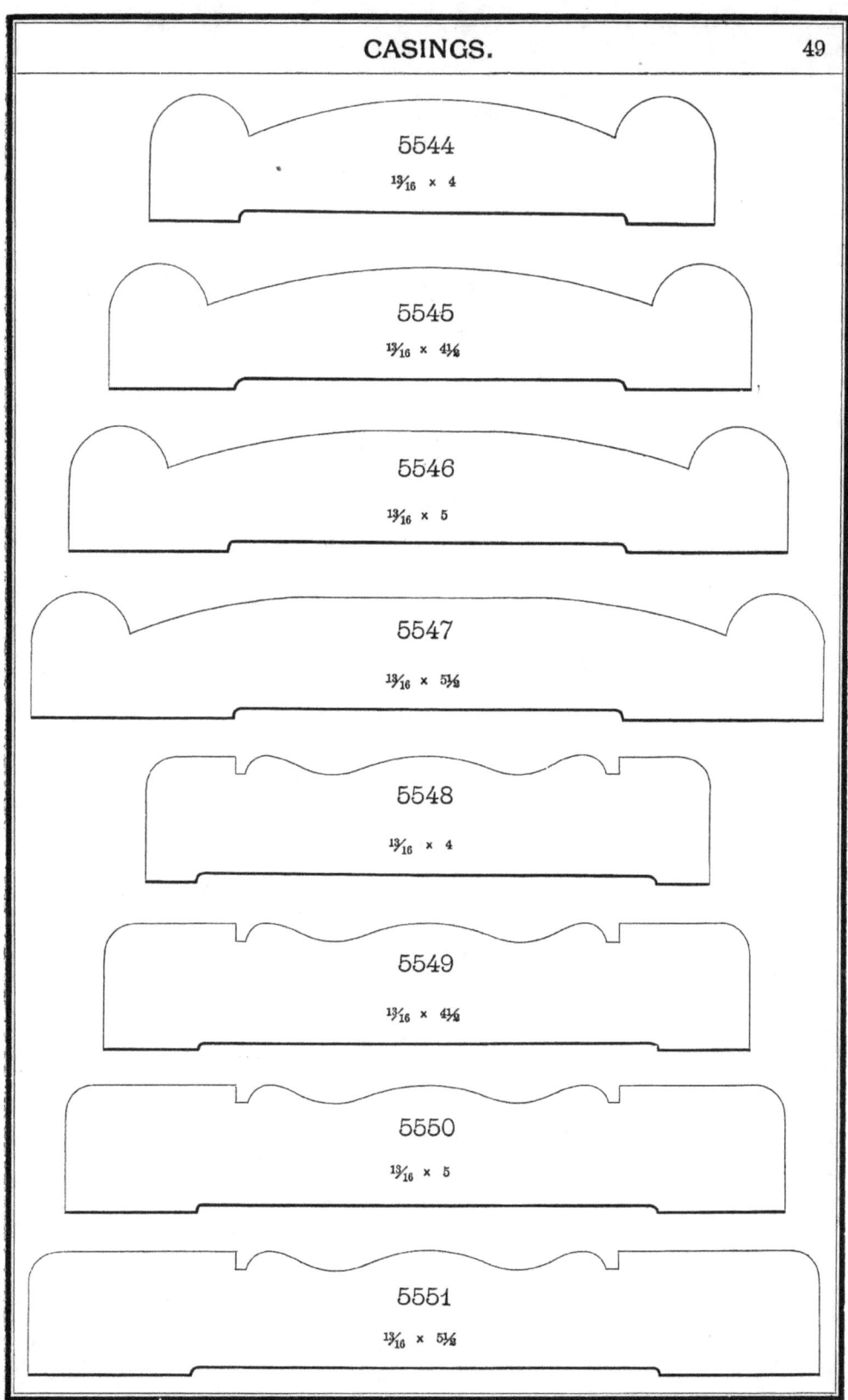

## CASINGS.

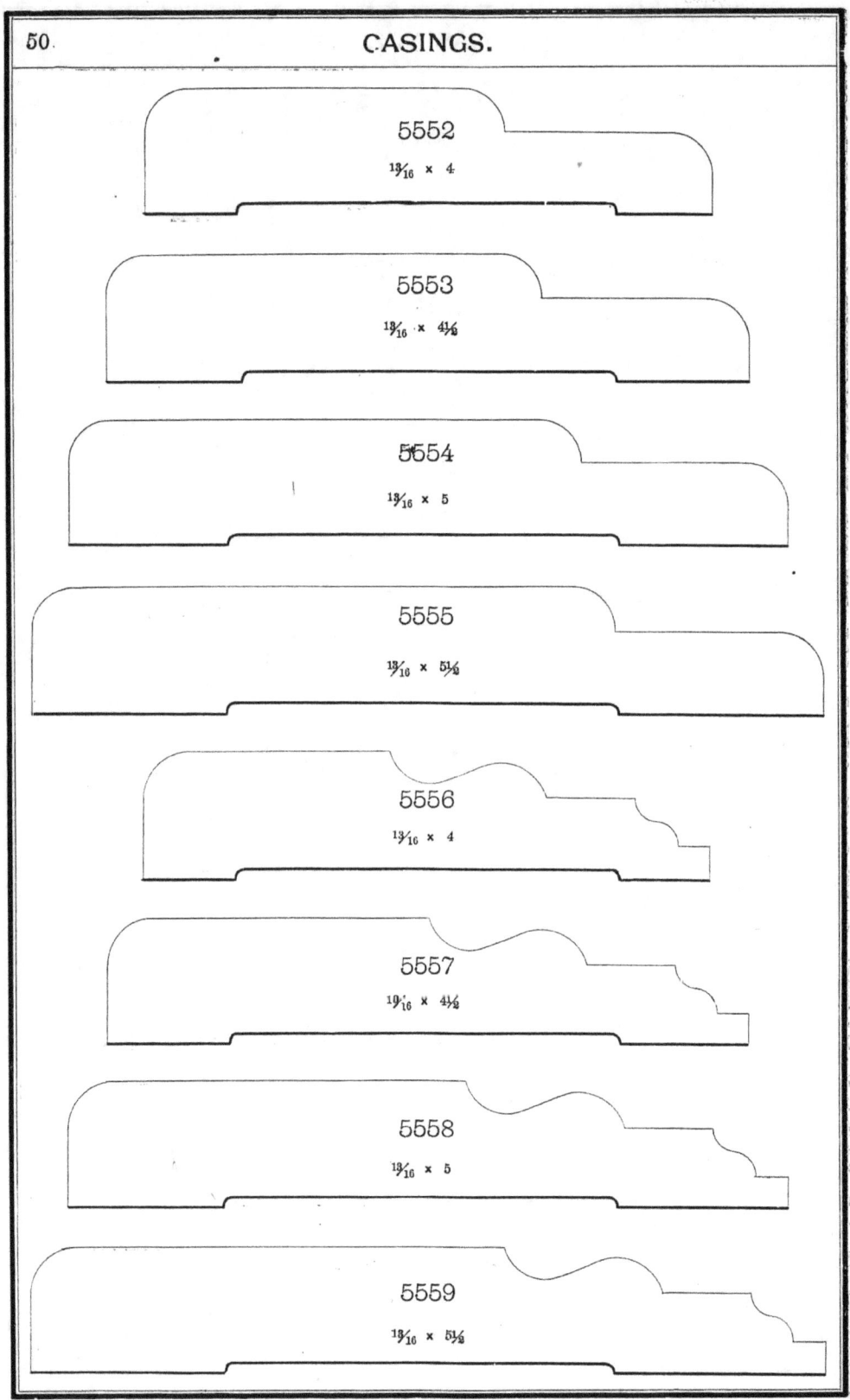

Mouldings made exact size of cuts. Figures represent the ripping width of Lumber.

## CASINGS.

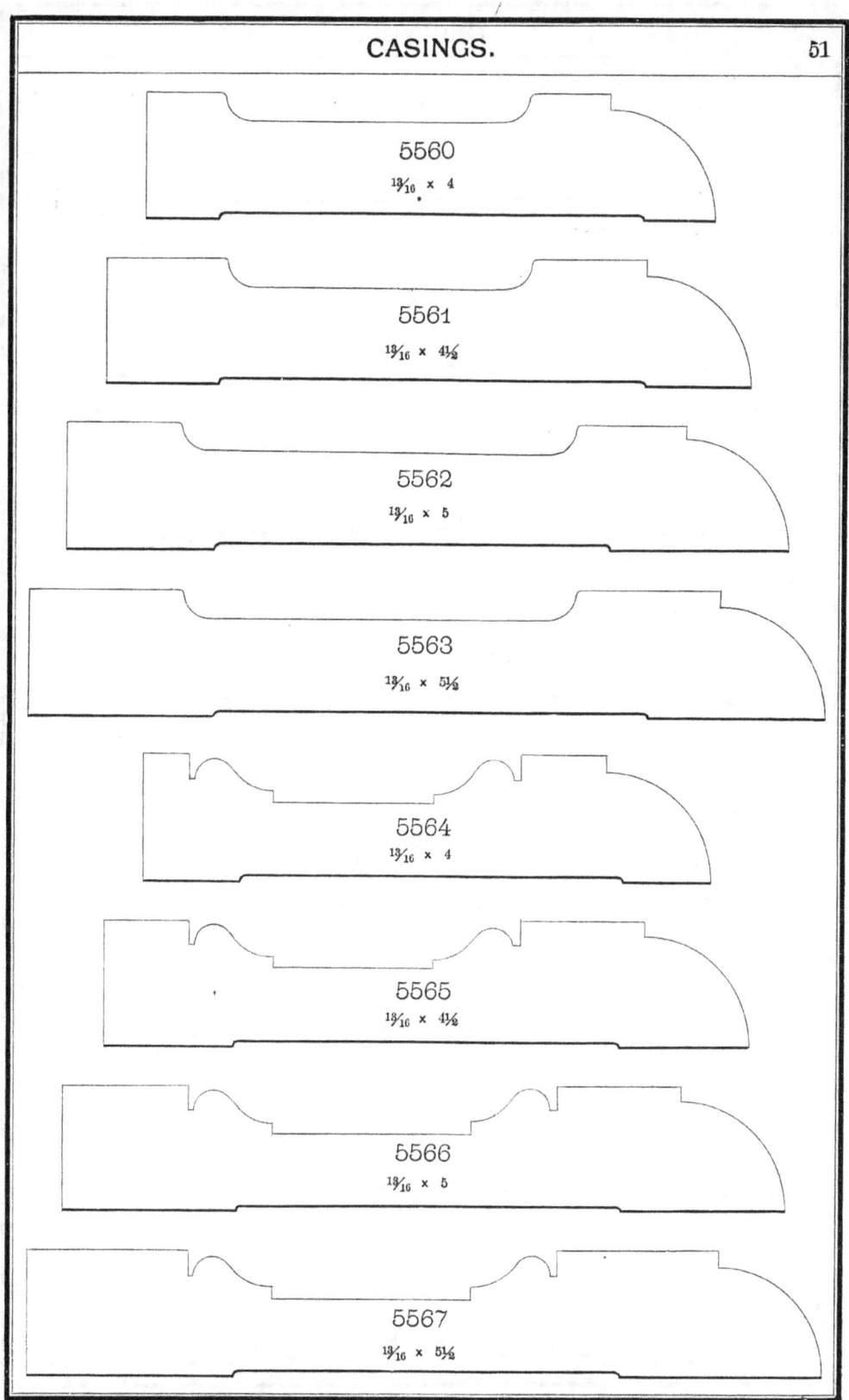

Mouldings made exact size of cuts. Figures represent the ripping width of Lumber.

## CASINGS.

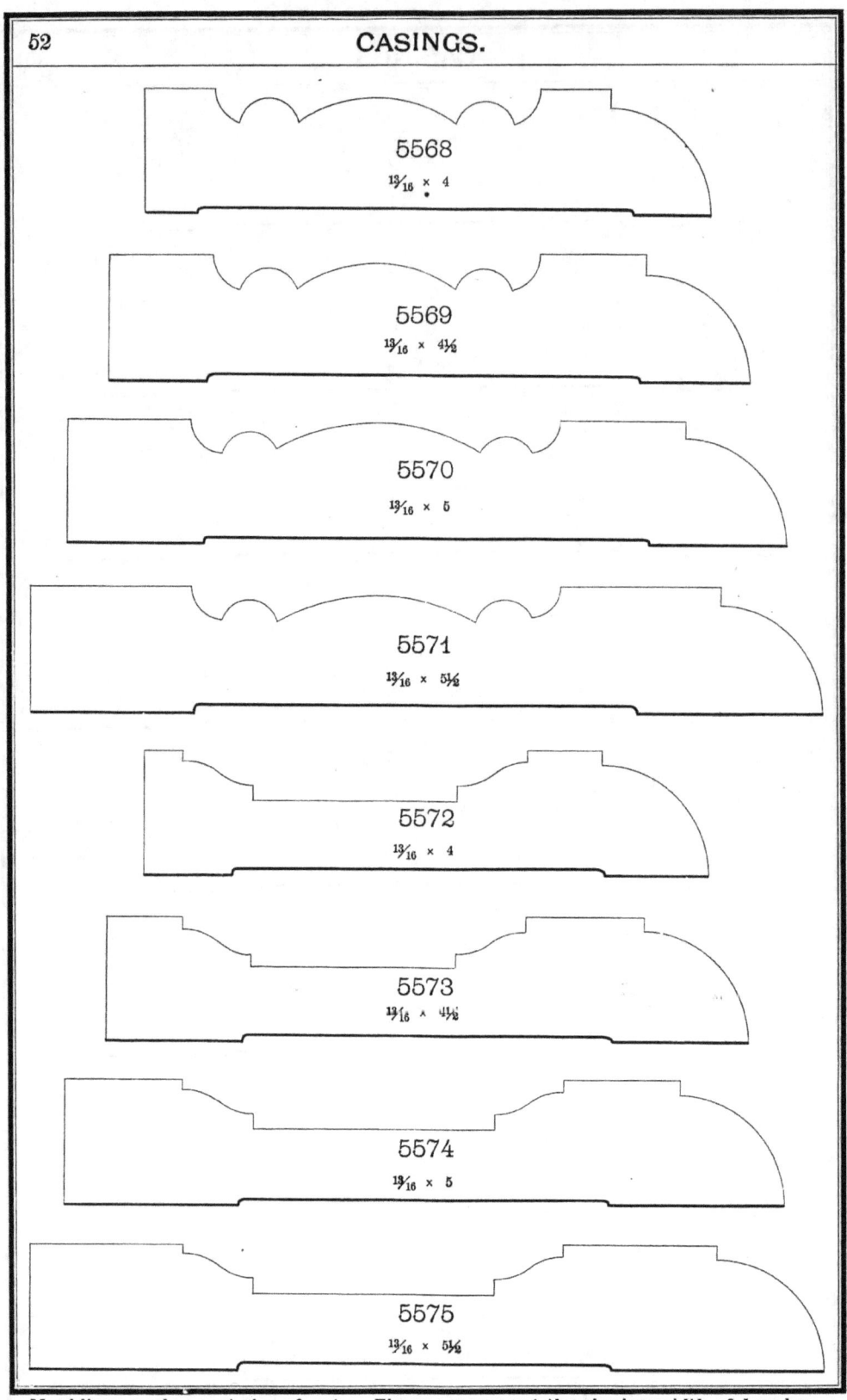

Mouldings made exact size of cuts. Figures represent the ripping width of Lumber.

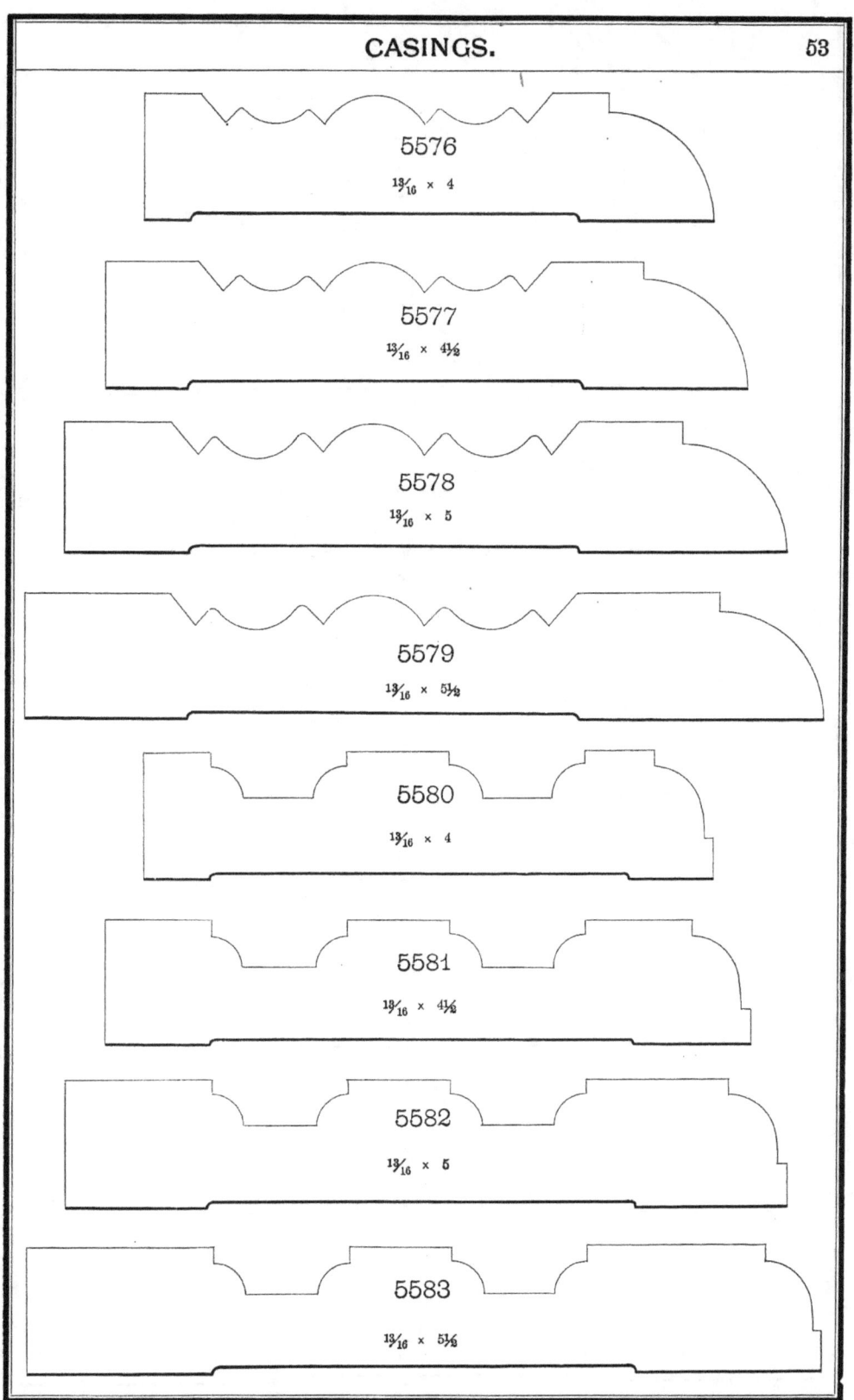

## CASINGS.

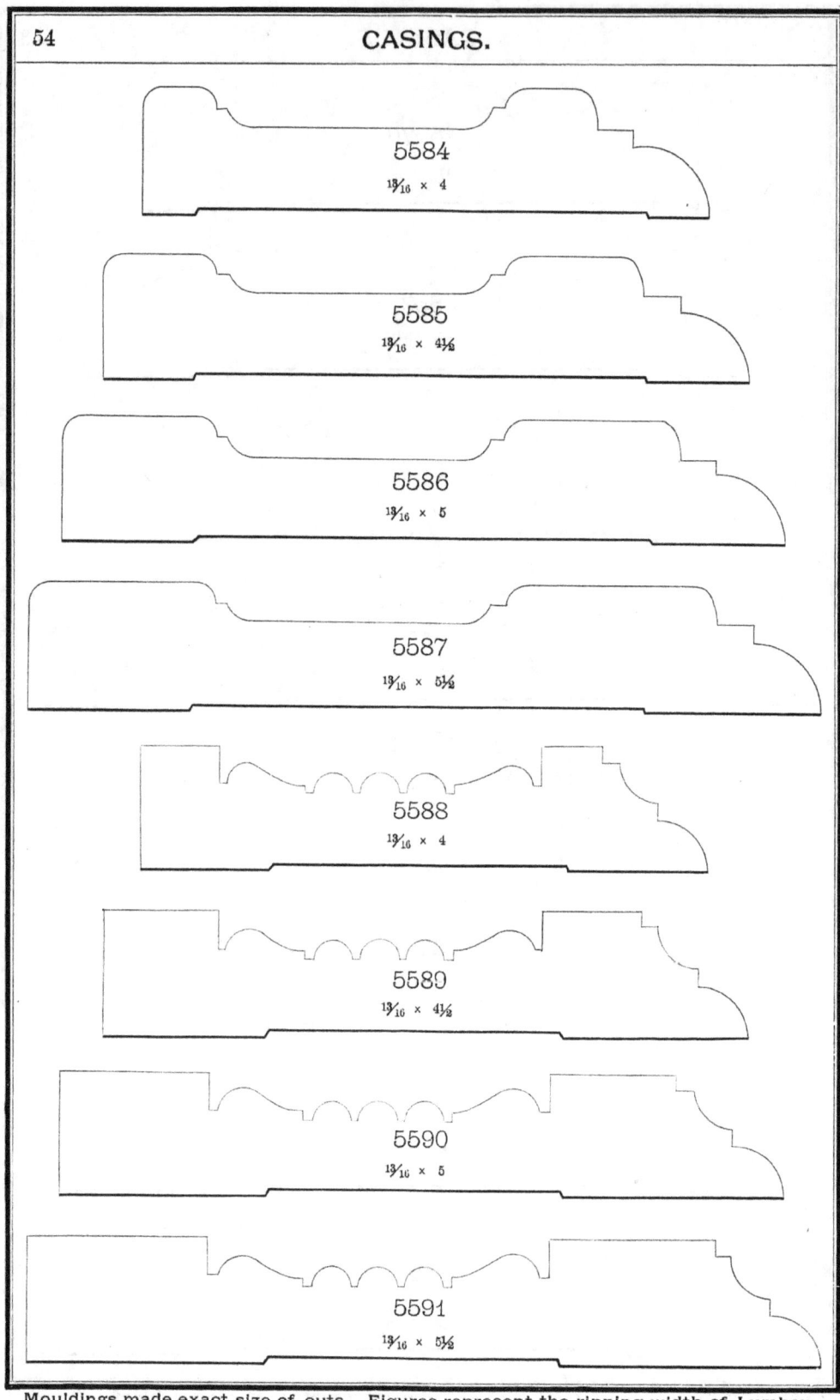

Mouldings made exact size of cuts. Figures represent the ripping width of Lumber.

# CASINGS.

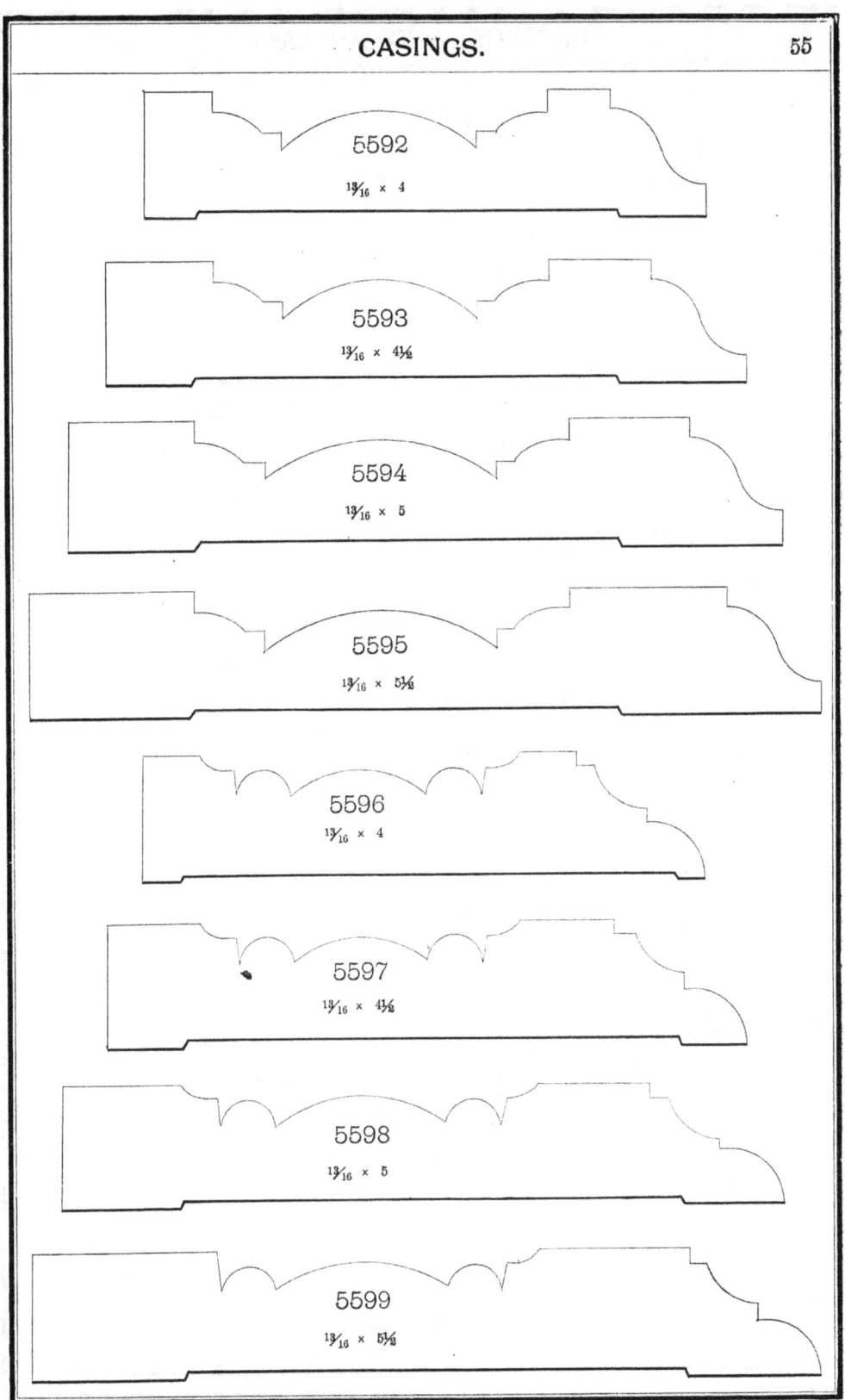

Mouldings made exact size of cuts. Figures represent the ripping width of Lumber.

## CASINGS AND APRONS.

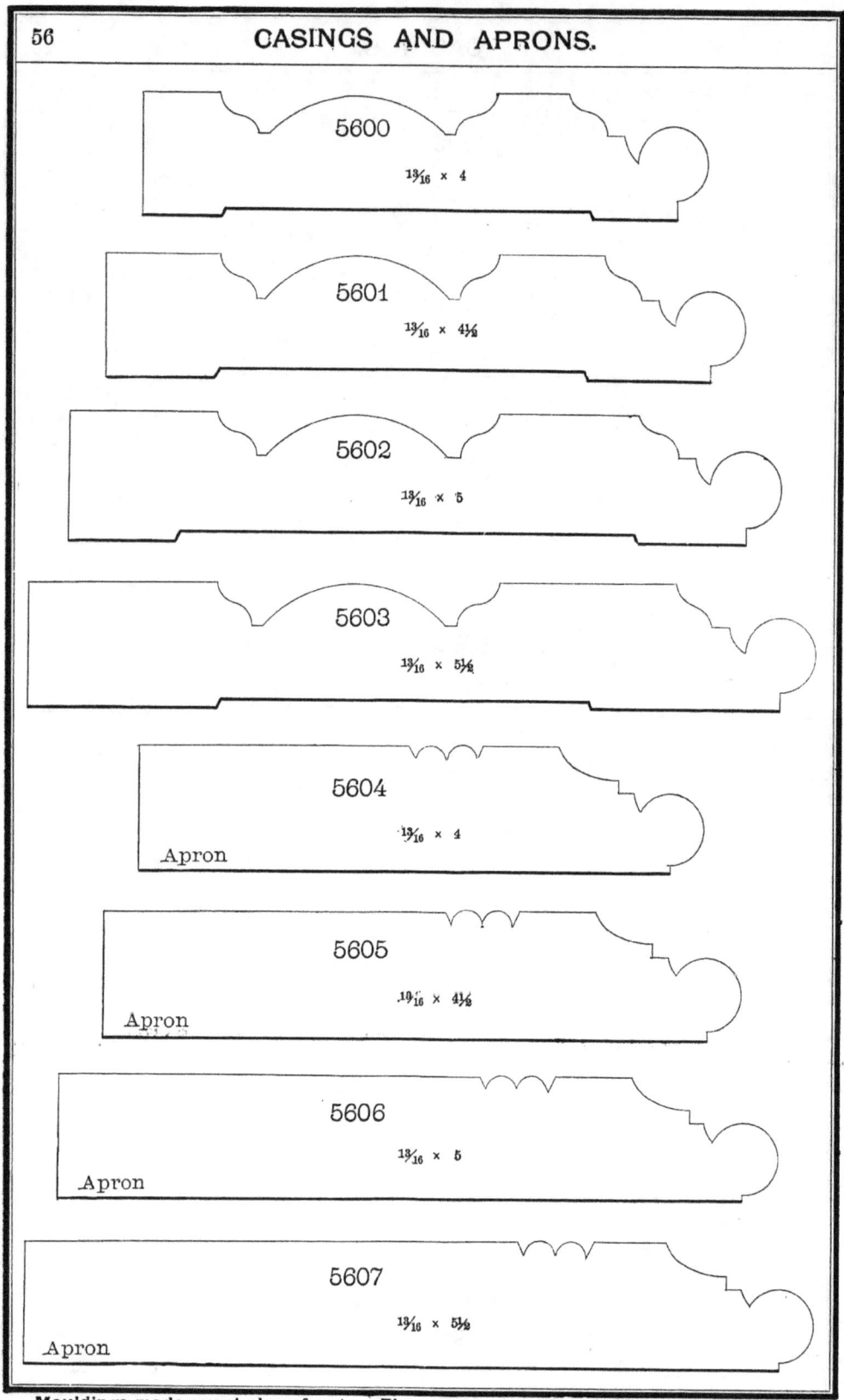

Mouldings made exact size of cuts. Figures represent the ripping width of Lumber.

# CASINGS.

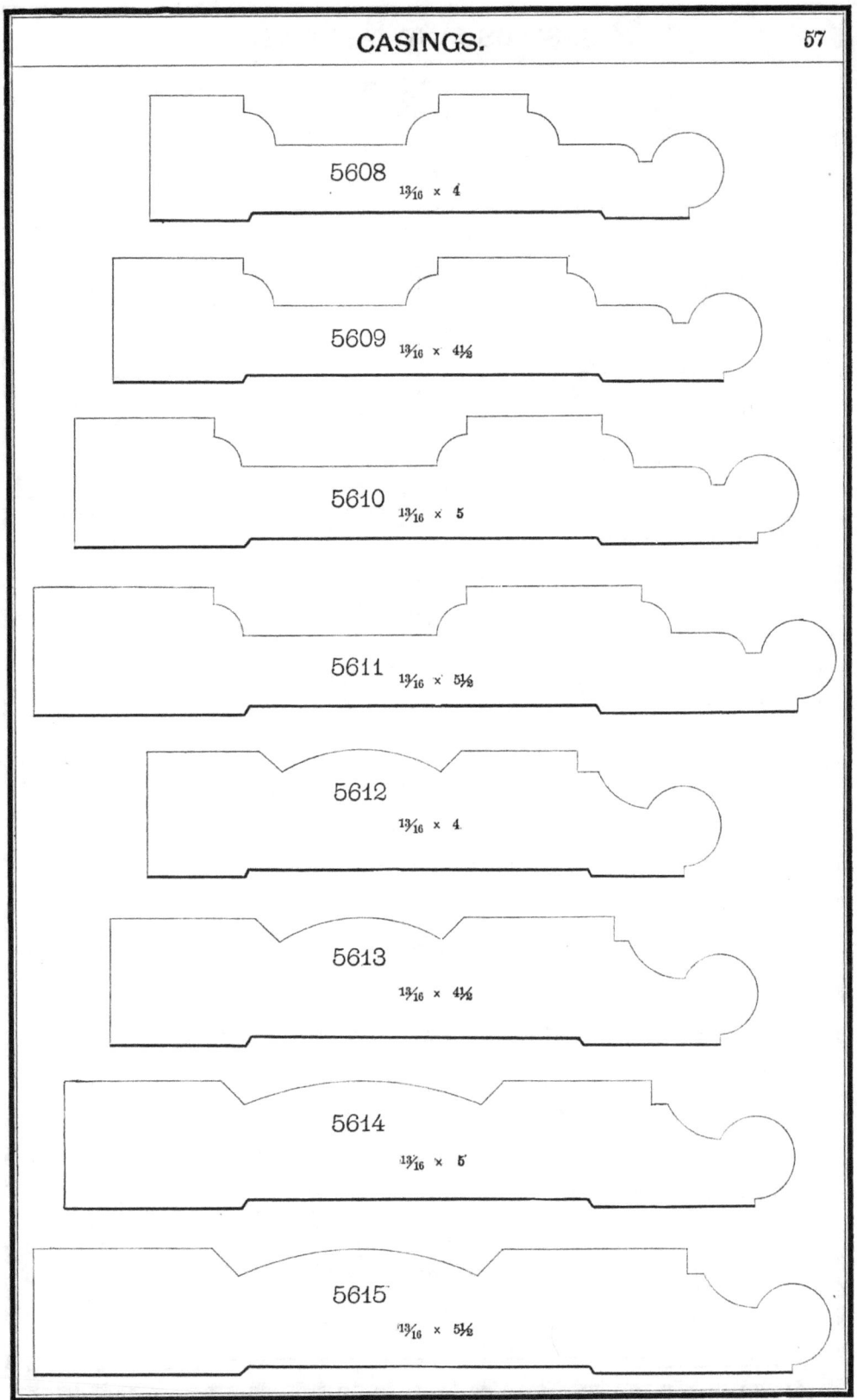

Mouldings made exact size of cuts. Figures represent the ripping width of Lumber.

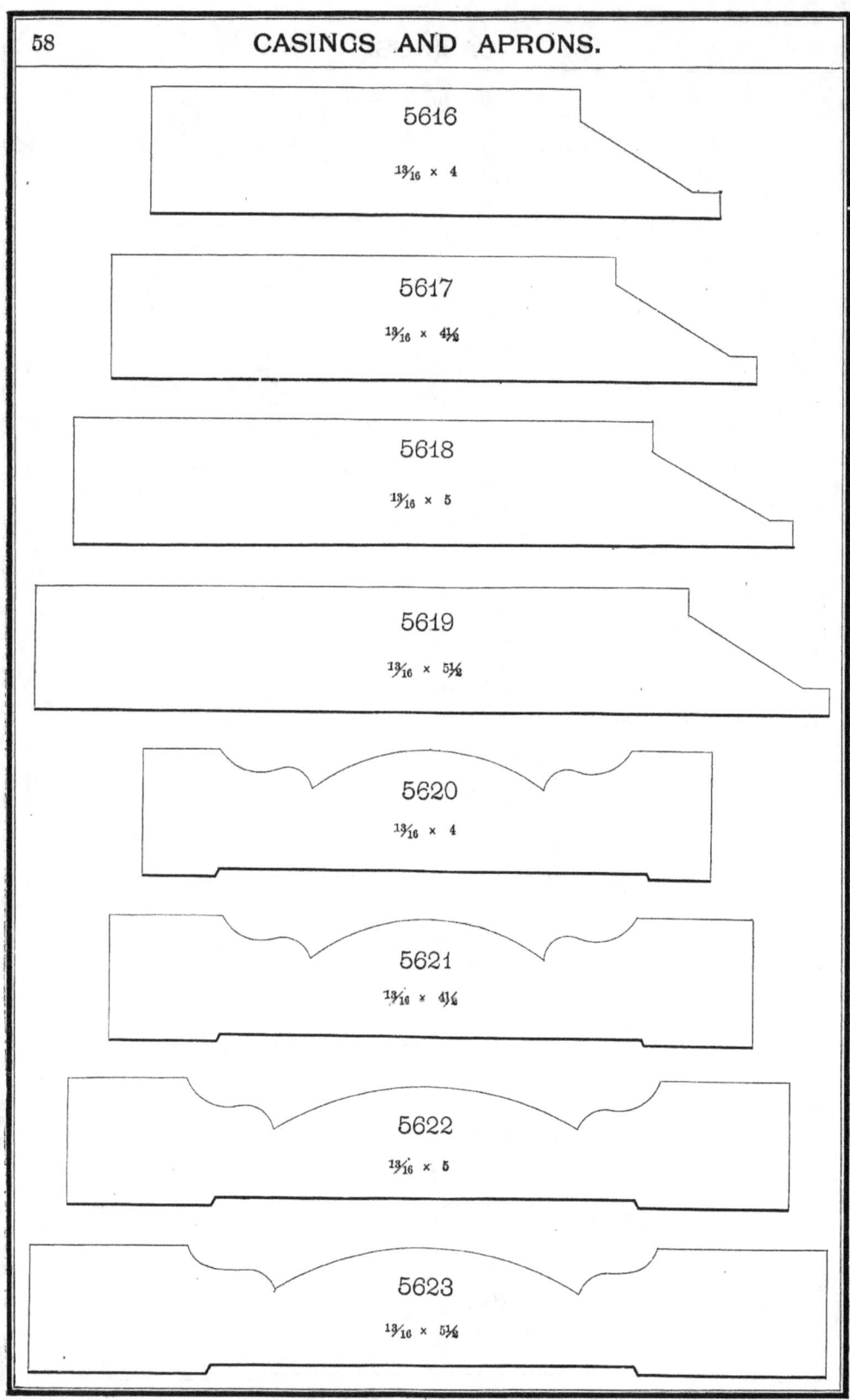

Mouldings made exact size of cuts. Figures represent the ripping width of Lumber.

# CASINGS.

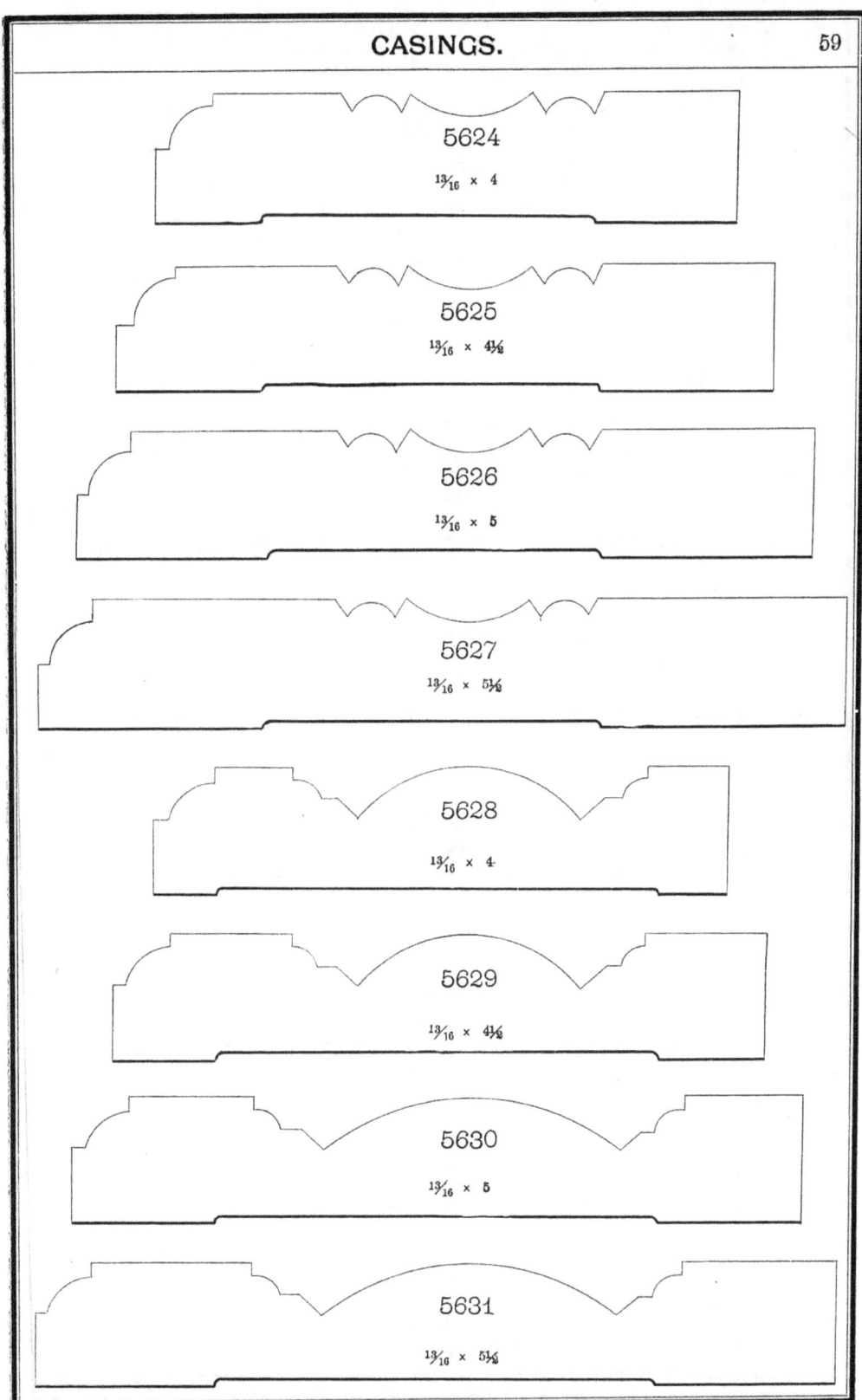

Mouldings made exact size of cuts. Figures represent the ripping width of Lumber.

# CASINGS.

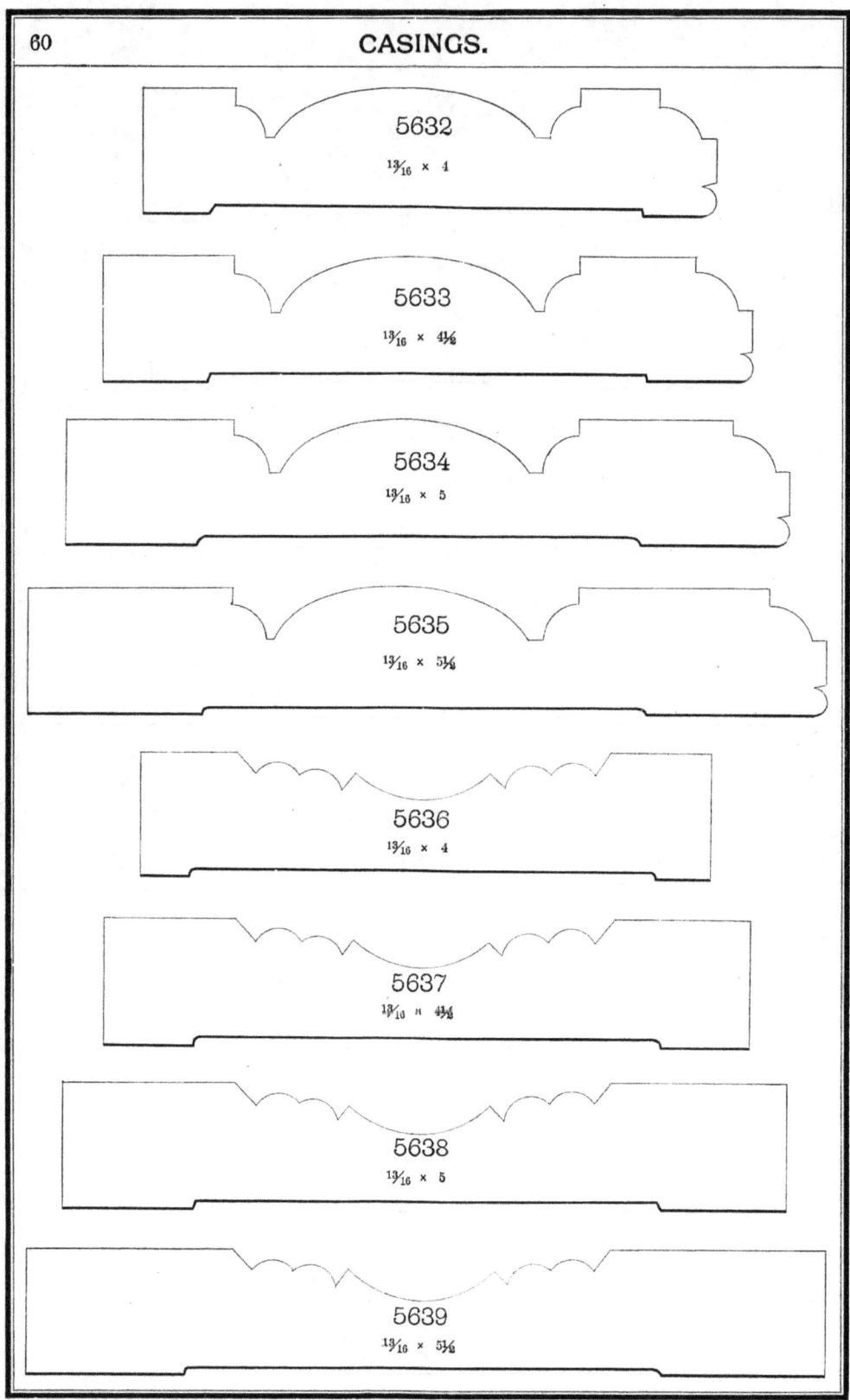

Mouldings made exact size of cuts.   Figures represent the ripping width of Lumber.

## CASINGS.

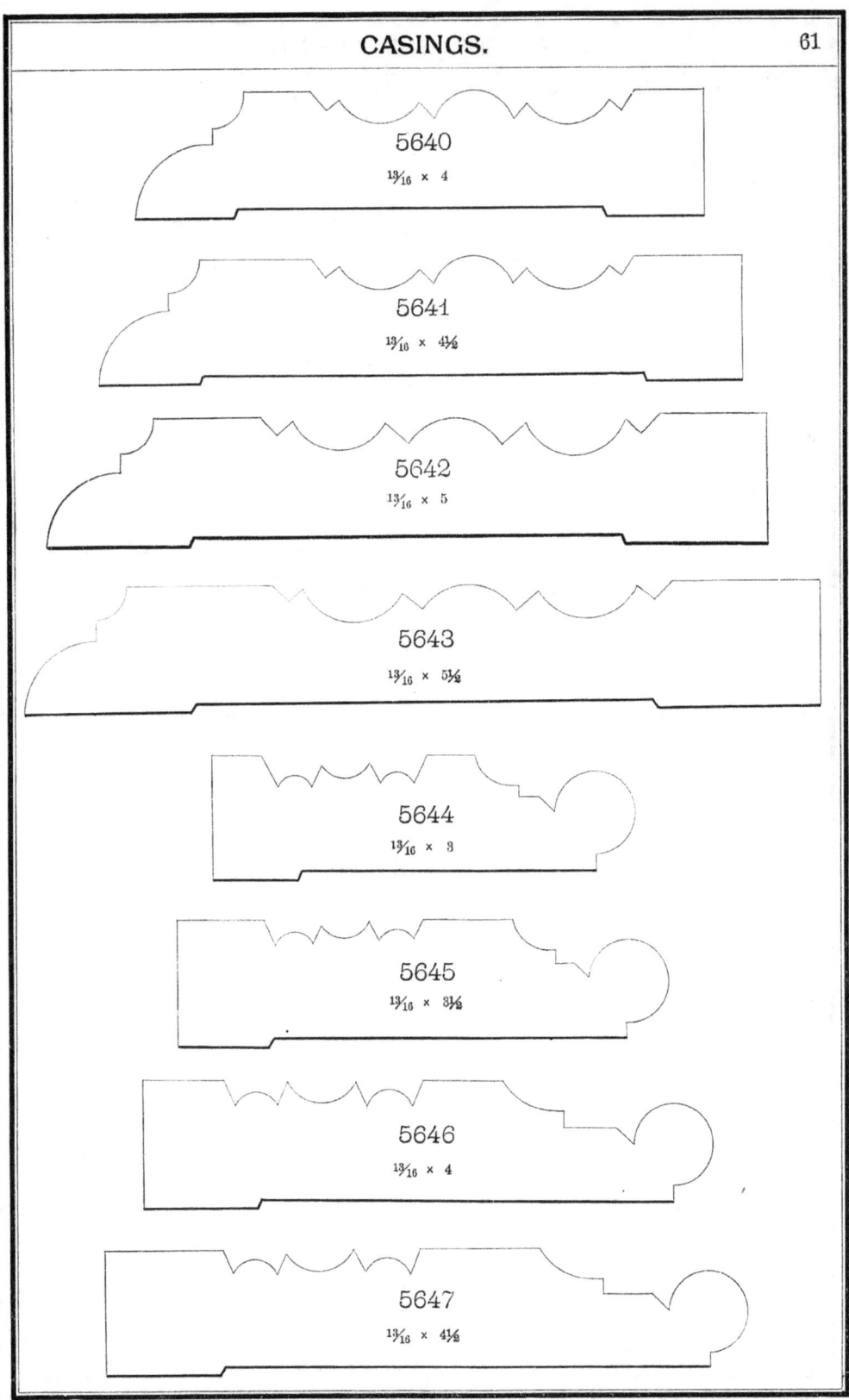

Mouldings made exact size of cuts. Figures represent the ripping width of Lumber.

## CASINGS AND APRONS.

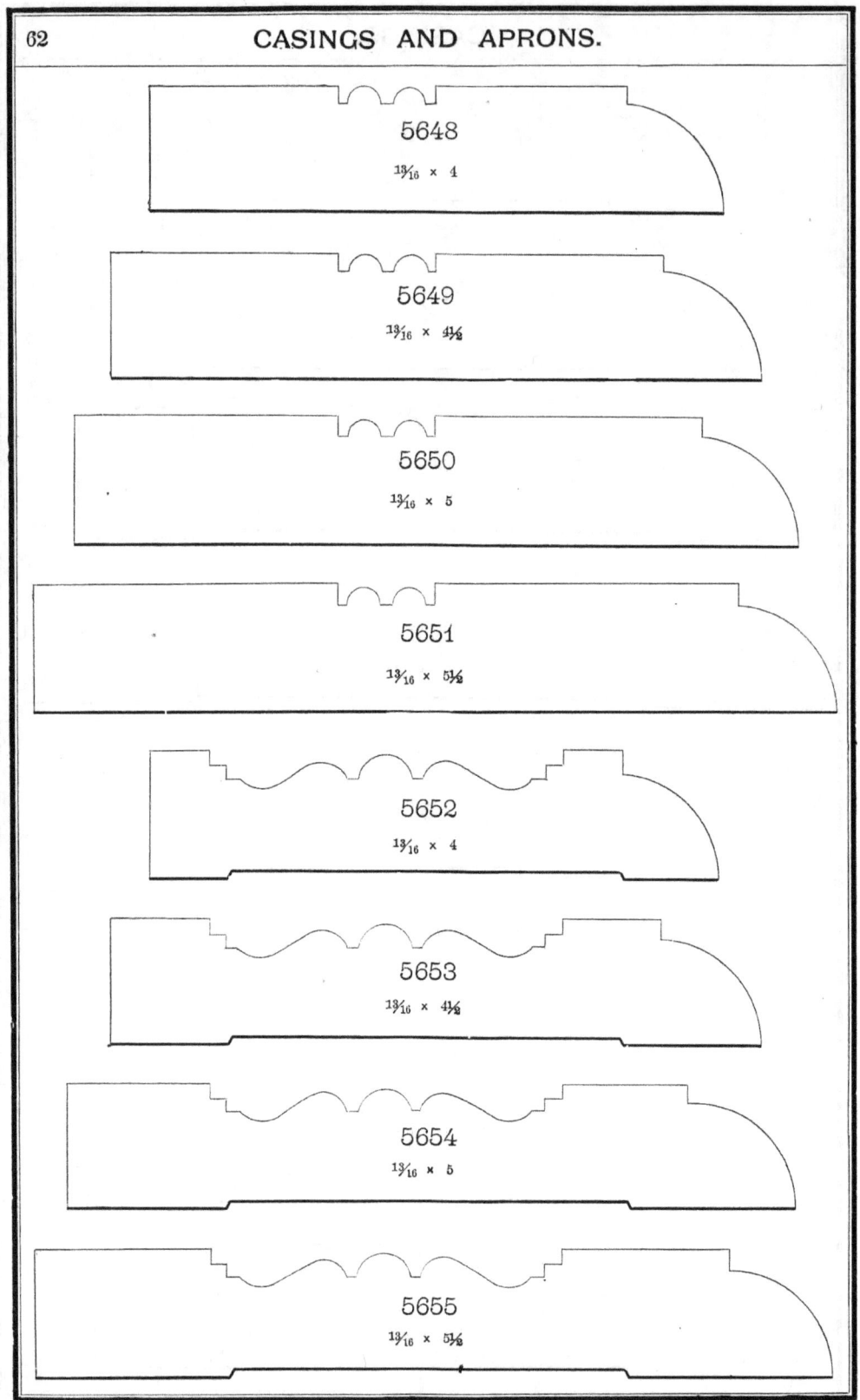

Mouldings made exact size of cuts. Figures represent the ripping width of Lumber.

## CASINGS.

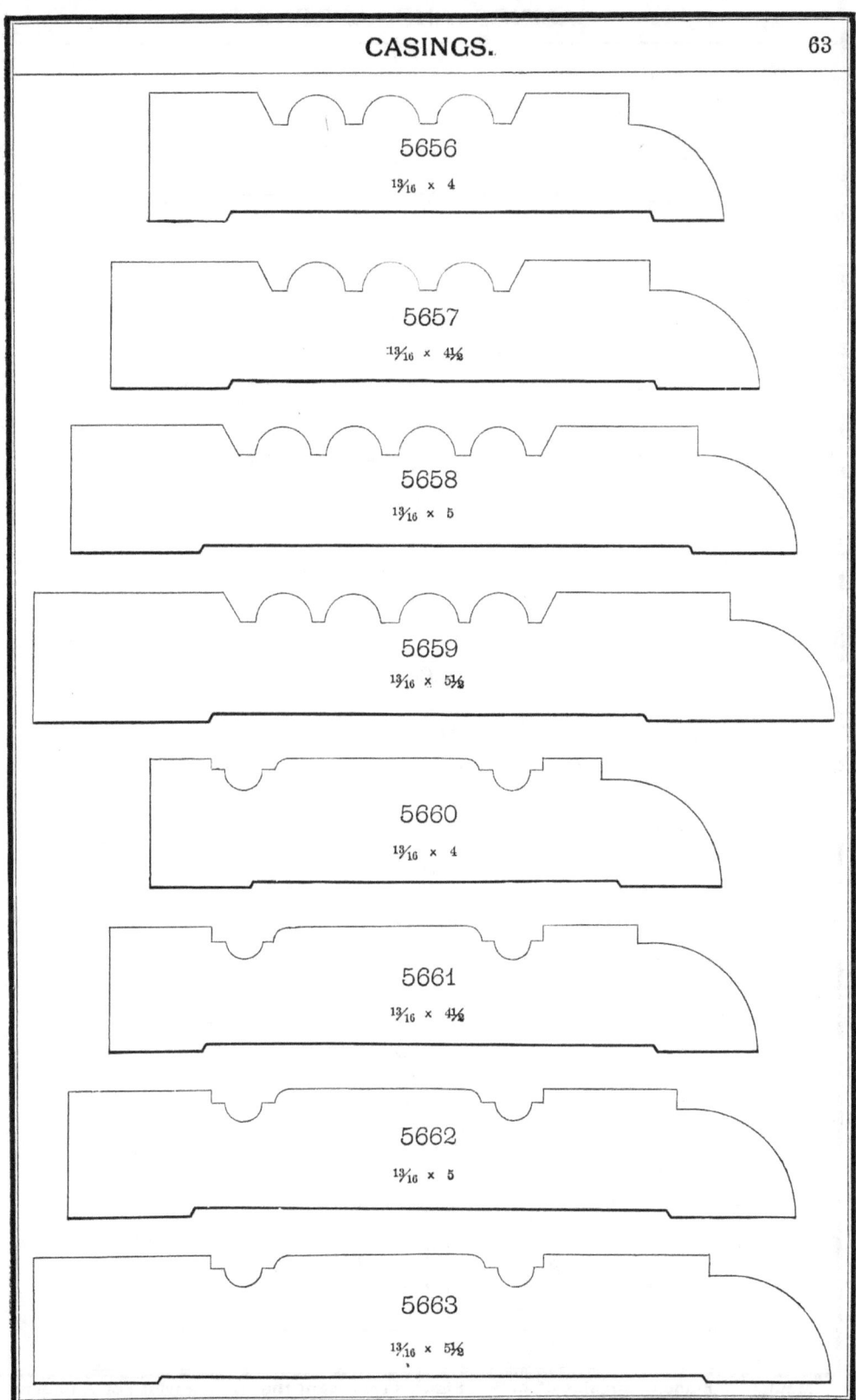

Mouldings made exact size of cuts. Figures represent the ripping width of Lumber.

## CASINGS AND APRONS.

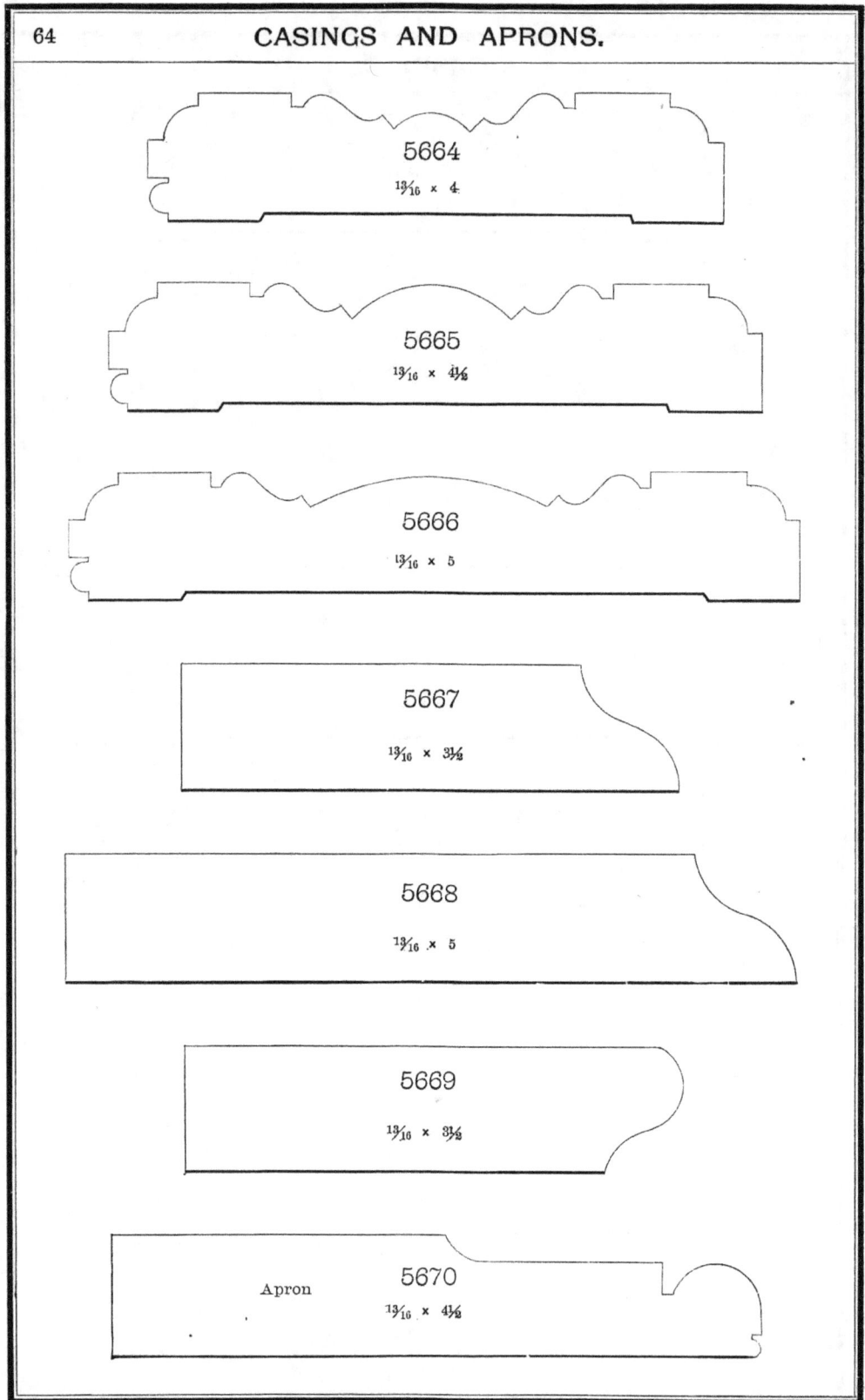

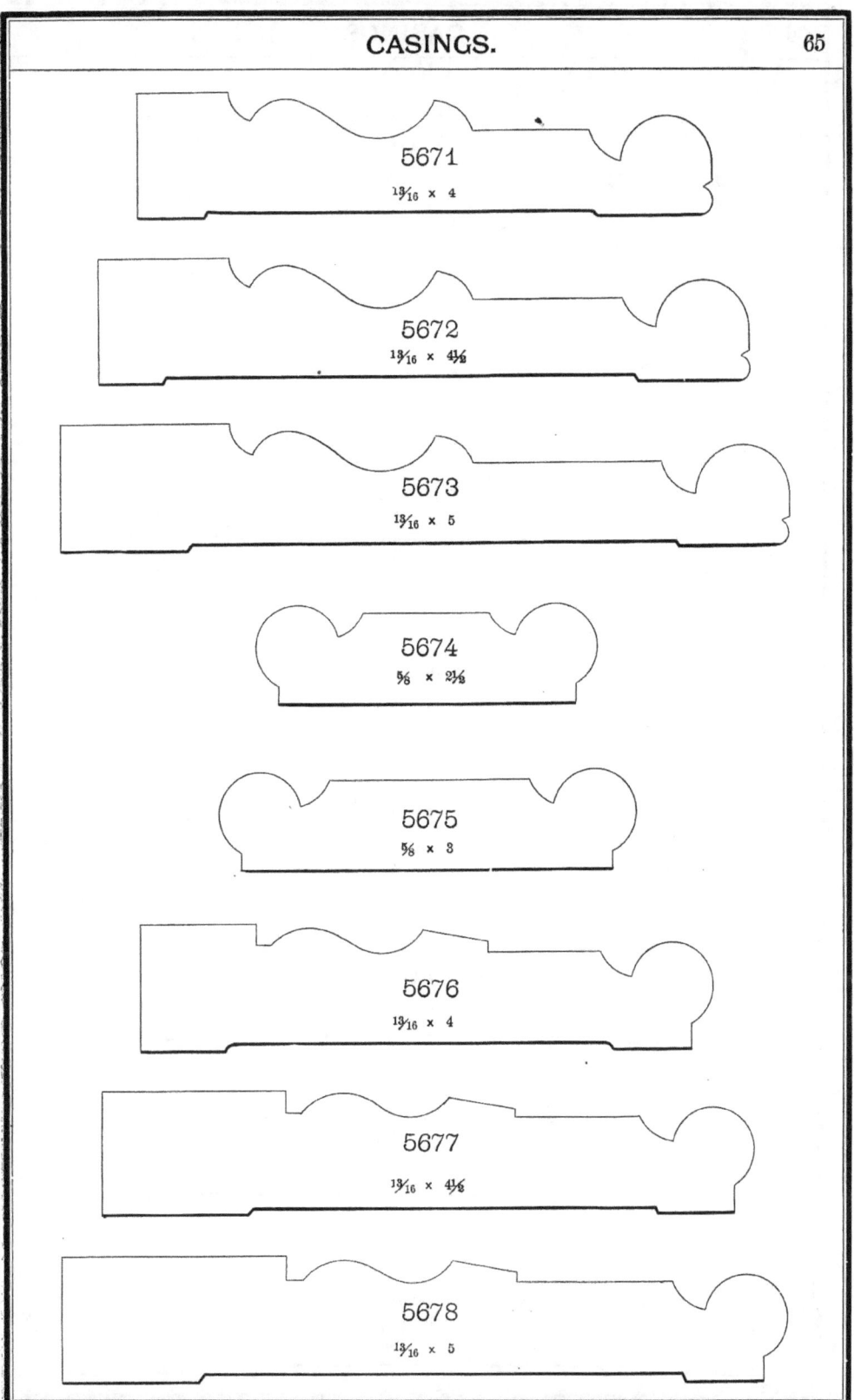

## CASINGS.

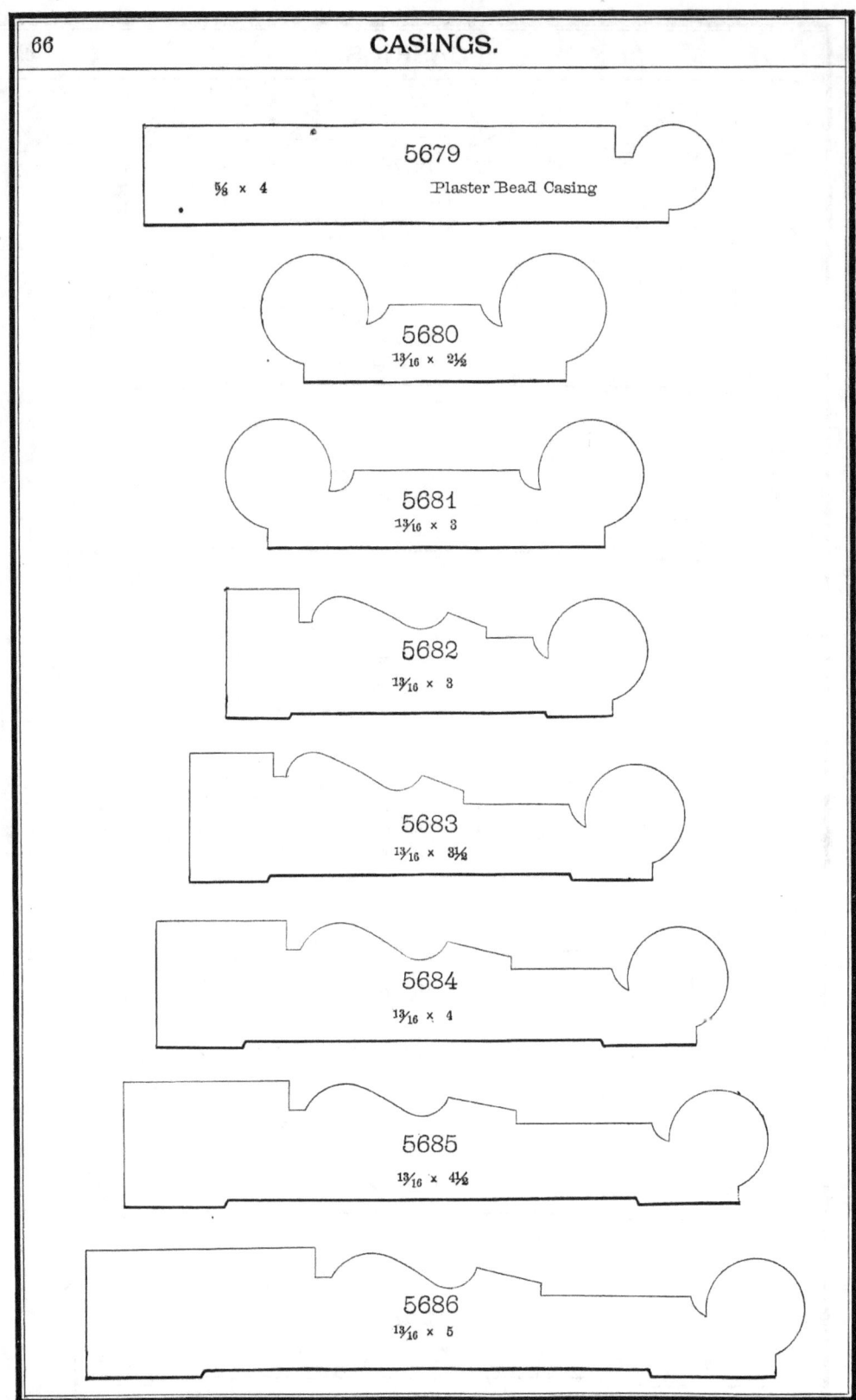

Mouldings made exact size of cuts. Figures represent the ripping width of Lumber.

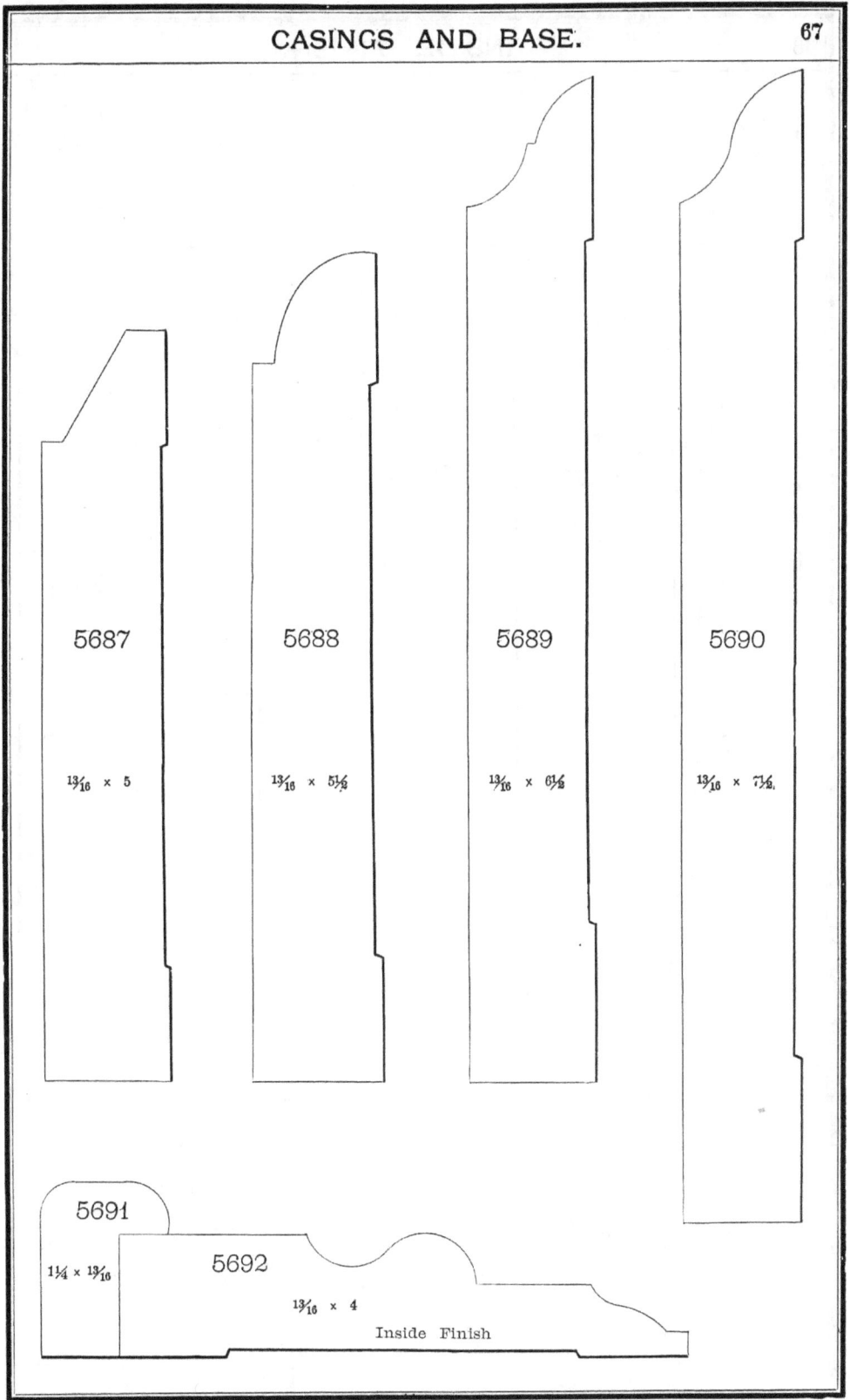

## INSIDE FINISH.

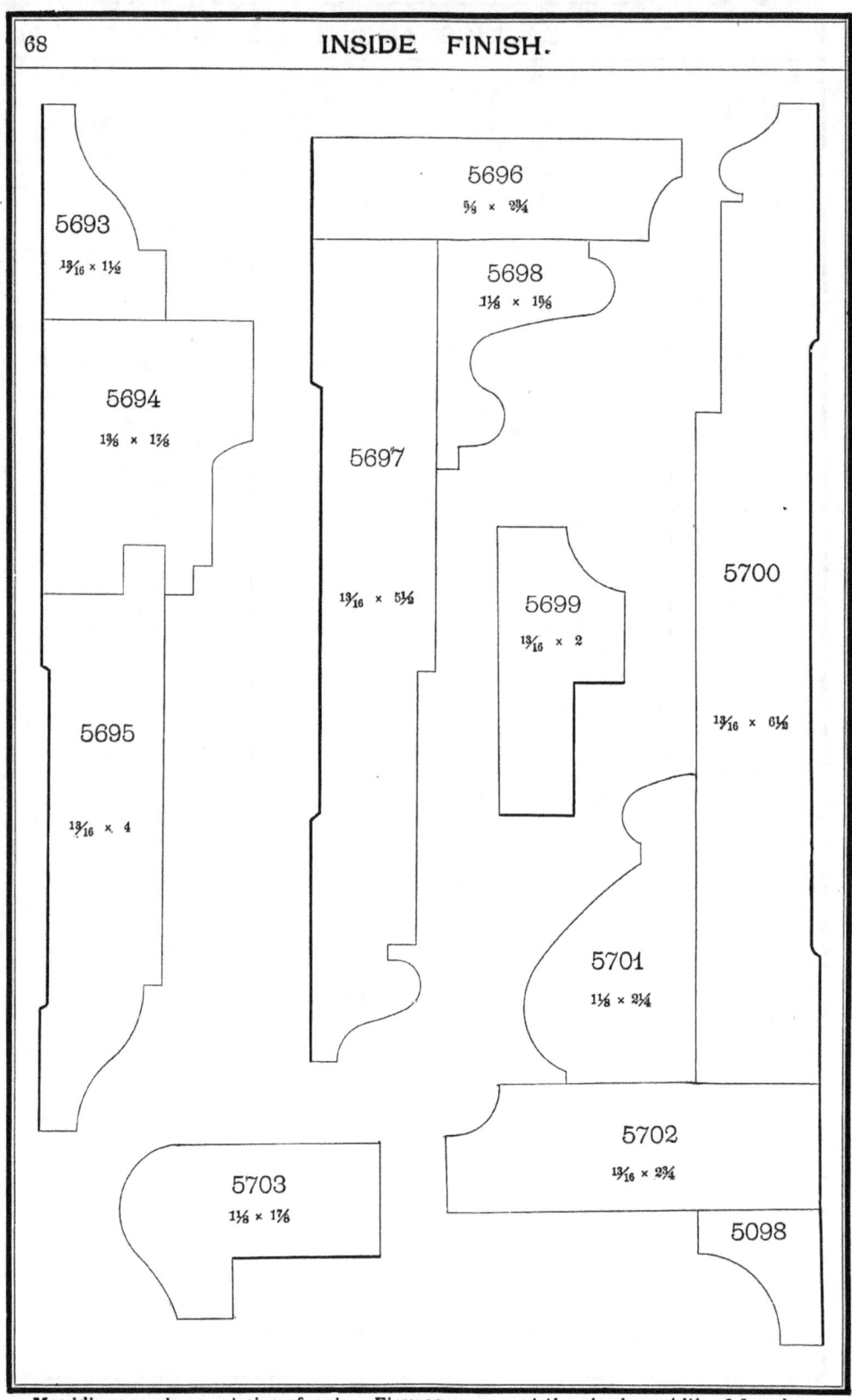

Mouldings made exact size of cuts. Figures represent the ripping width of Lumber.

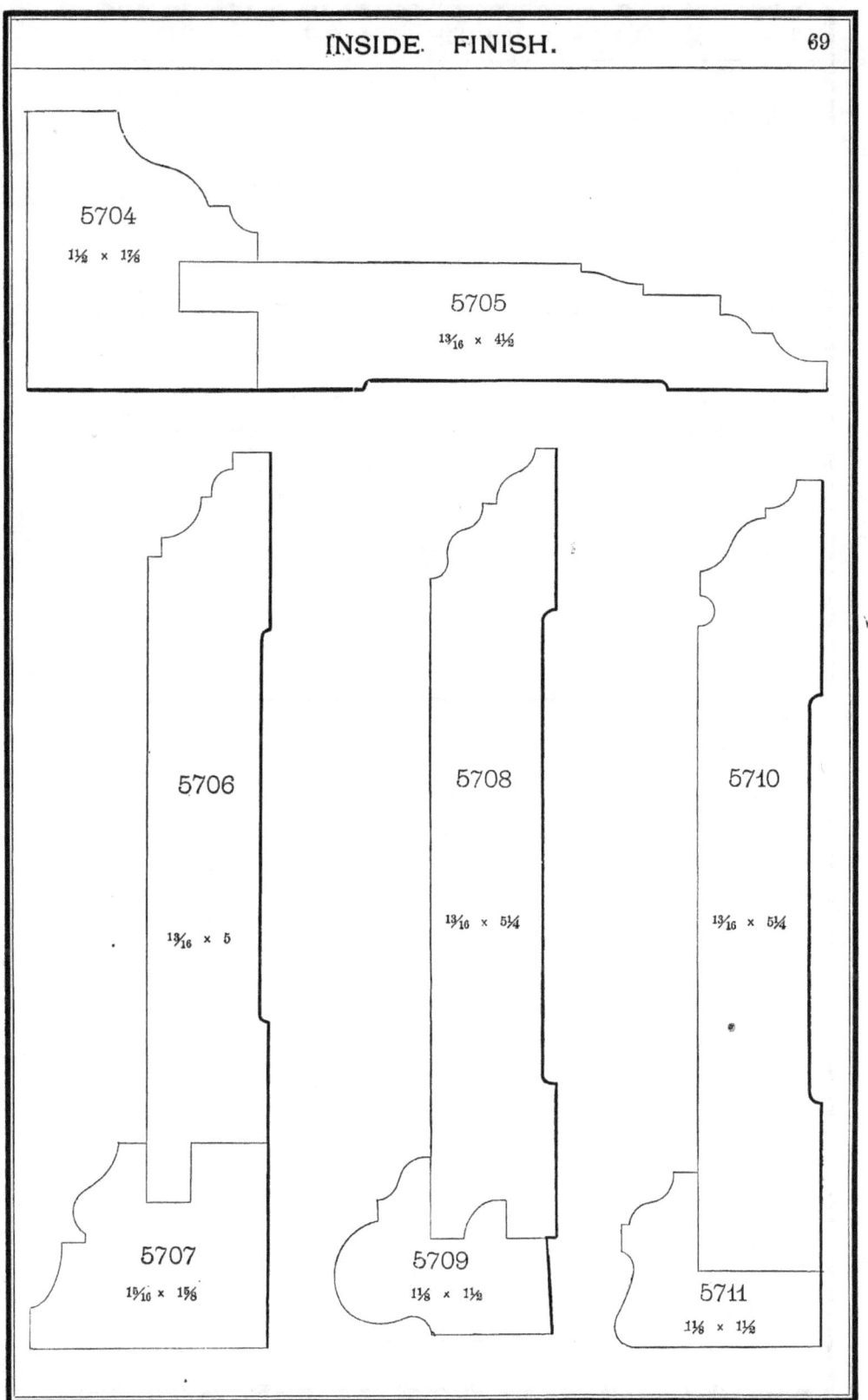

## INSIDE FINISH

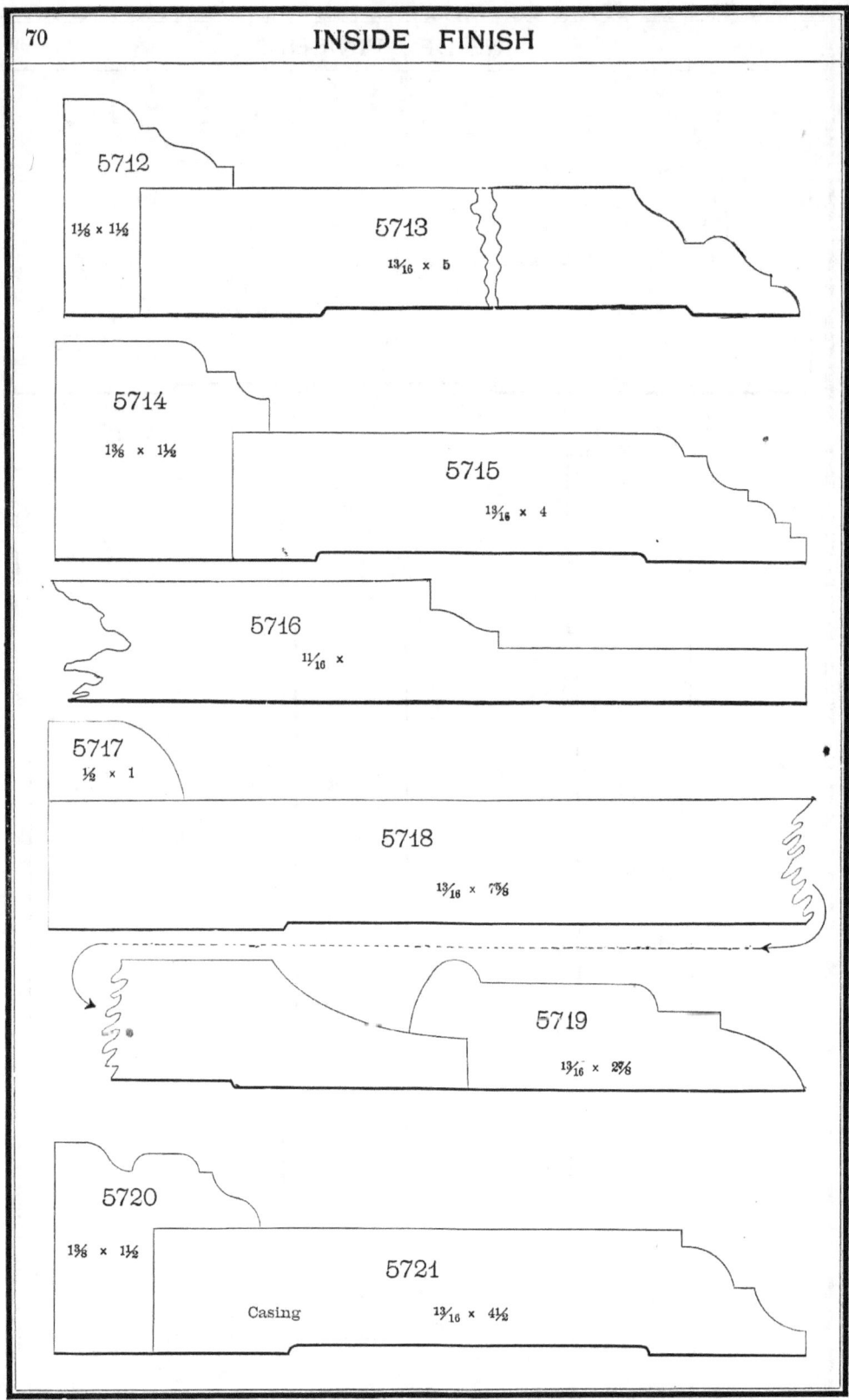

Mouldings made exact size of cuts. Figures represent the ripping width of Lumber.

# INSIDE FINISH.

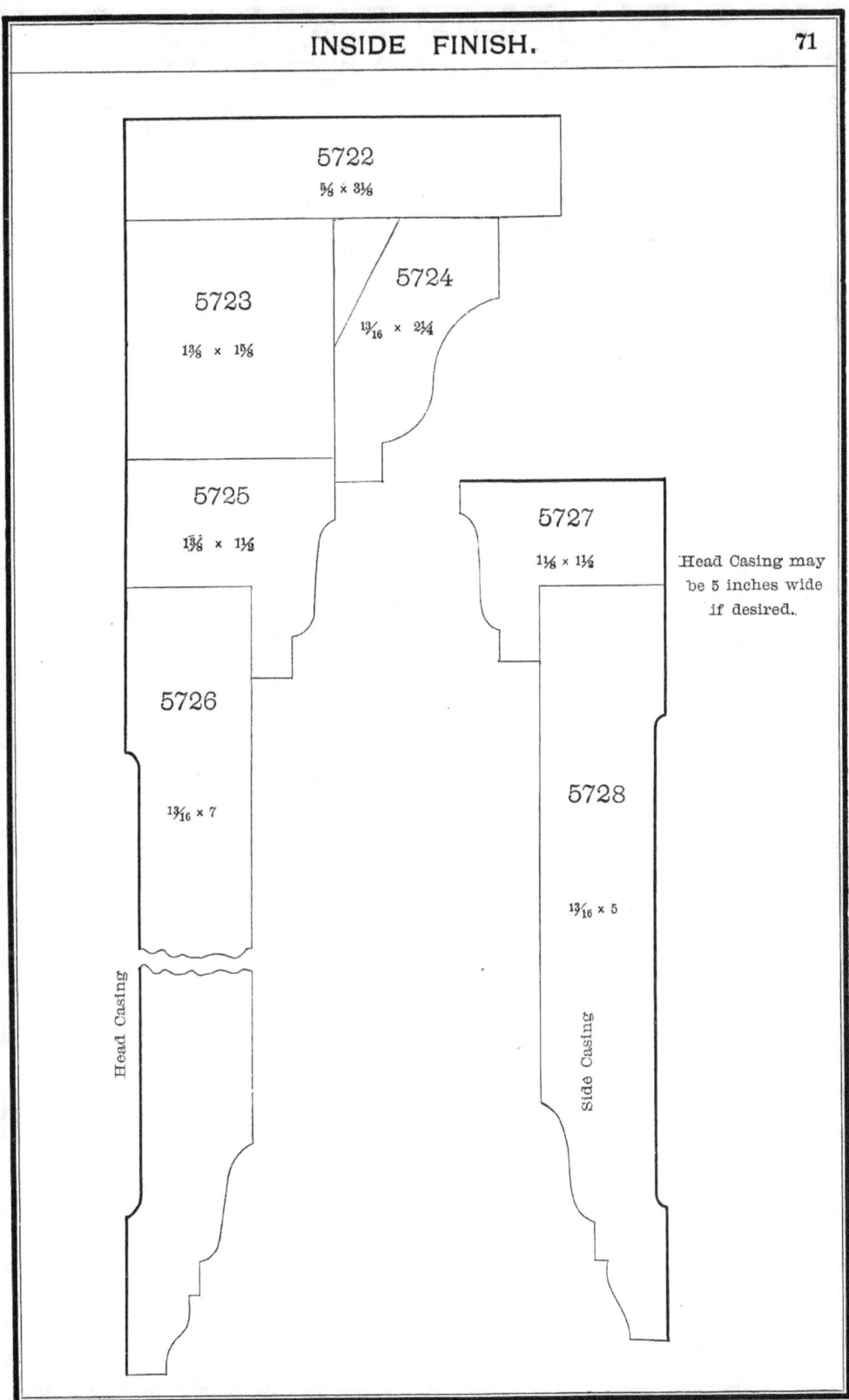

Mouldings made exact size of cuts.  Figures represent the ripping width of Lumber.

## INSIDE FINISH.

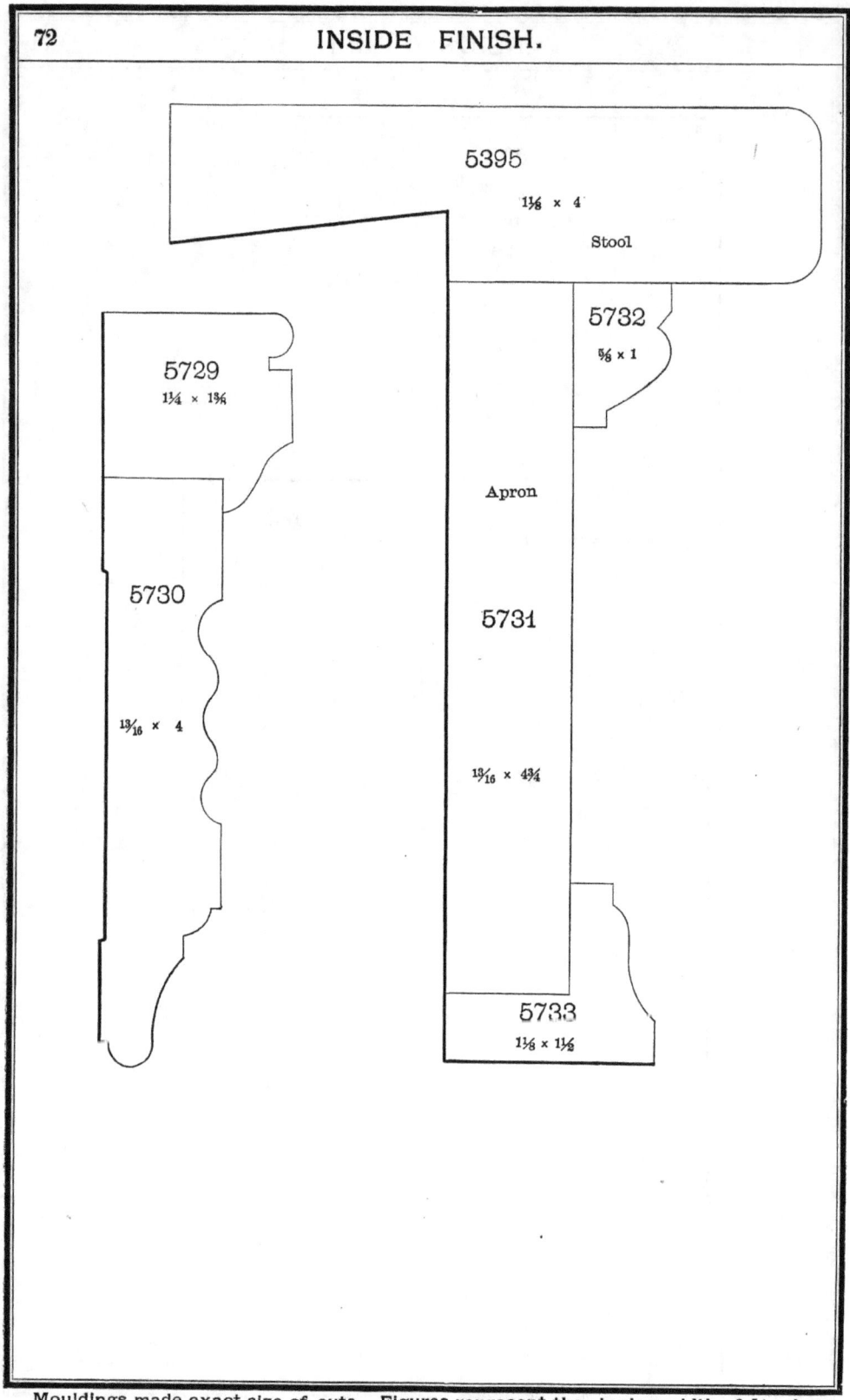

Mouldings made exact size of cuts. Figures represent the ripping width of Lumber.

# BASE.

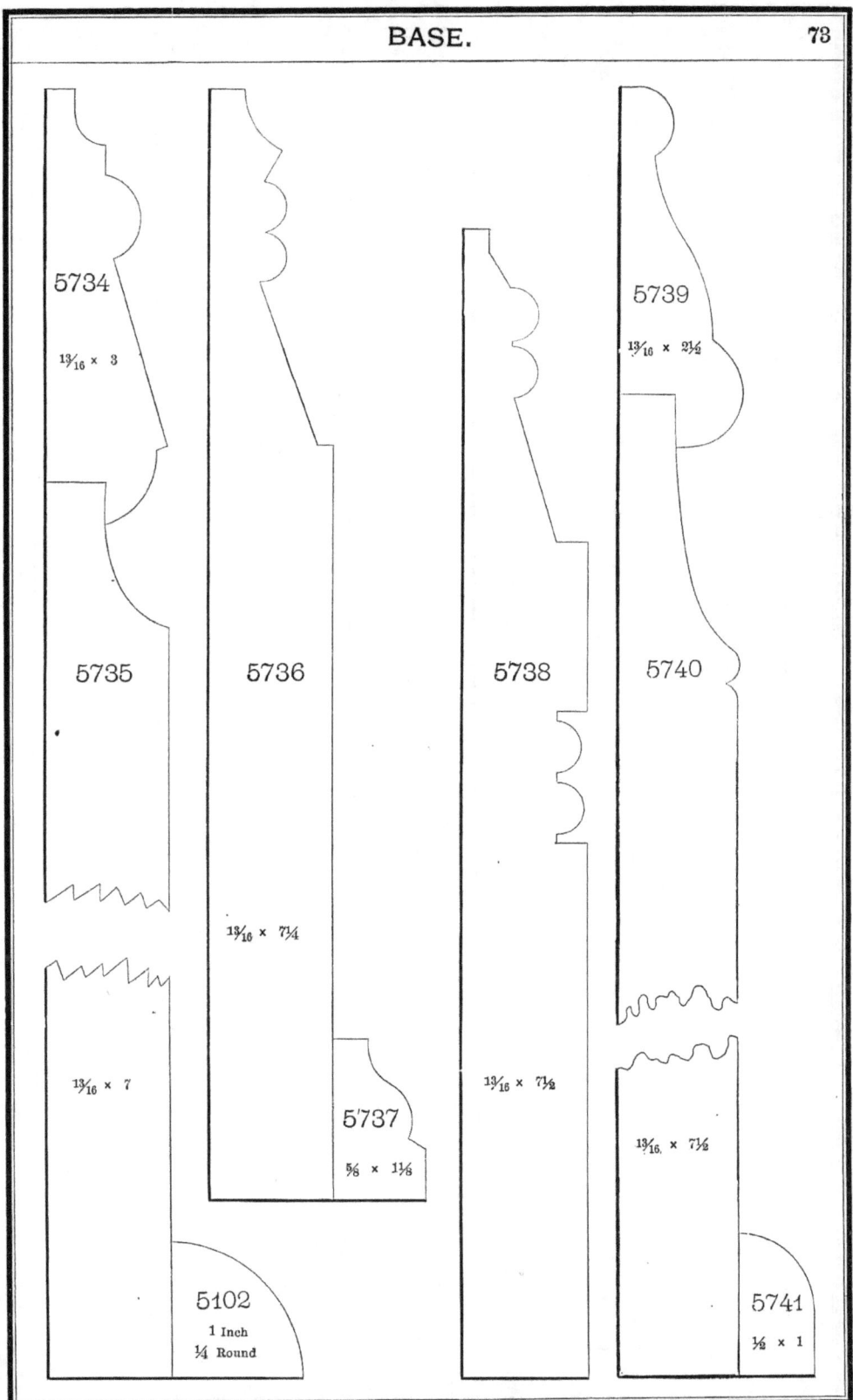

Mouldings made exact size of cuts. Figures represent the ripping width of Lumber.

## BASE.

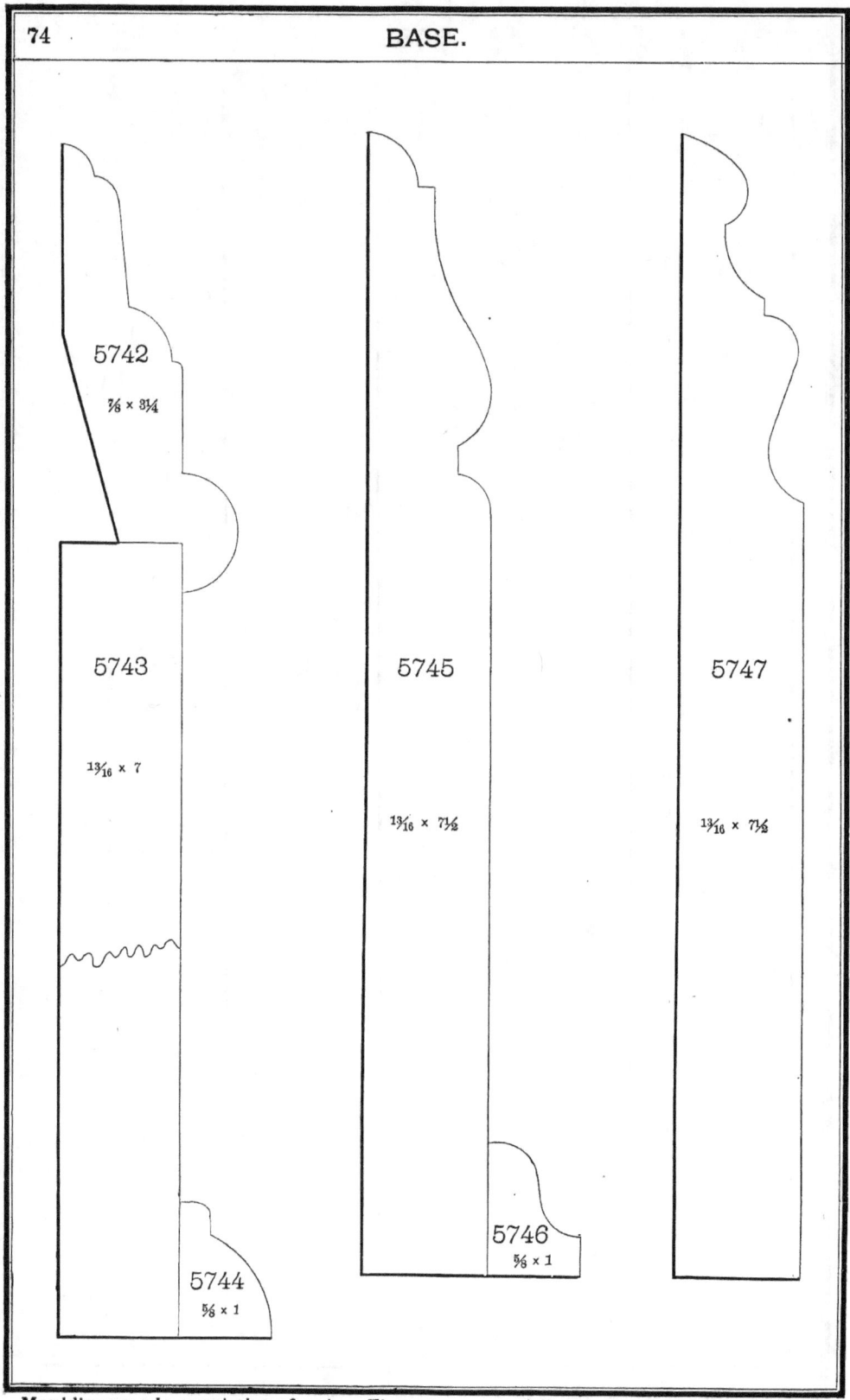

Mouldings made exact size of cuts. Figures represent the ripping width of Lumber.

## BASES, EXTENSION WINDOW JAMBS. 75

5748—13/16 x 6
5749—13/16 x 7
5750—13/16 x 8

5751—13/16 x 6
5752—13/16 x 7
5753—13/16 x 8

5754—13/16 x 6
5755—13/16 x 7
5756—13/16 x 8

5757—13/16 x 6
5758—13/16 x 7
5759—13/16 x 8

5760—13/16 x 6
5761—13/16 x 7
5762—13/16 x 8

5763—13/16 x 6
5764—13/16 x 7
5765—13/16 x 8

Plain Window Jambs

5766—13/16 x 4½
5767—13/16 x 5

5768—13/16 x 4½
5769—13/16 x 5

Mouldings made exact size of cuts. Figures represent the ripping width of Lumber.

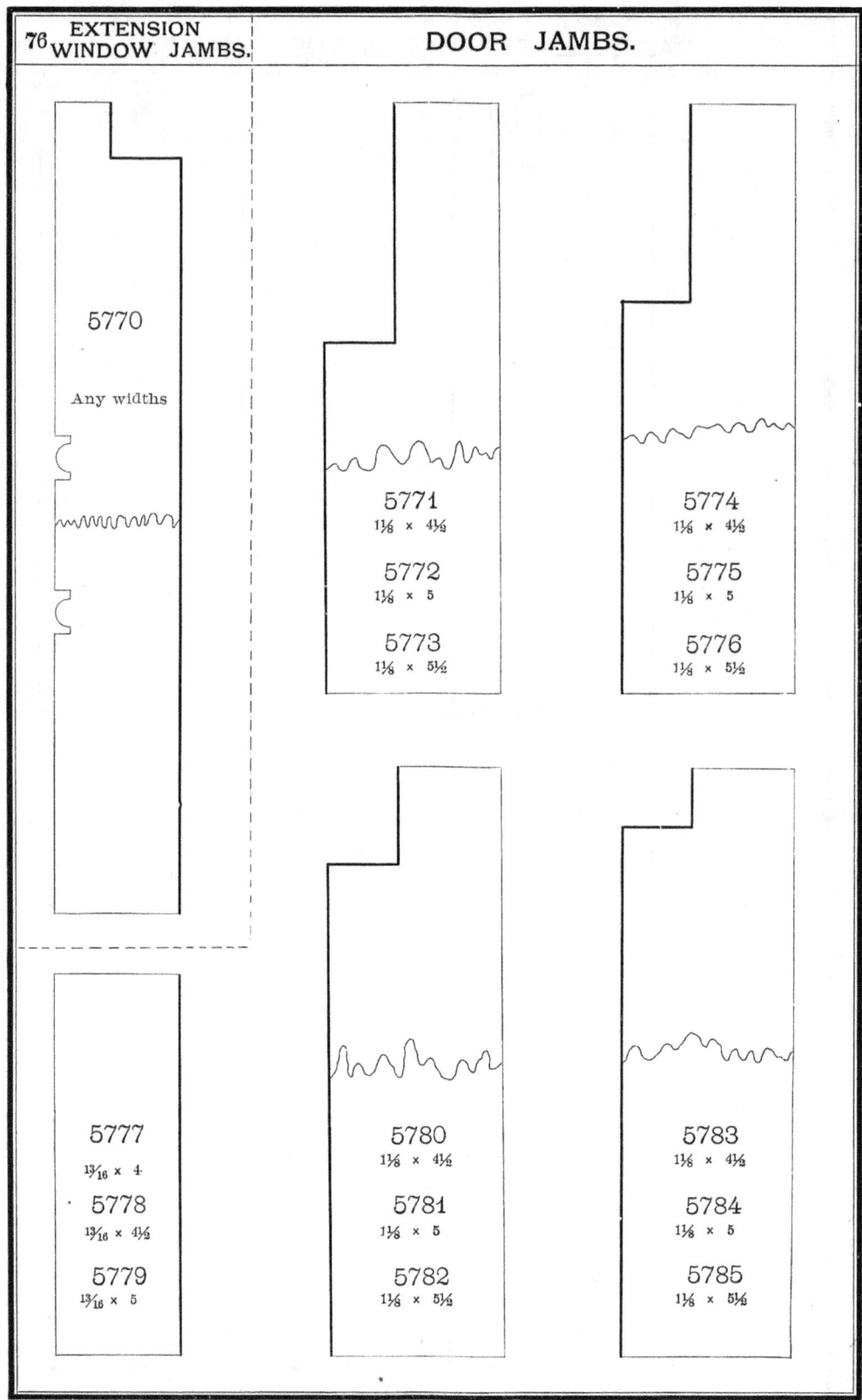

## BELT COURSE AND BASE.

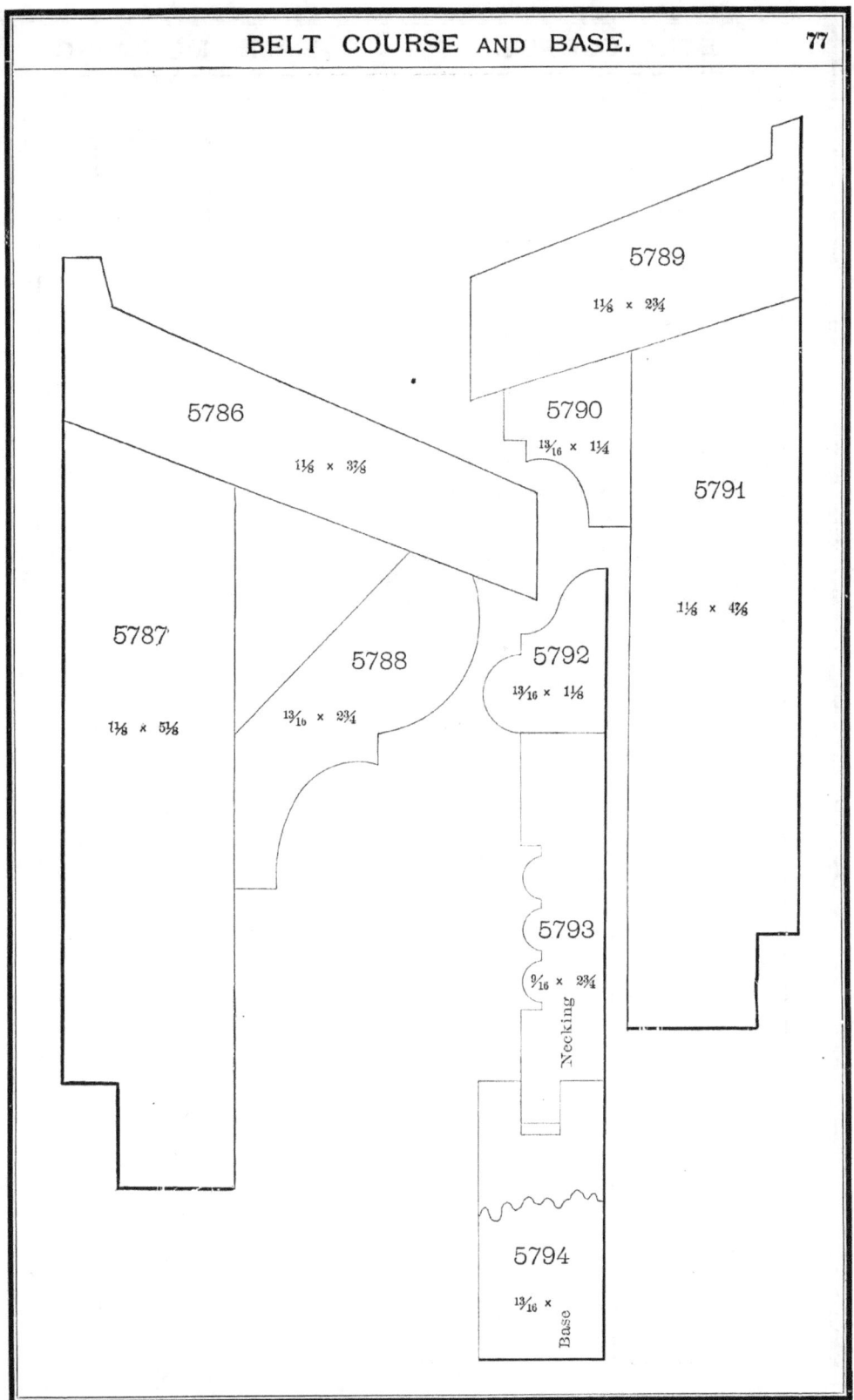

Mouldings made exact size of cuts. Figures represent the ripping width of Lumber.

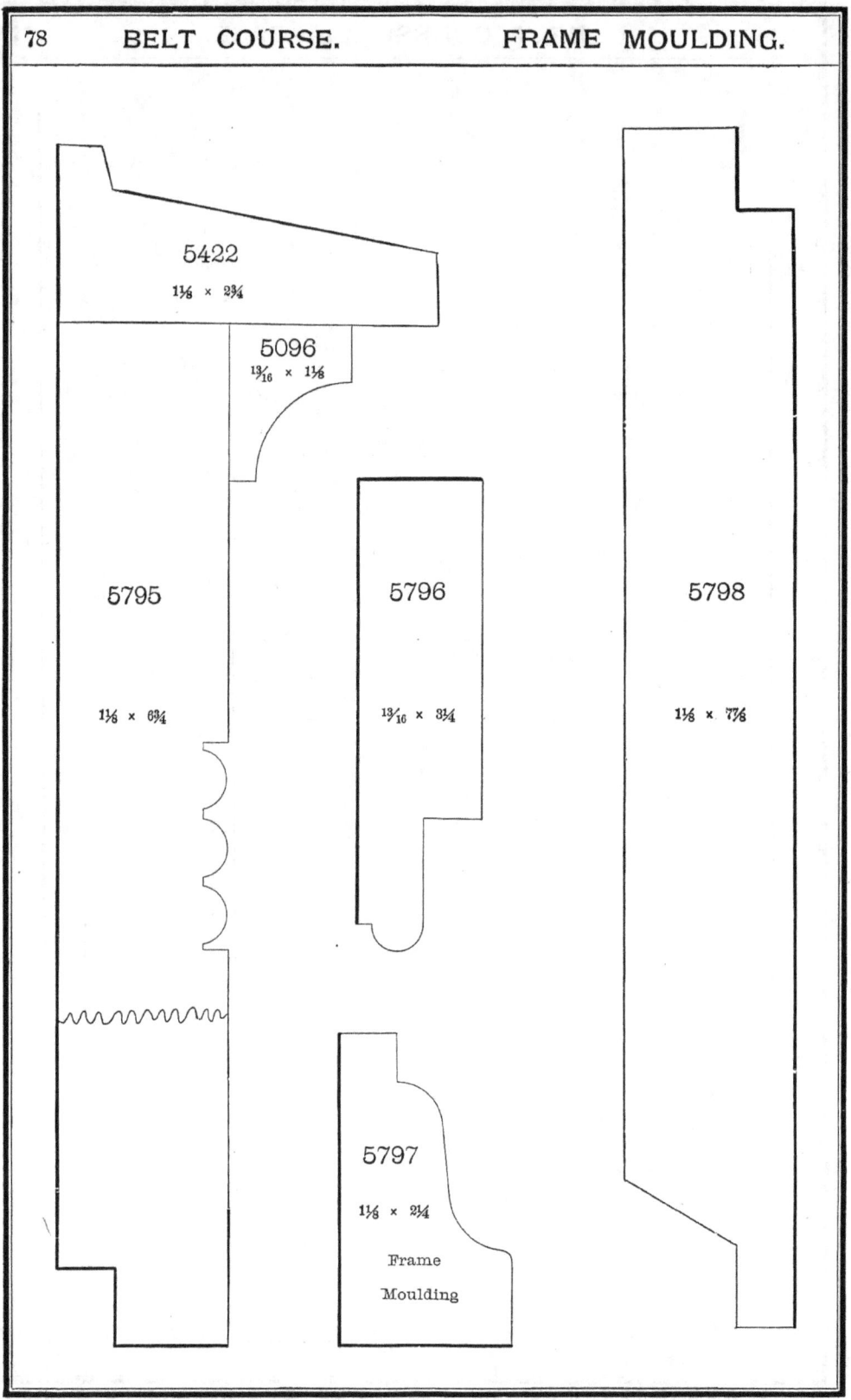

## REVEAL FRAME FOR 1⅜ INCH SASH. (Philadelphia.)

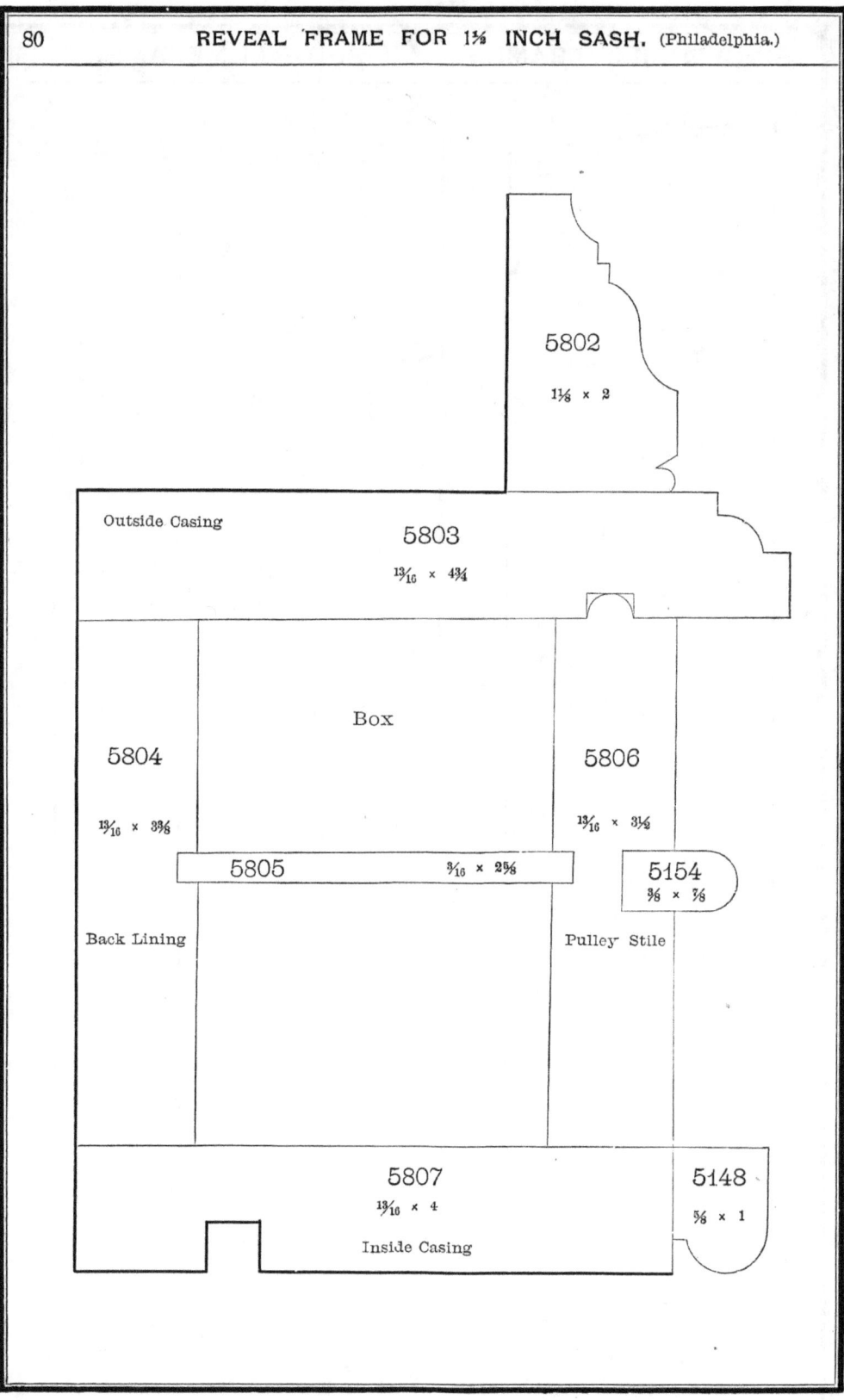

## REVEAL FRAME FOR 1½ INCH SASH. (Philadelphia.)

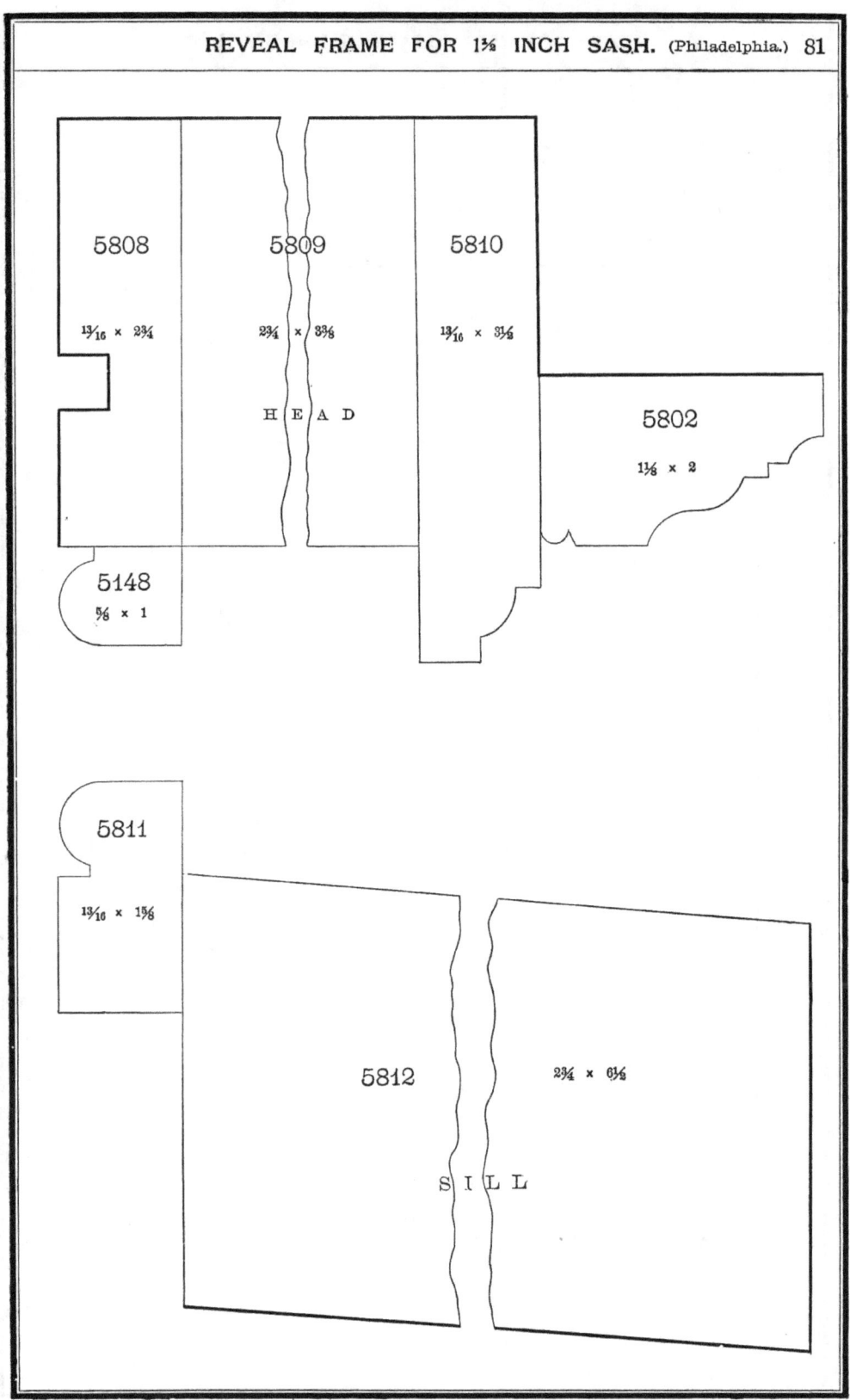

# PLANK FRAME FOR 1⅜ INCH SASH. (Philadelphia.)

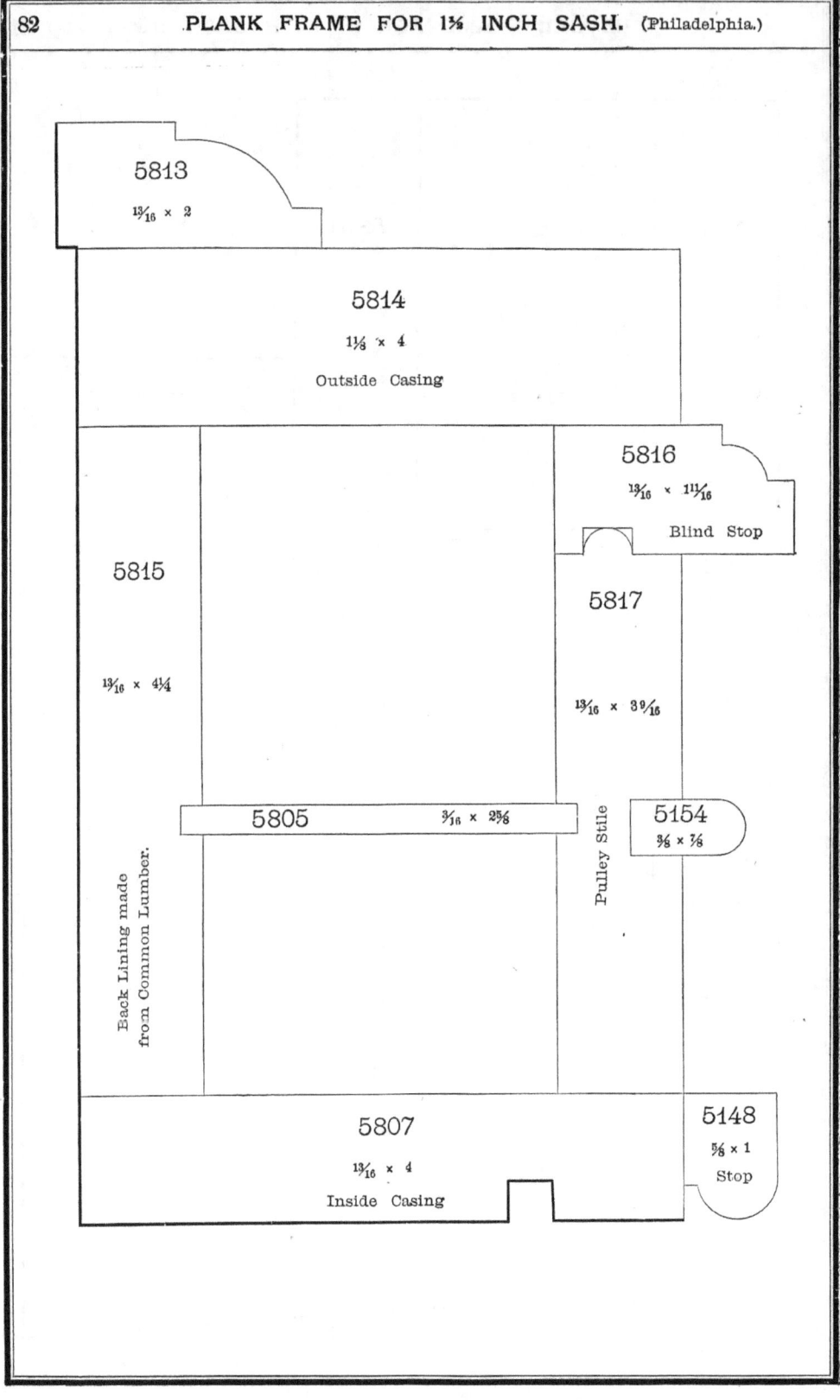

# PLANK FRAME FOR 1⅜ INCH SASH. (Philadelphia.) 83

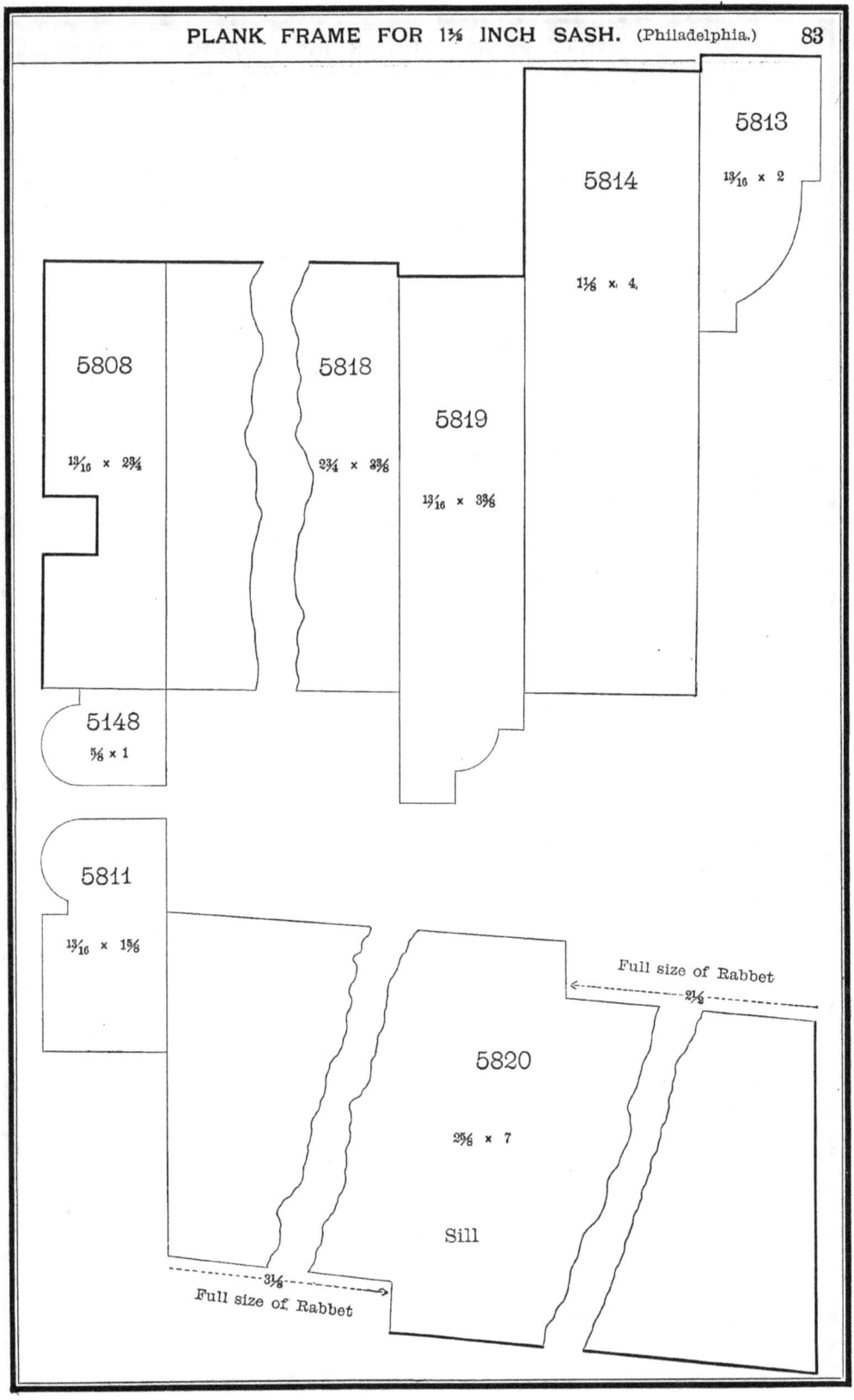

BAY FRAME FOR 1⅜ INCH SASH. (Philadelphia.)

**5803**
13/16 × 4¾
Outside Casing

**5804**
13/16 × 3⅜

BOX

**5806**
13/16 × 3½

5805    3/16 × 2⅝

**5154**
3/8 × 7/8

Back Lining made from Common Lumber

**5821**
13/16 × 4
Inside Casing

**5148**
5/8 × 1

BAY FRAME FOR 1½ INCH SASH. (Philadelphia.) 85

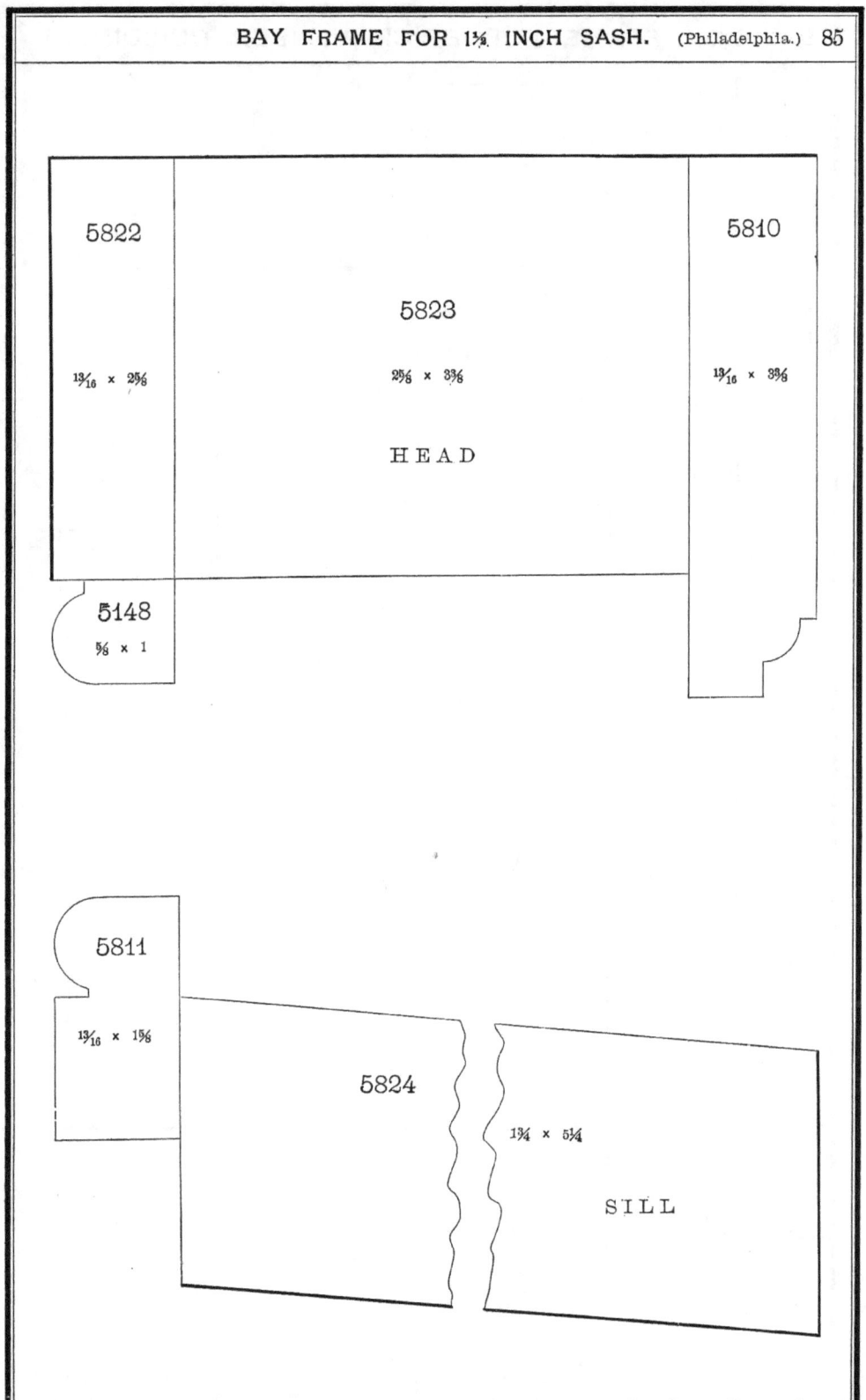

## 86 BOX FRAME FOR BRICK VENEER BUILDING.

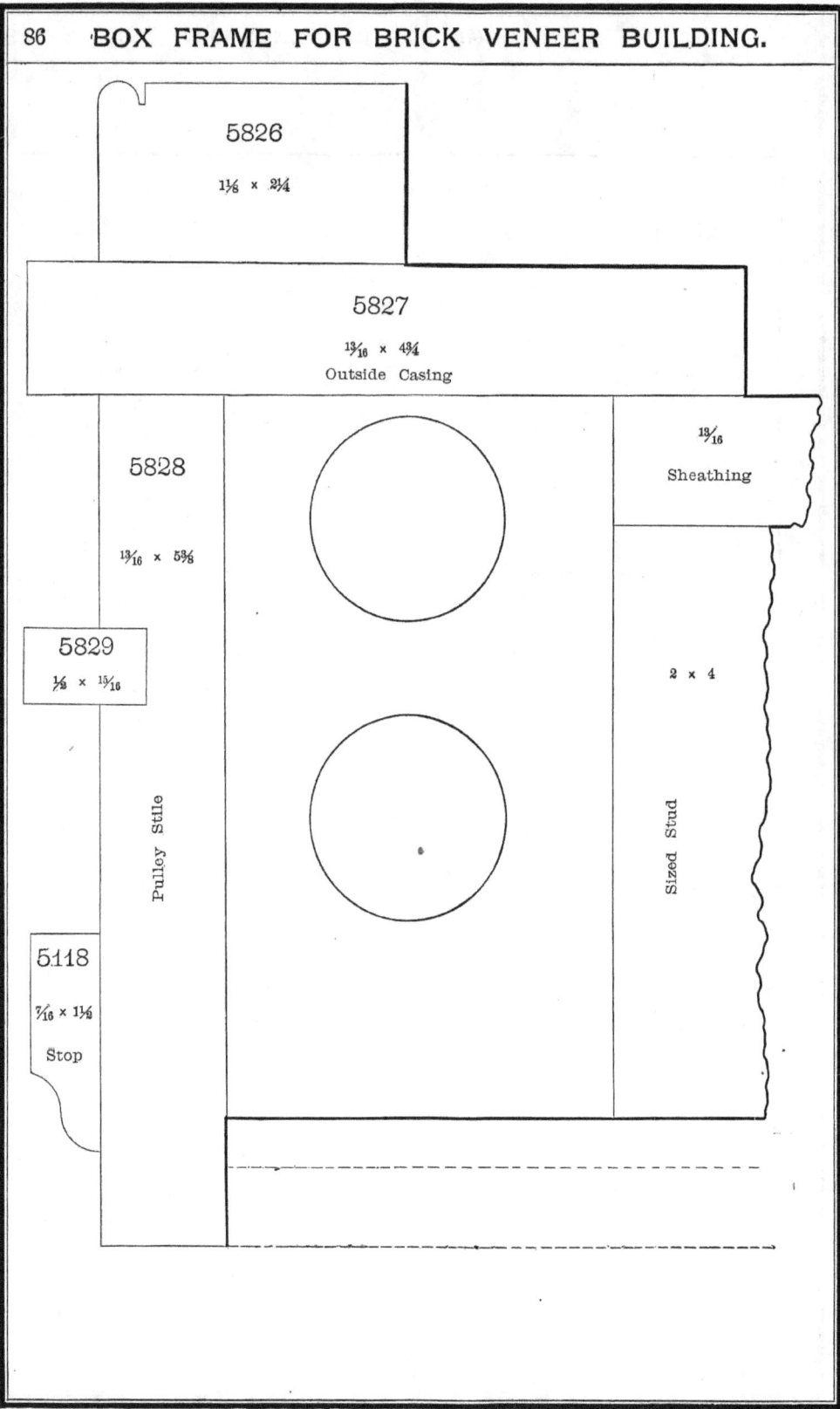

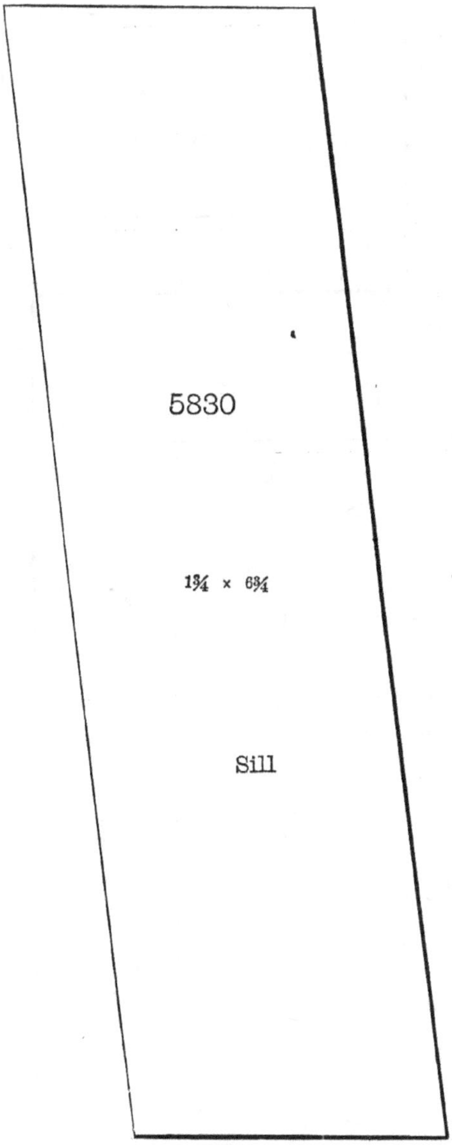

# BOX FRAME FOR BRICK VENEER BUILDING.

5830

1¾ × 6¾

Sill

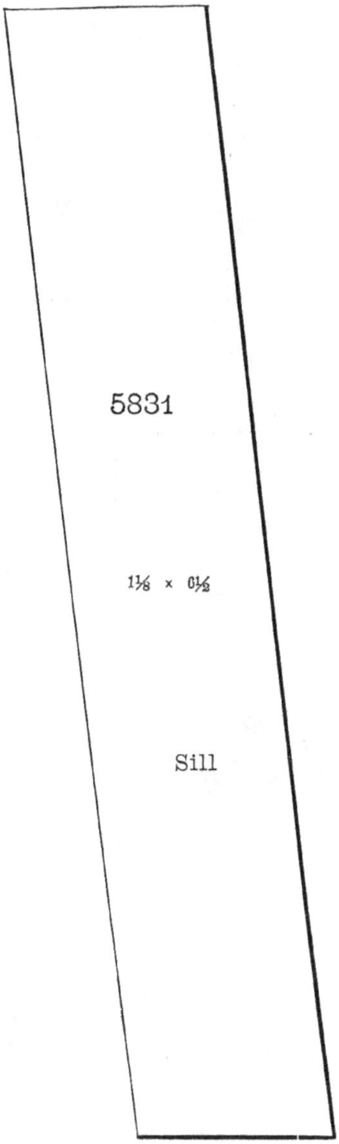

5831

1⅛ × 6½

Sill

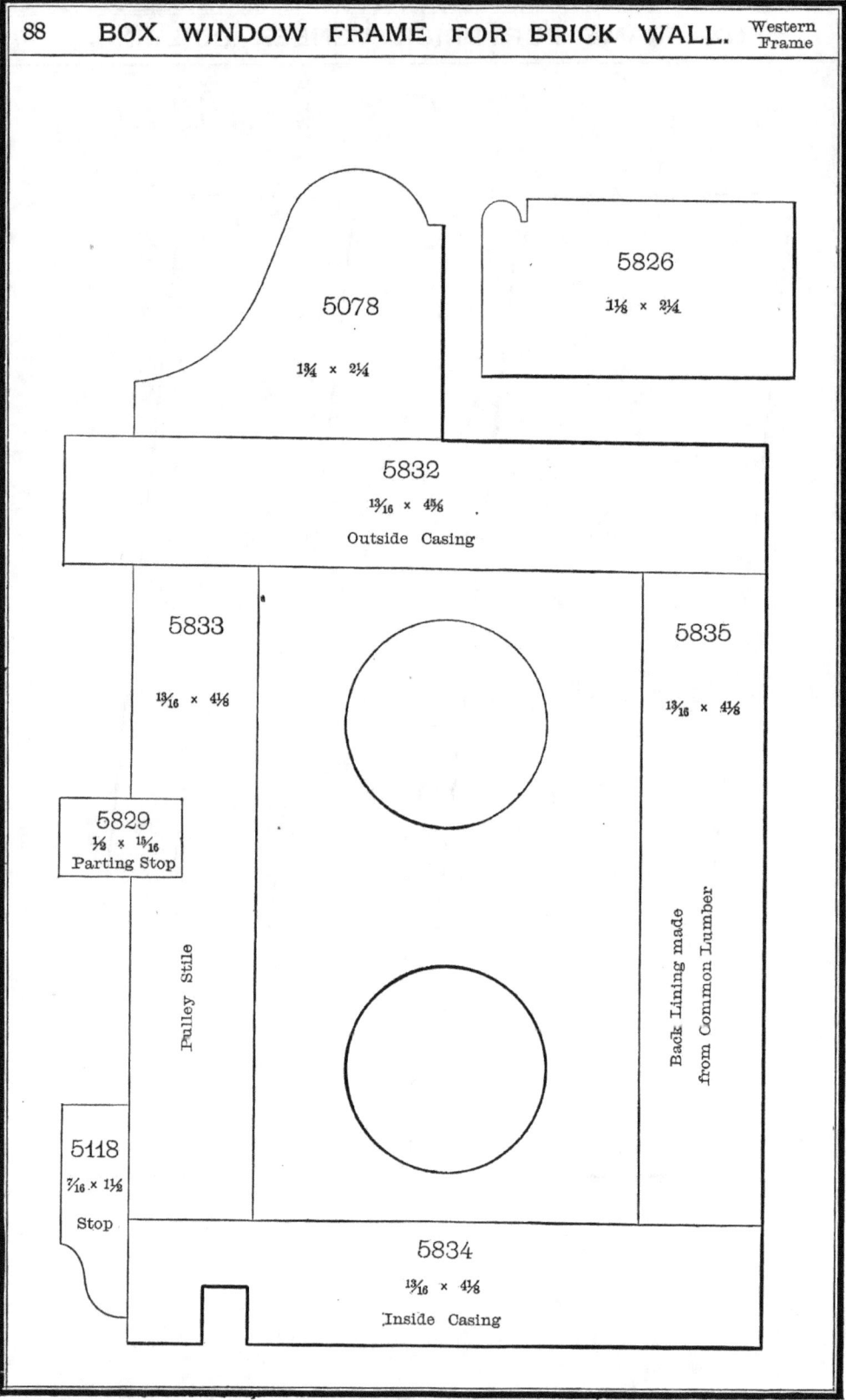

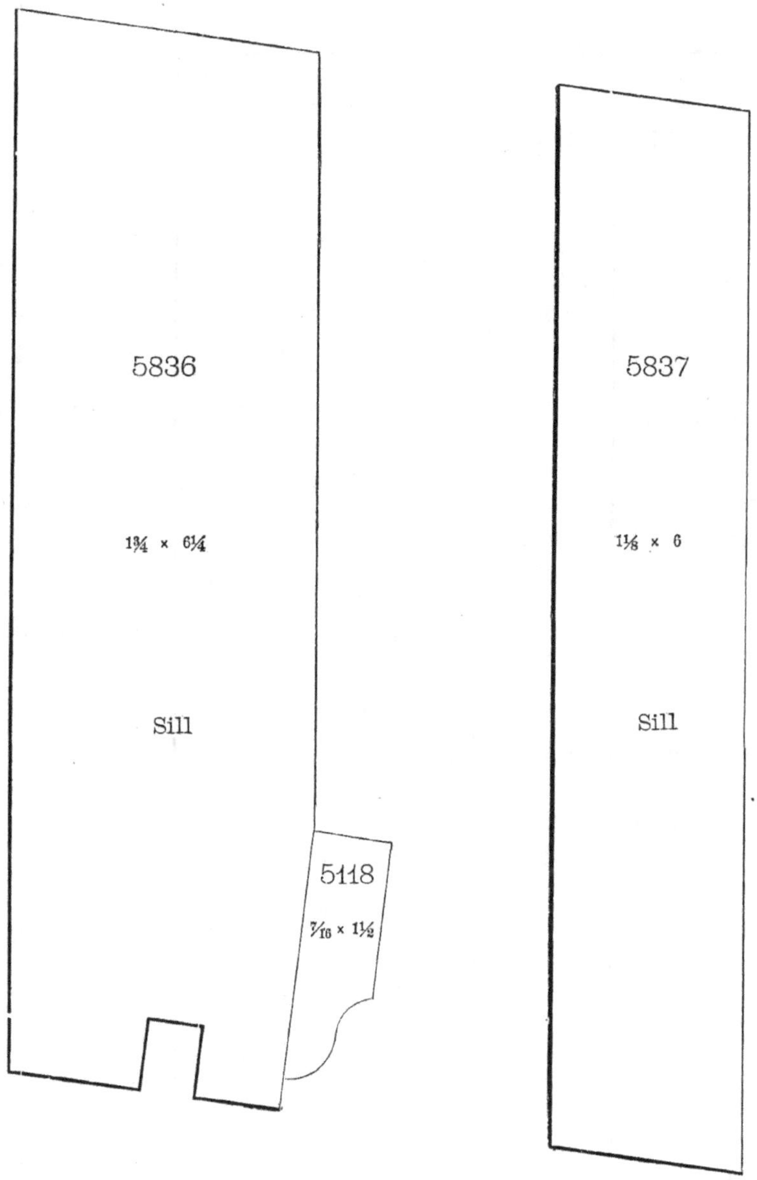

# BOX WINDOW FRAME FOR BRICK WALL. 89

5836

1¾ × 6¼

Sill

5118

7/16 × 1½

5837

1⅛ × 6

Sill

## OUTSIDE DOOR FRAME—FRAME BUILDING.

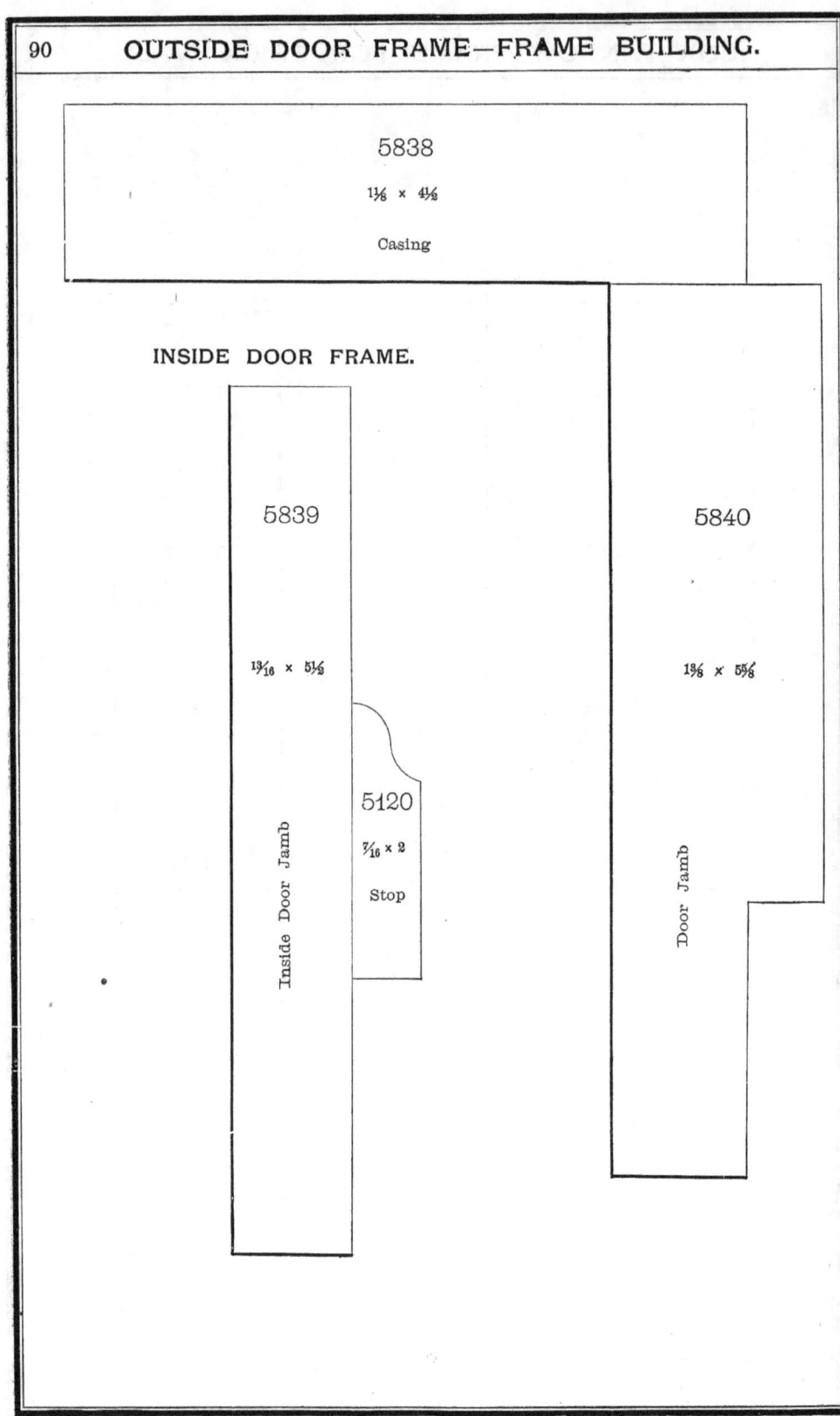

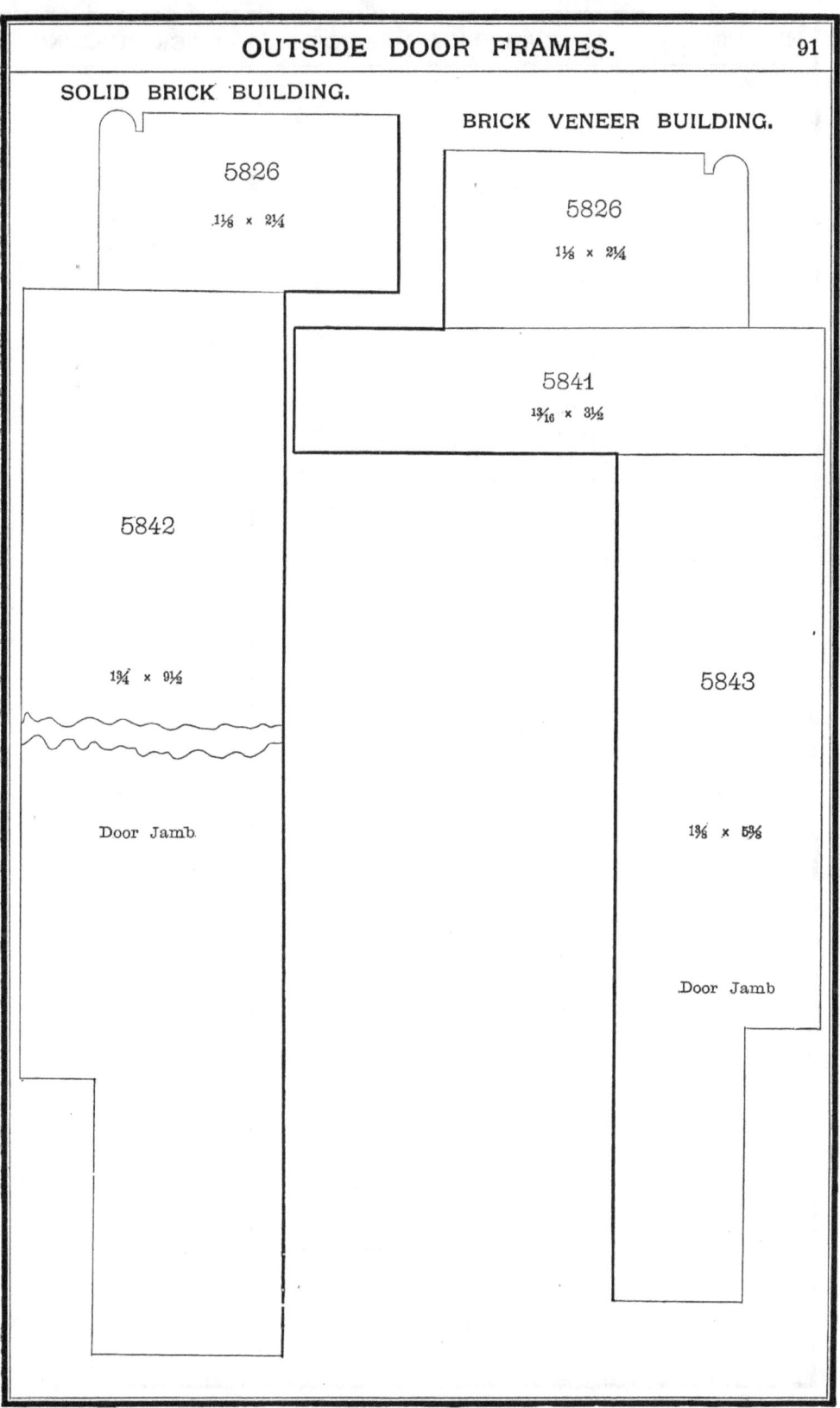

## 92 WINDOW FRAMES—PLANK JAMBS FOR SOLID BRICK BUILDING.

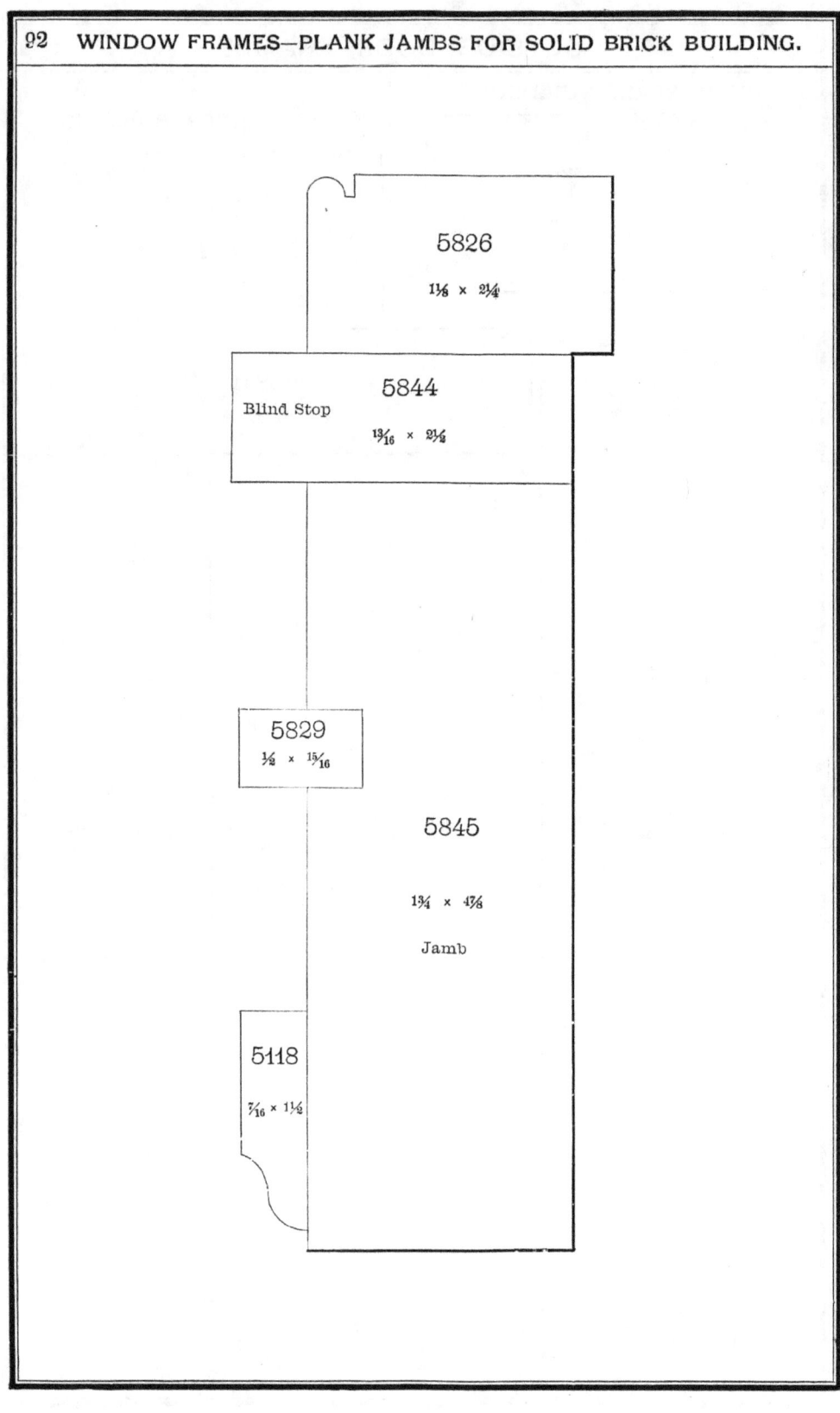

# WINDOW FRAME—FRAME BUILDING—PLAIN RAIL SASH
## 1⅛ INCH SIDE JAMBS.

## 94 WINDOW FRAME FOR FRAME BUILDING—Check rail Sash 1⅜ Inches.

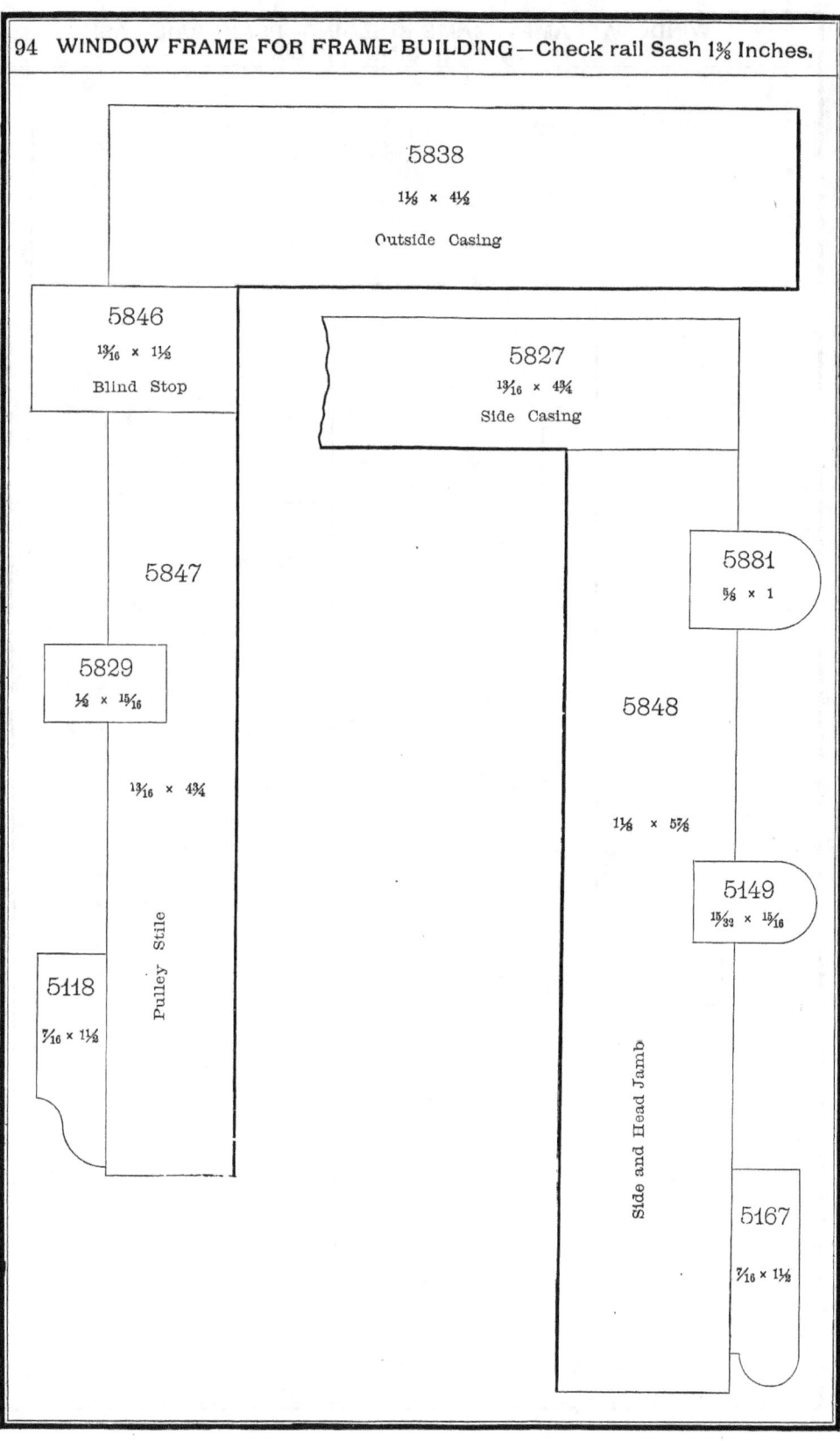

# SKELETON CHECK FRAME. (New England.) 95

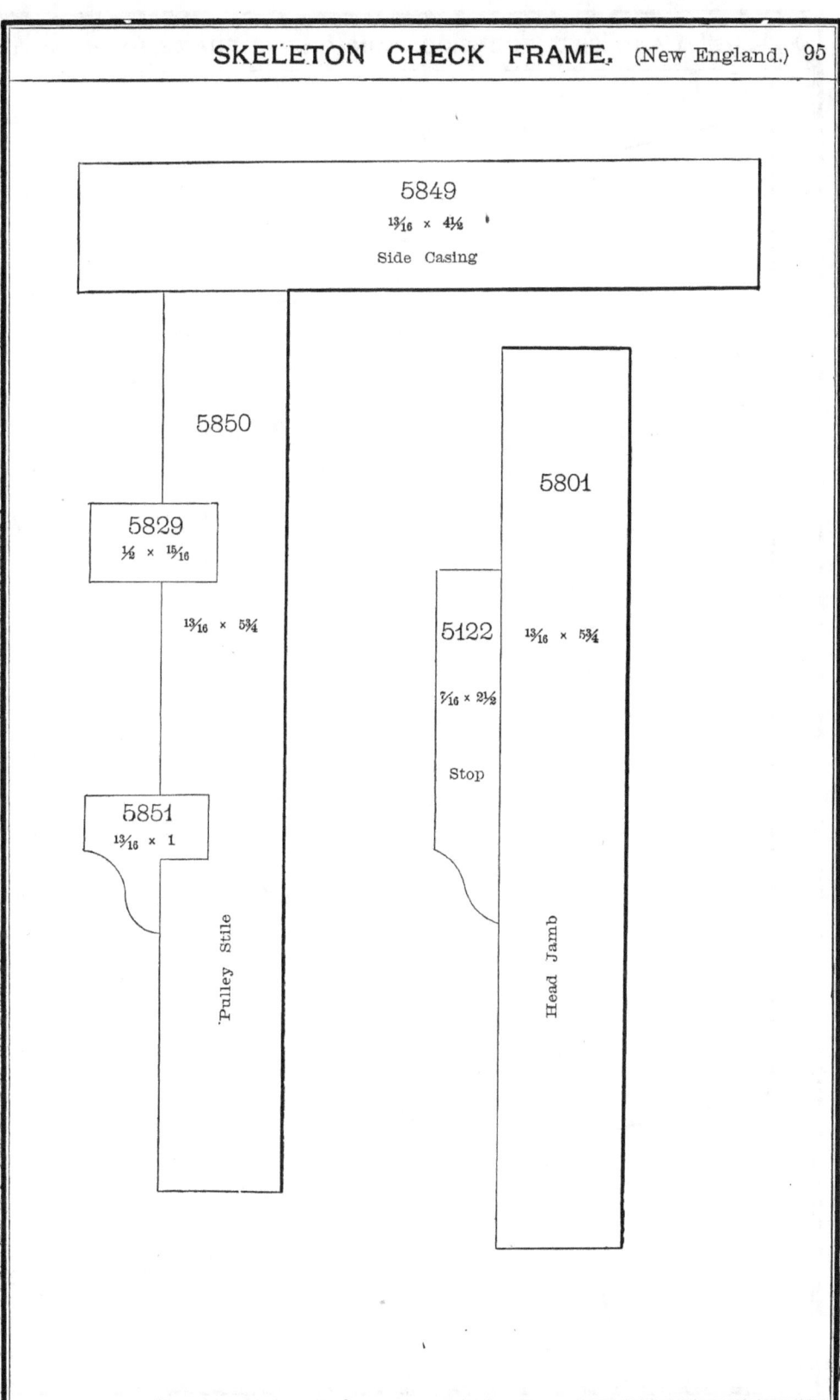

## HEAD AND SILL FOR SKELETON CHECK FRAME. (New England)

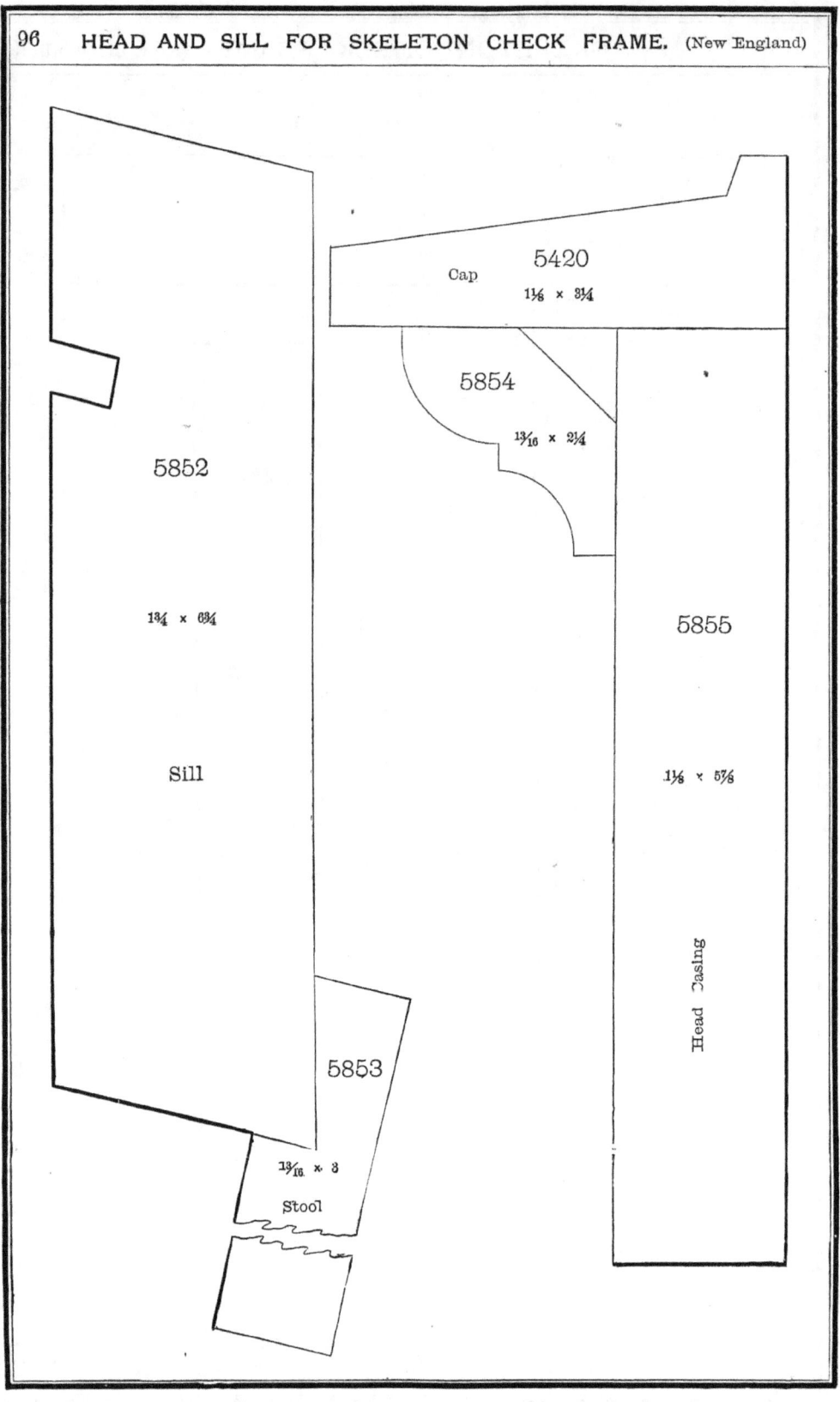

## BOX WINDOW FRAME—BRICK BUILDING. (Western New York) 97

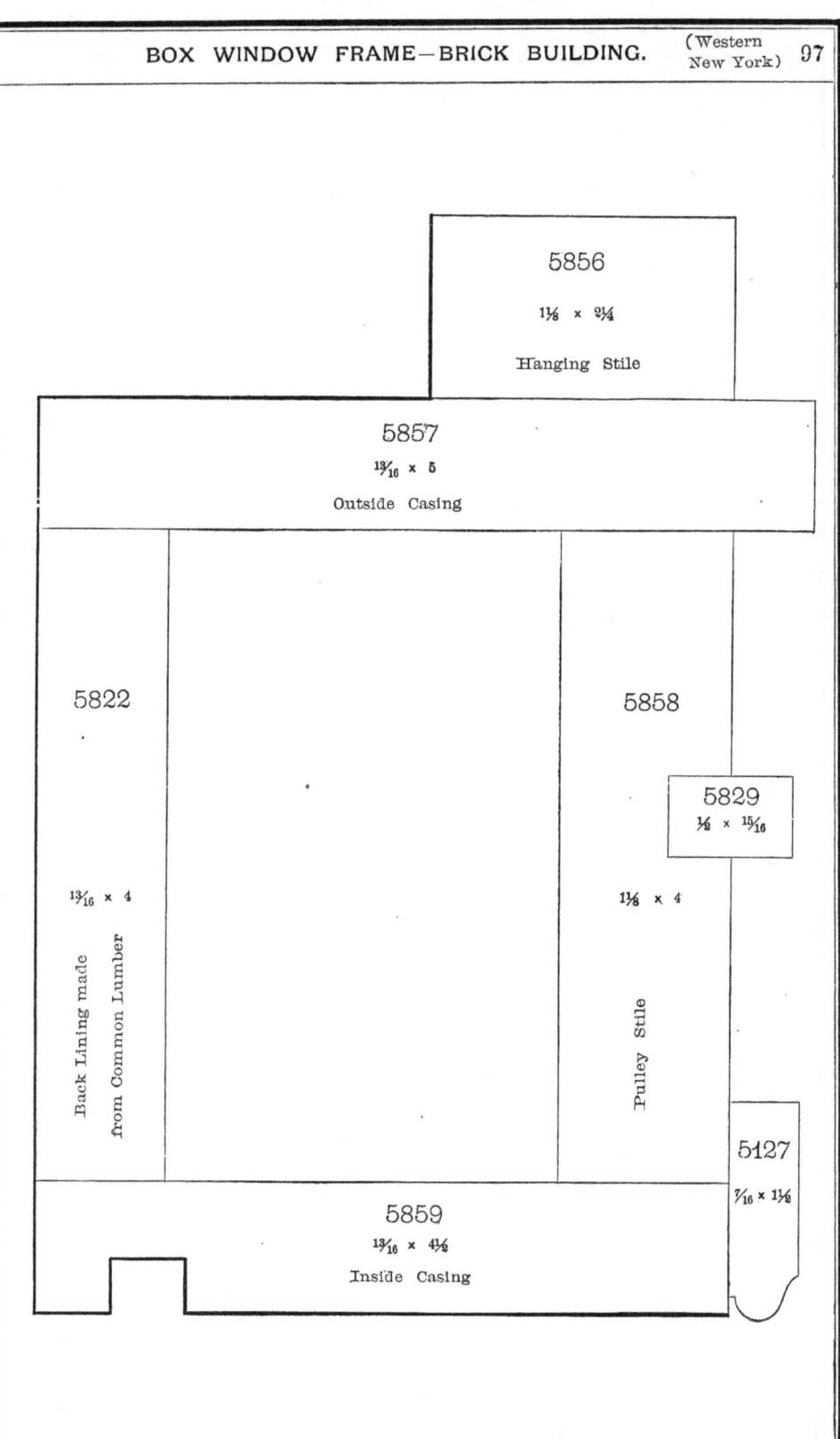

## 98 HEAD AND SILL FOR BOX WINDOW FRAME—Brick Building.

(New York and Brooklyn)

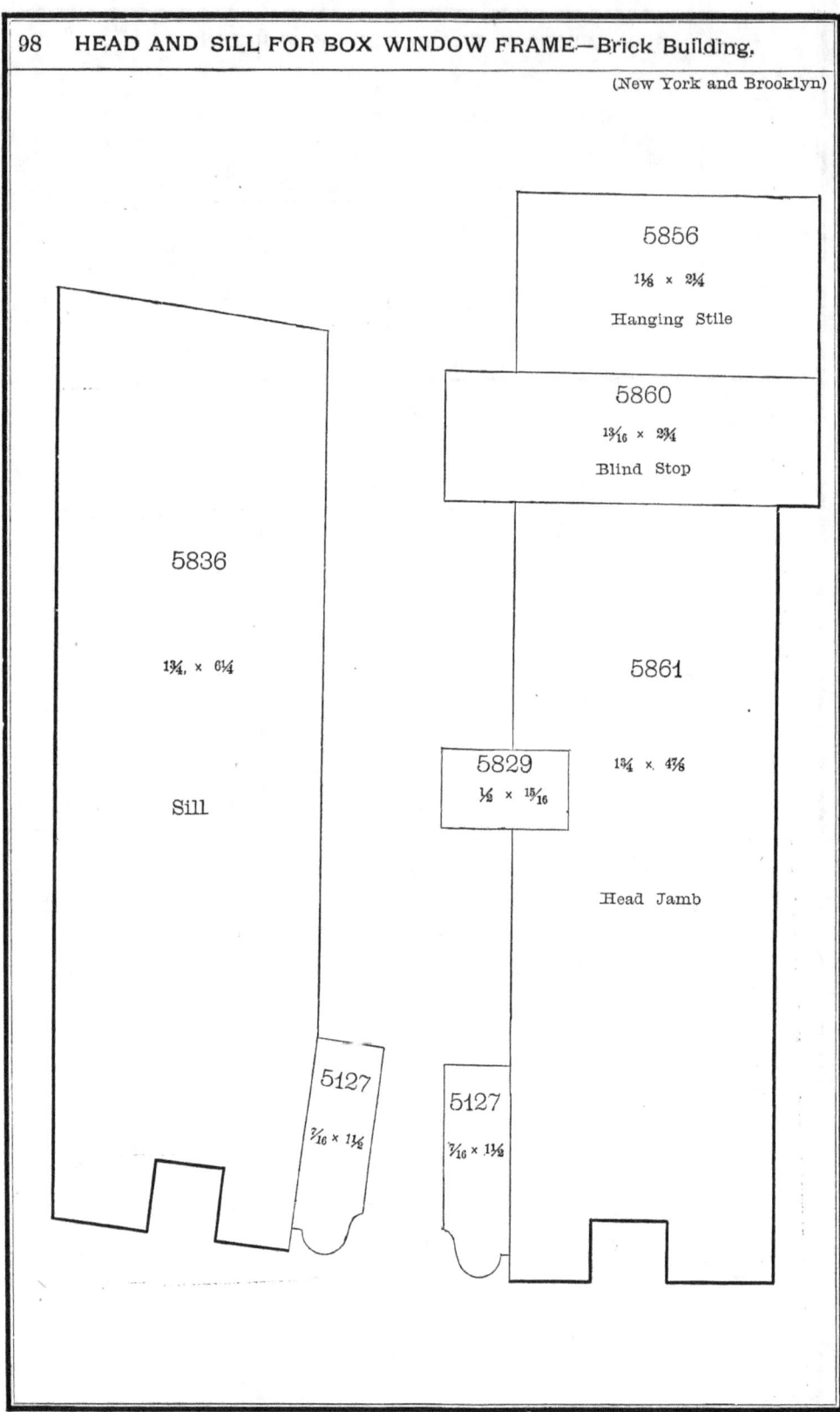

# BOX WINDOW FRAME FOR BRICK BUILDING.

(New York and Brooklyn)

5826
1⅛ × 2¼

5849
13/16 × 4½
Outside Casing

5822

13/16 × 4

Back Lining made
from Common Lumber

5863

5829
½ × 15/16

13/16 × 4

Pulley Stile

5167
3/16 × 1½

5862
13/16 × 4
Inside Casing

100  HEAD AND SILL FOR BOX WINDOW FRAME—Brick Building.

(New York and Brooklyn)

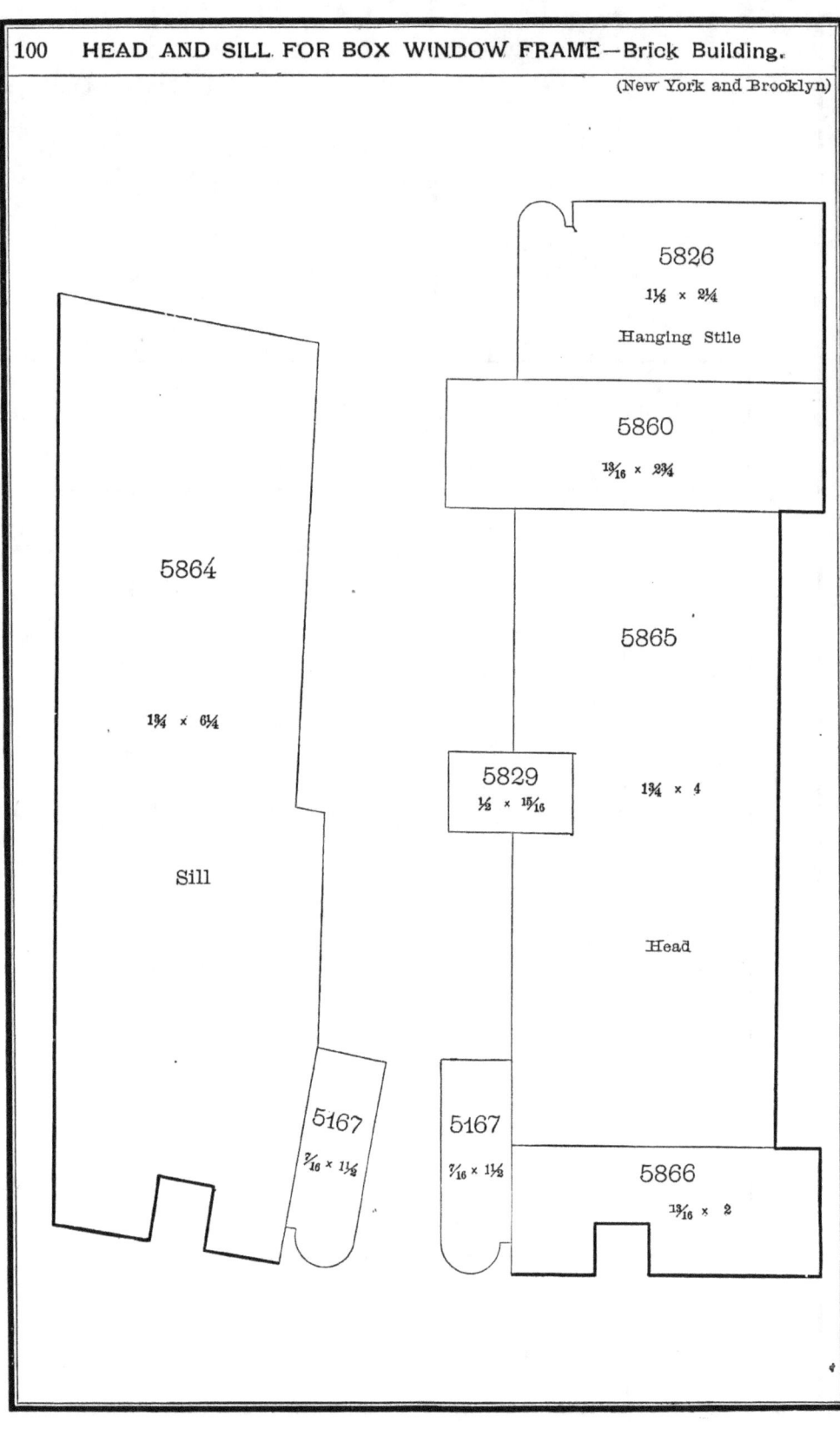

# BOX WINDOW FRAME FOR BRICK BUILDING. 101

(New England)

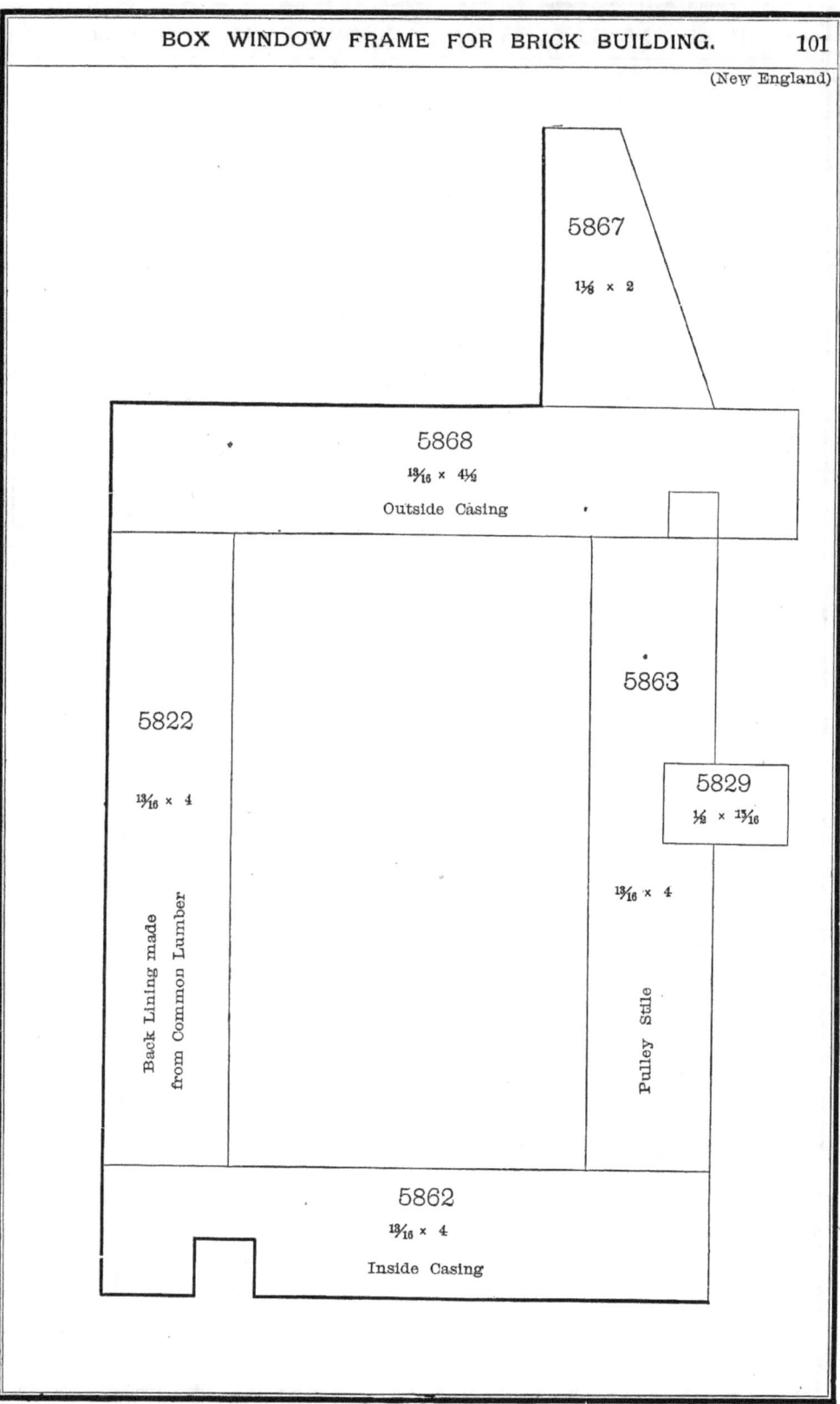

## 102   HEAD AND SILL FOR BOX WINDOW FRAME—Brick Building.

(New England)

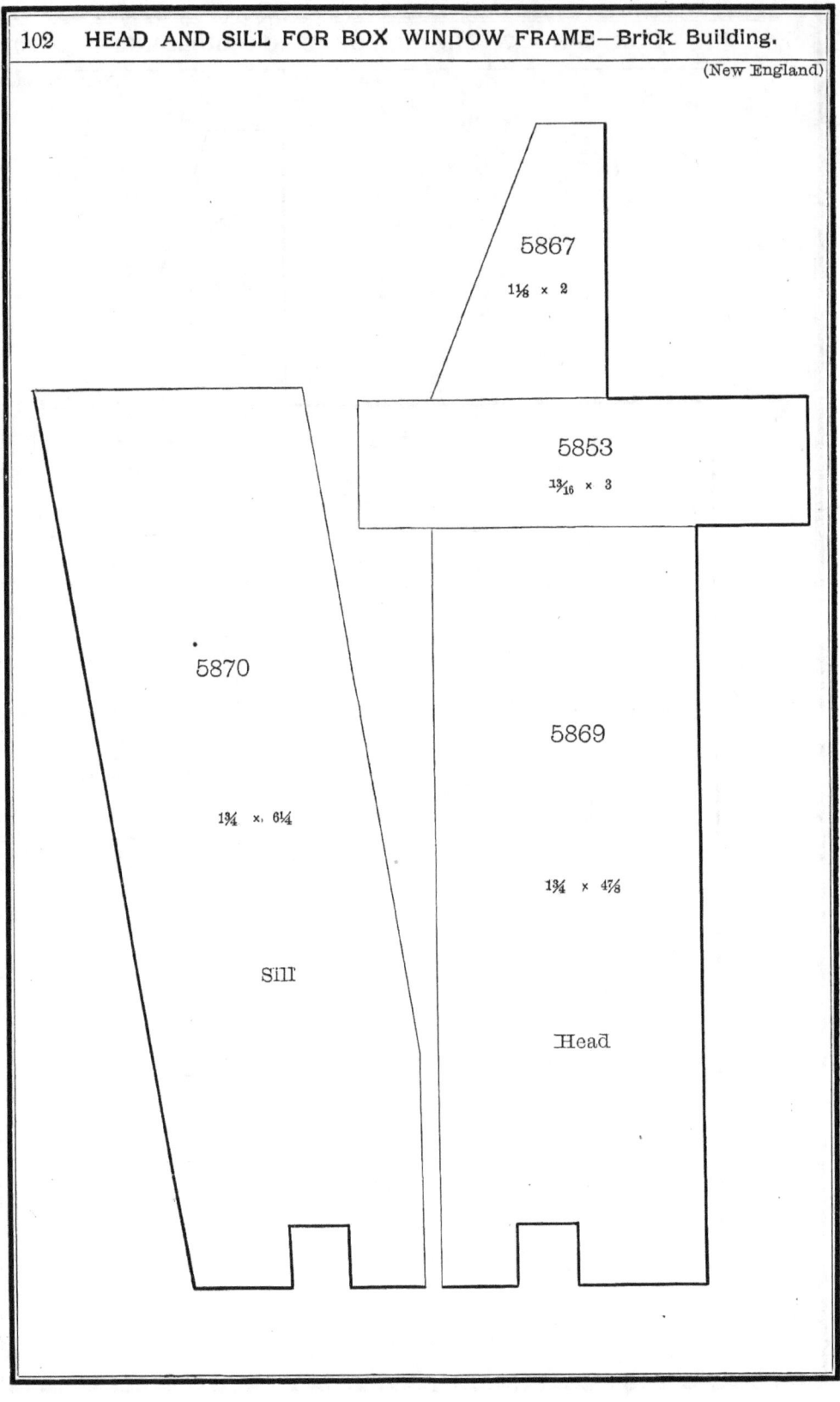

# SKELETON CHECK FRAME. (New England) 103

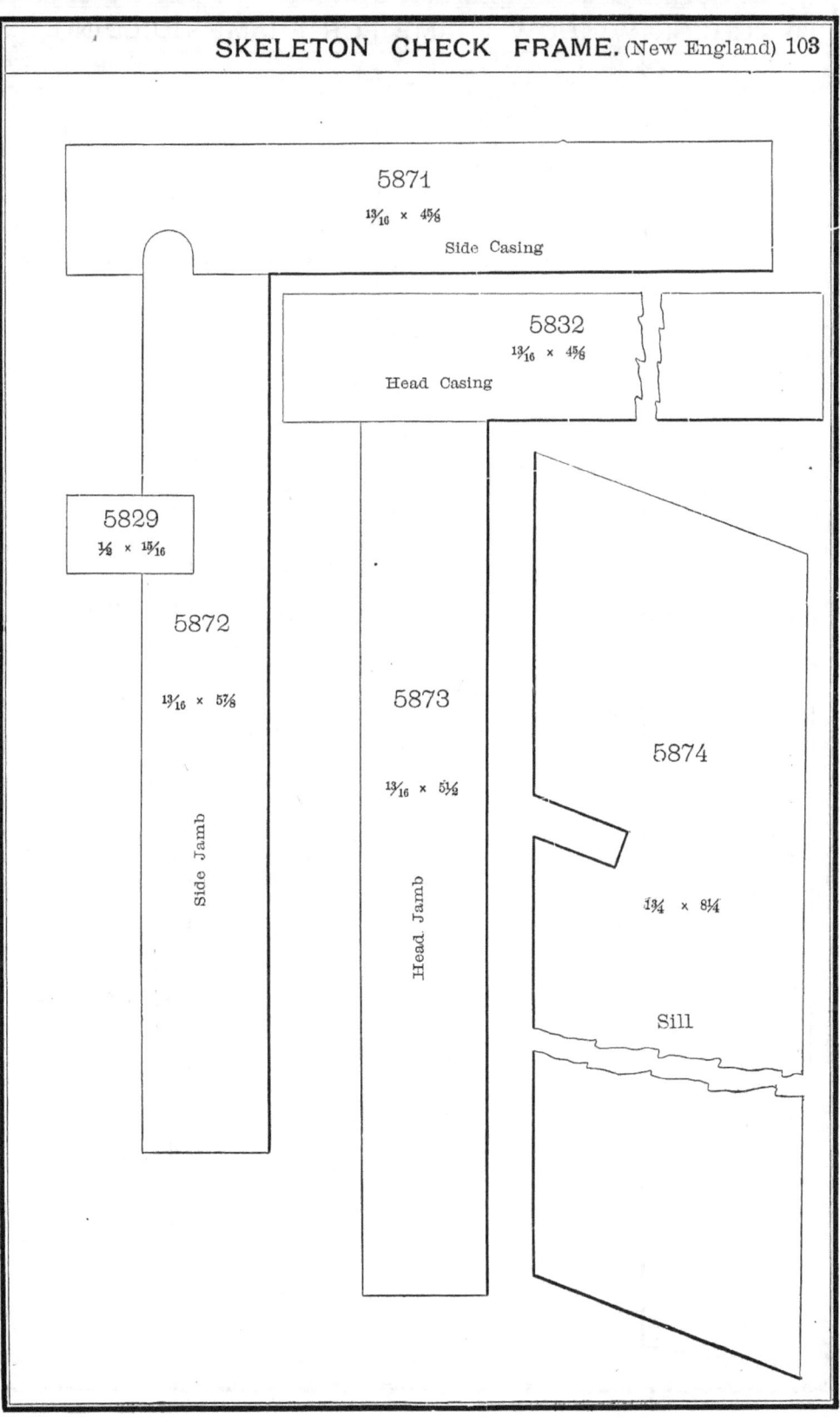

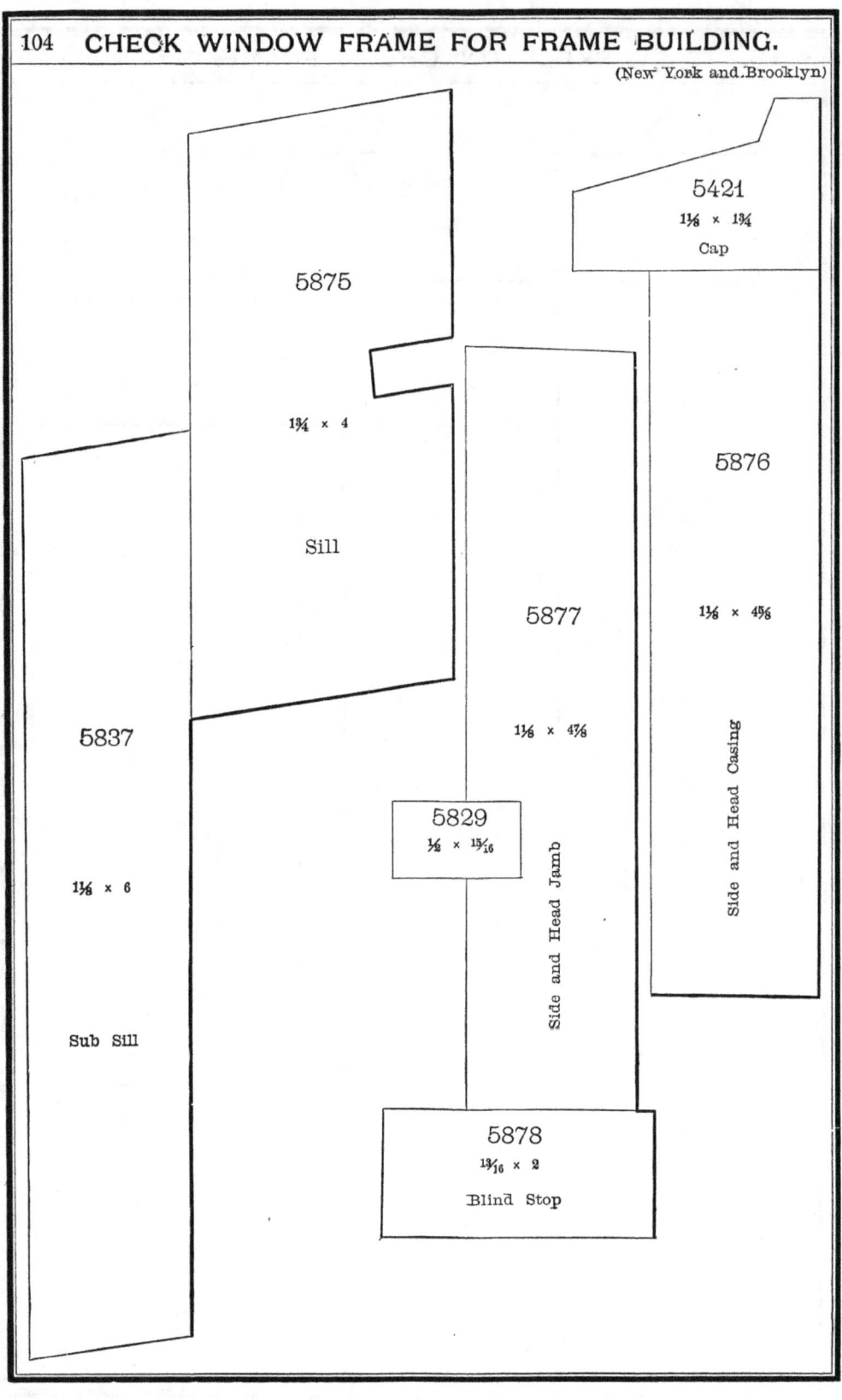

# CHECK WINDOW FRAME FOR FRAME BUILDING. 105
(Western New York)

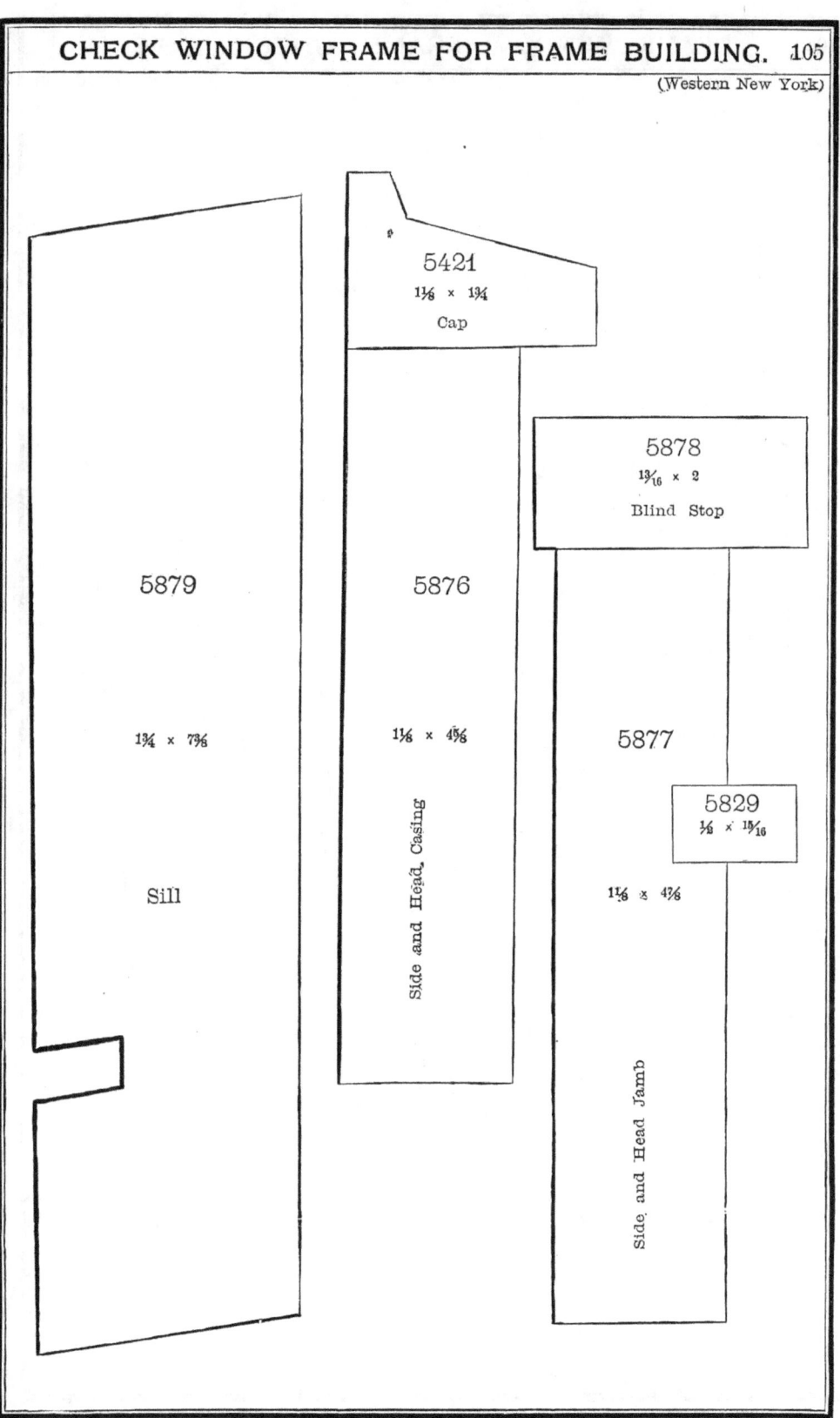

## 106    PLANK WINDOW FRAME—CHECK SASH.

(New England)

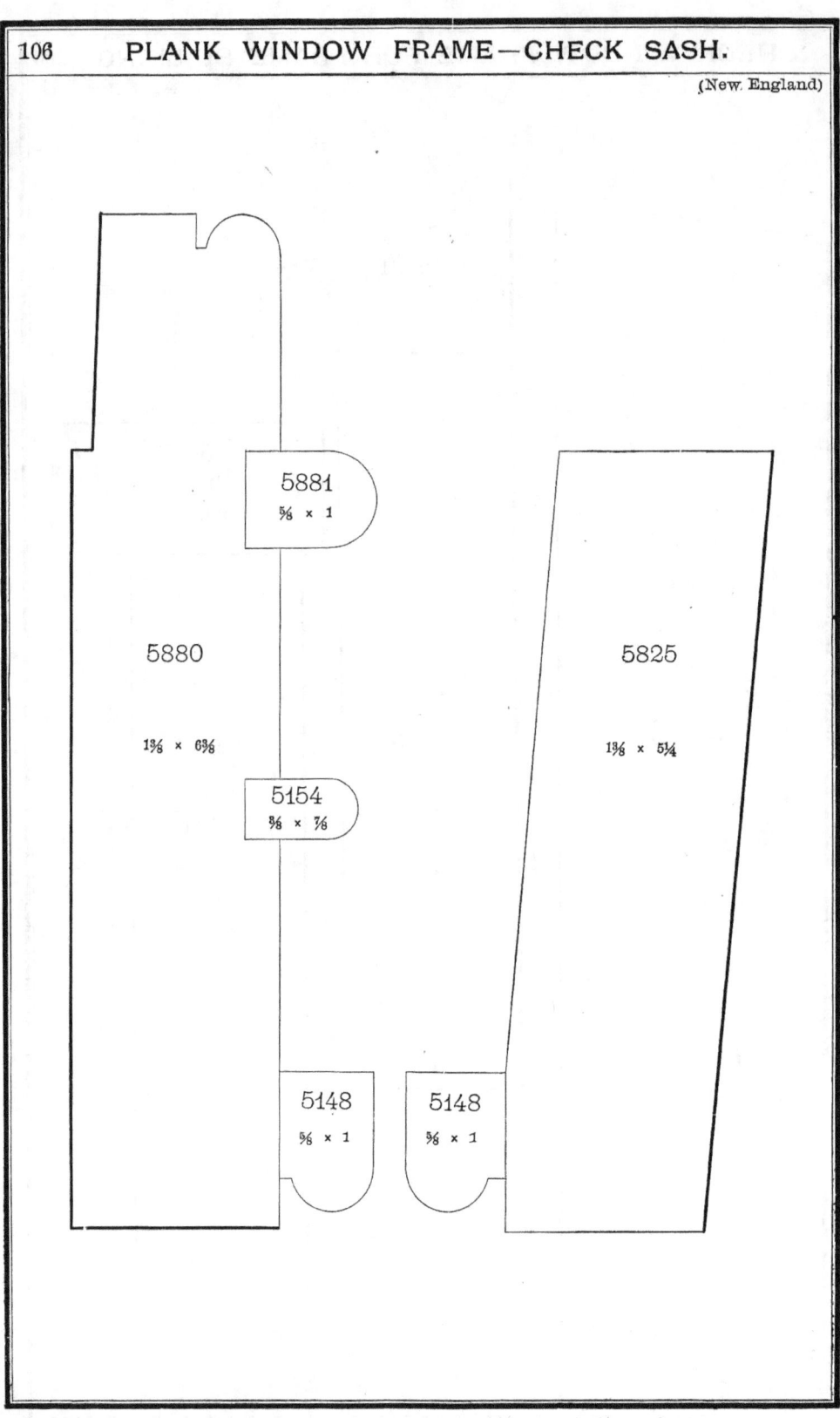

# PLANK WINDOW FRAME — PLAIN RAIL SASH. 107

(New England)

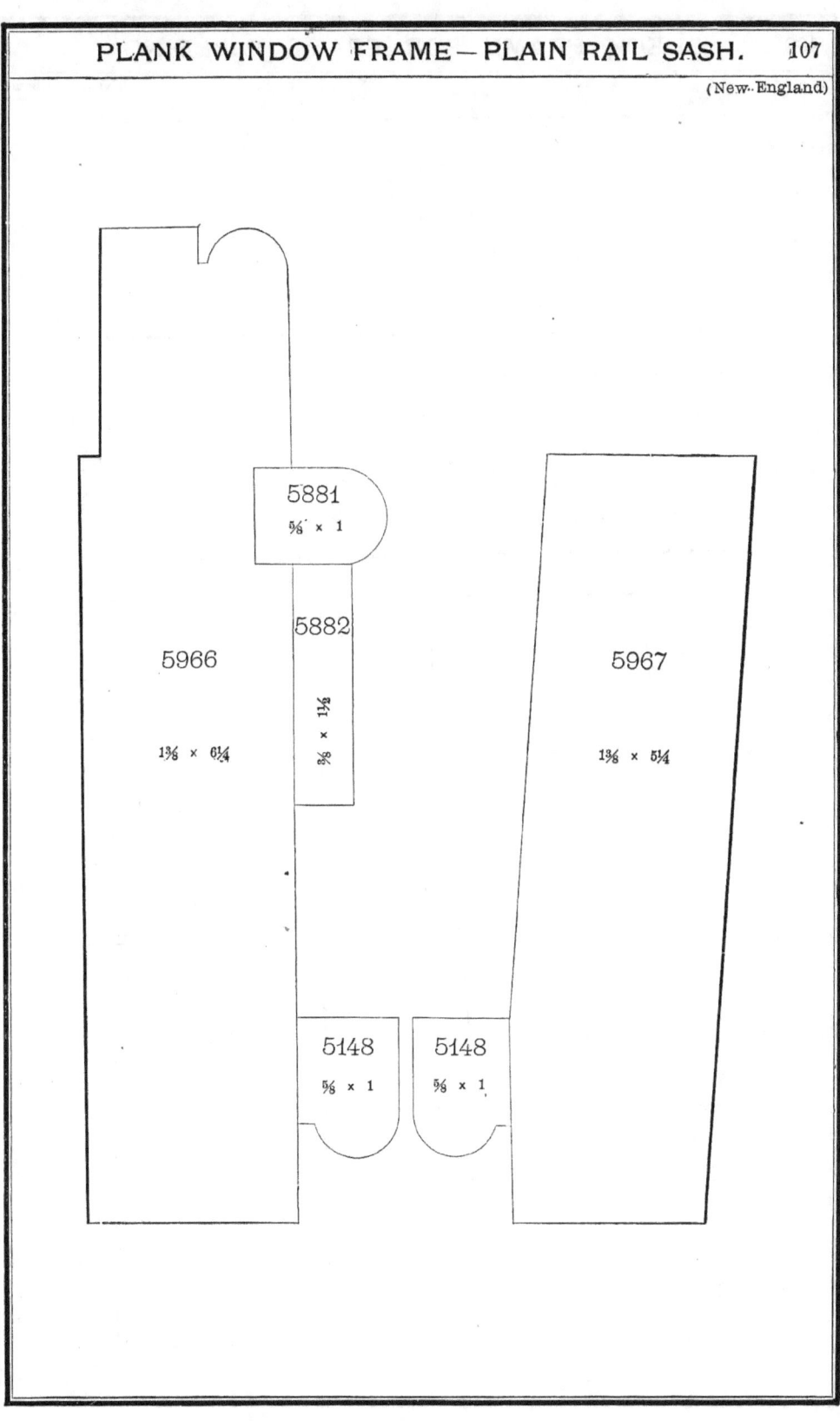

## CHECK FRAME FOR FRAME BUILDING.

(New England)

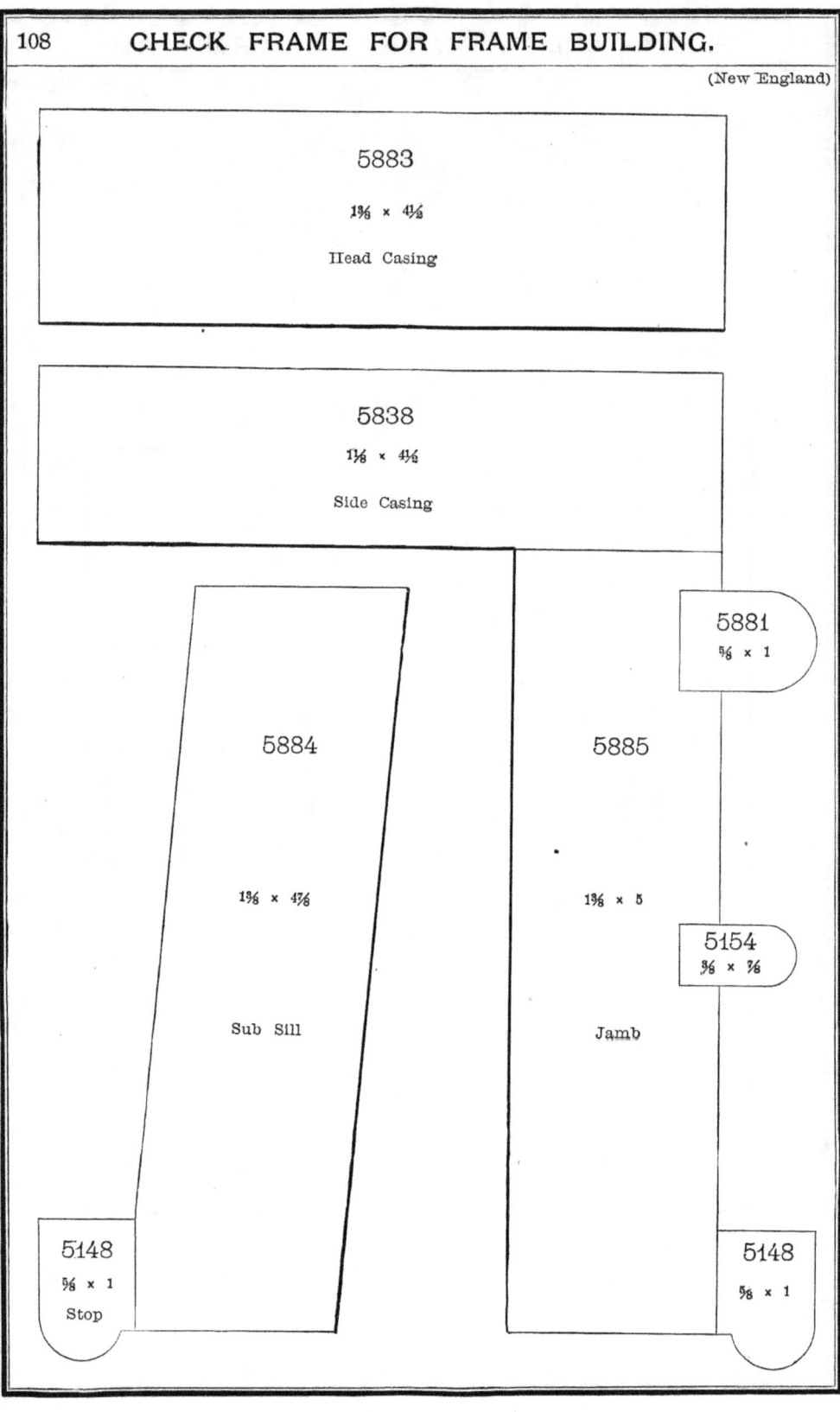

# PLANK WINDOW FRAME FOR PLAIN SASH. 109

(New England)

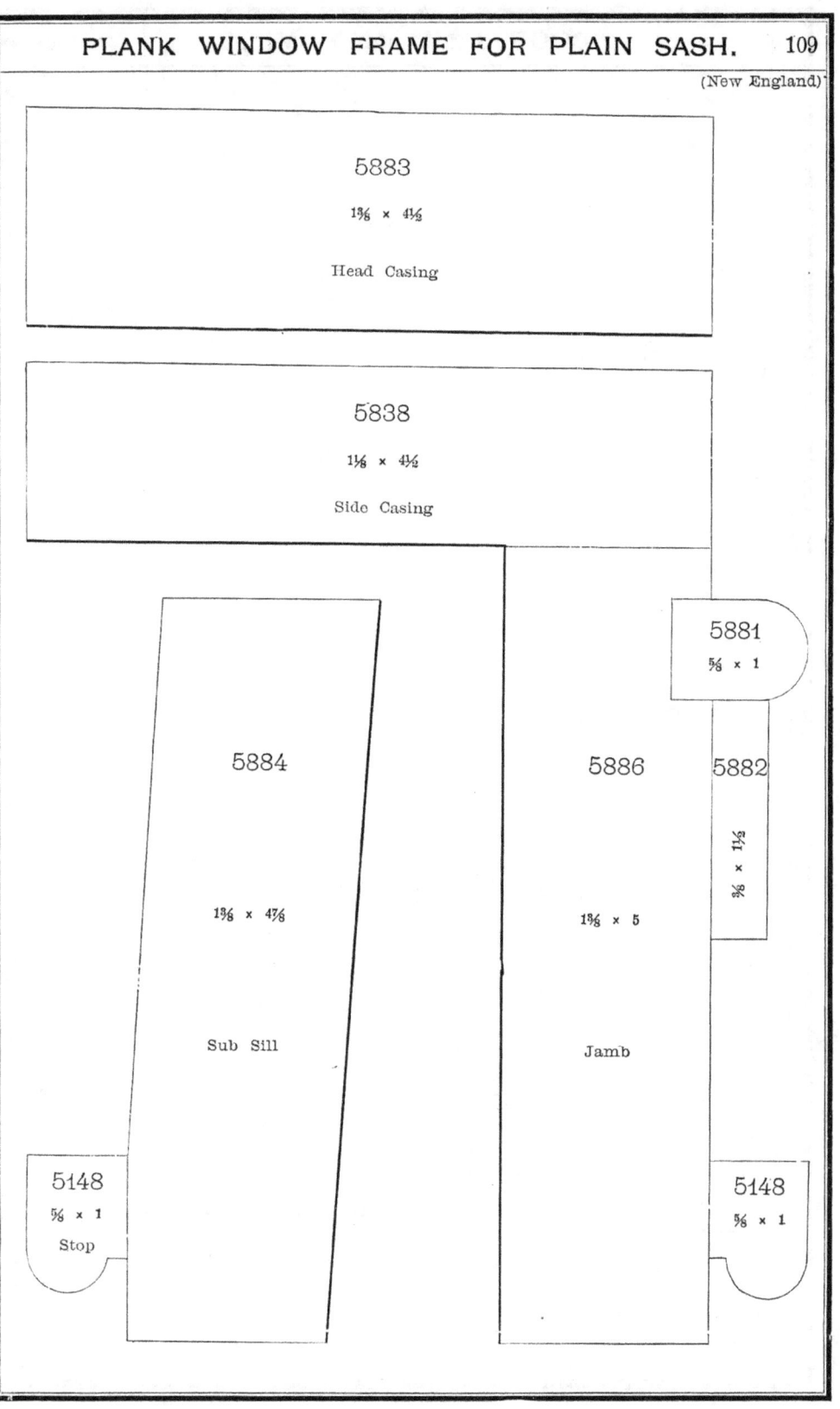

# DOOR JAMB AND IMPOST. (New England)

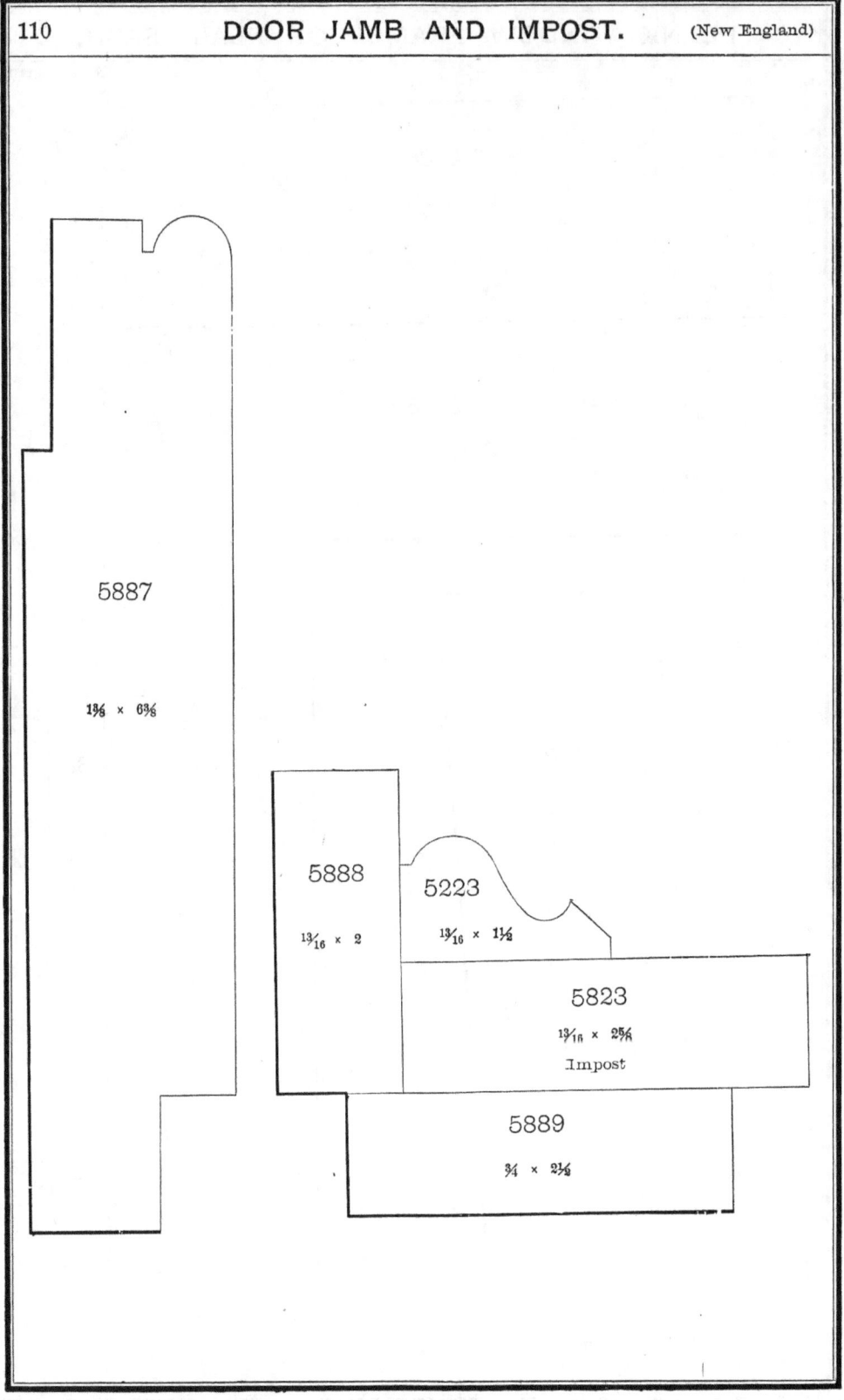

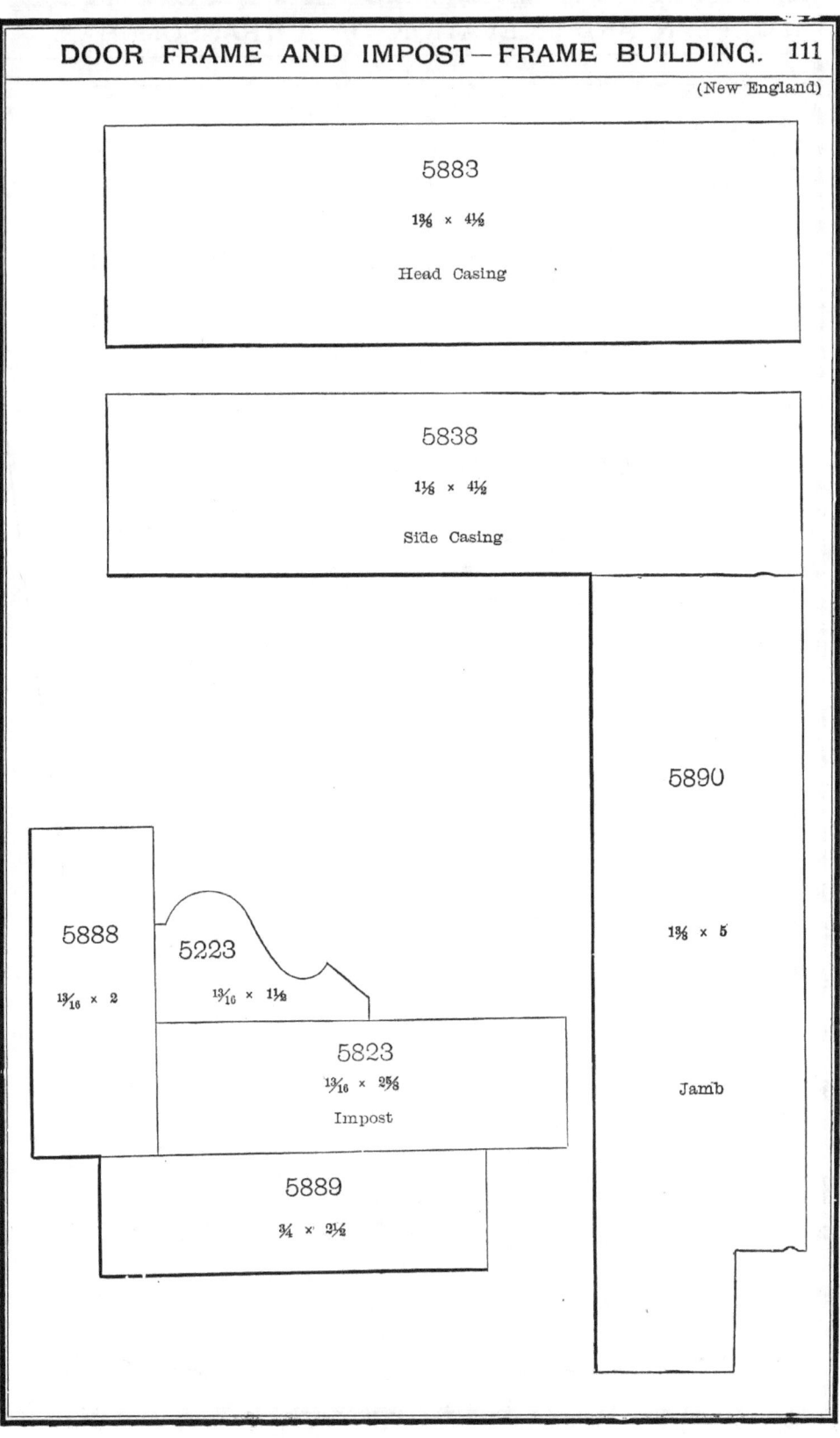

## 112 PLAN AND ELEVATION OF A TRANSOM BAR.

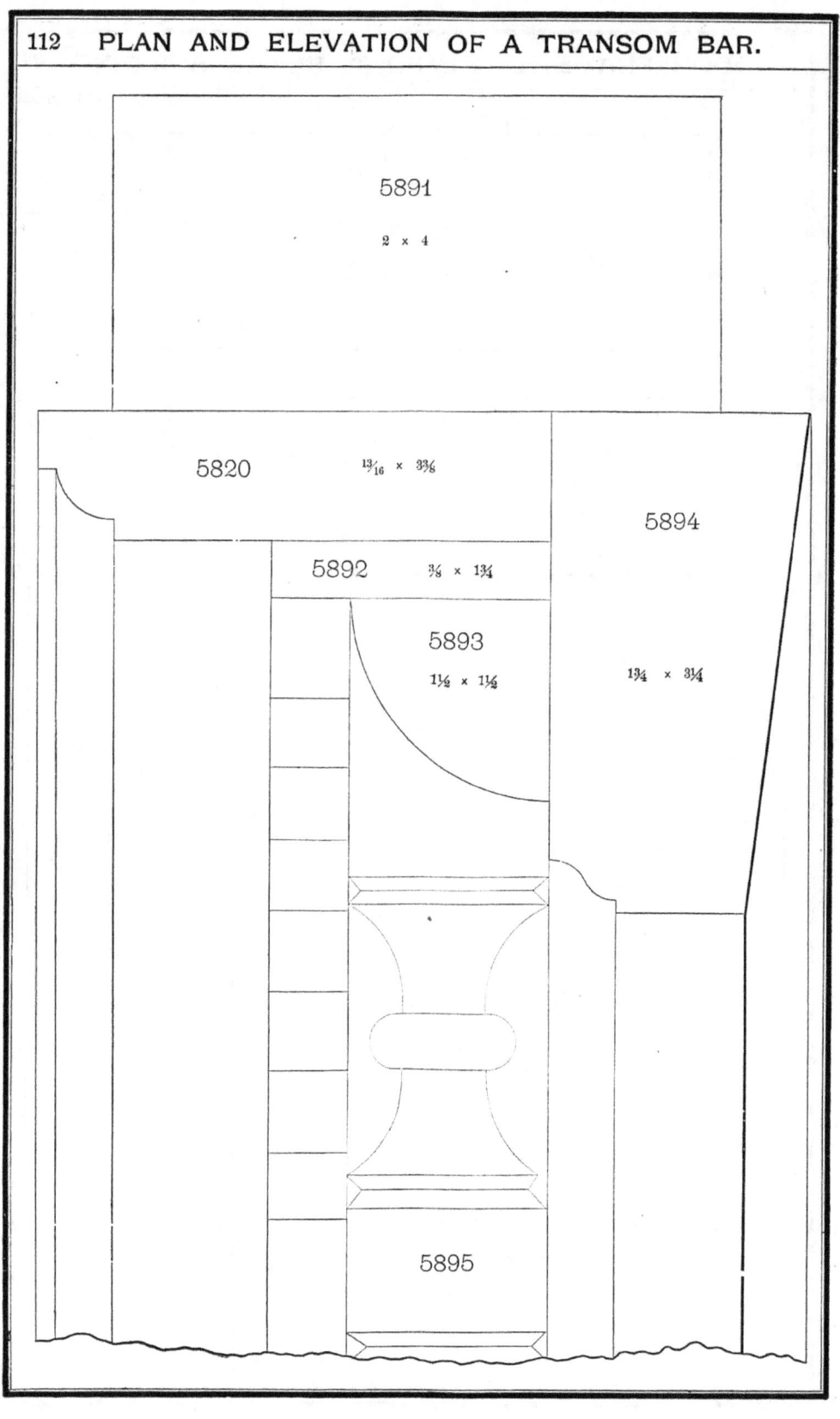

# PITTSBURG FRAME. 113

Inside Bead

Sash

5896

Parting Bead

$13/16 \times 5\frac{1}{4}$

Sash

Sub Sill

5831

$1\frac{3}{8} \times 6\frac{1}{2}$

Outside Bead

Sill

Jamb

Outside Casing

Let Sill extend
past Casing about
Two Inches.

## PITTSBURG FRAME.

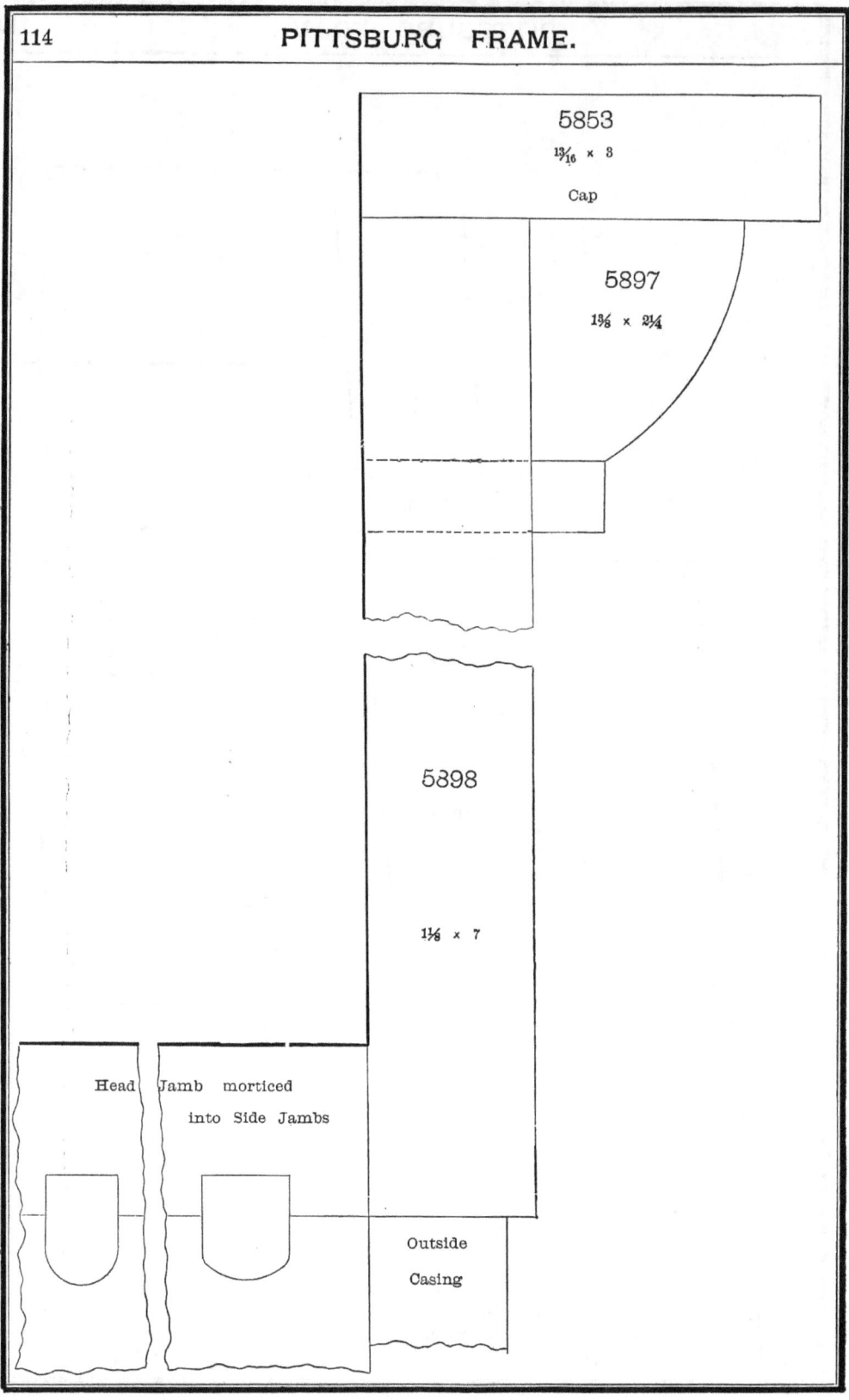

# FRAMES. (Washington) 115

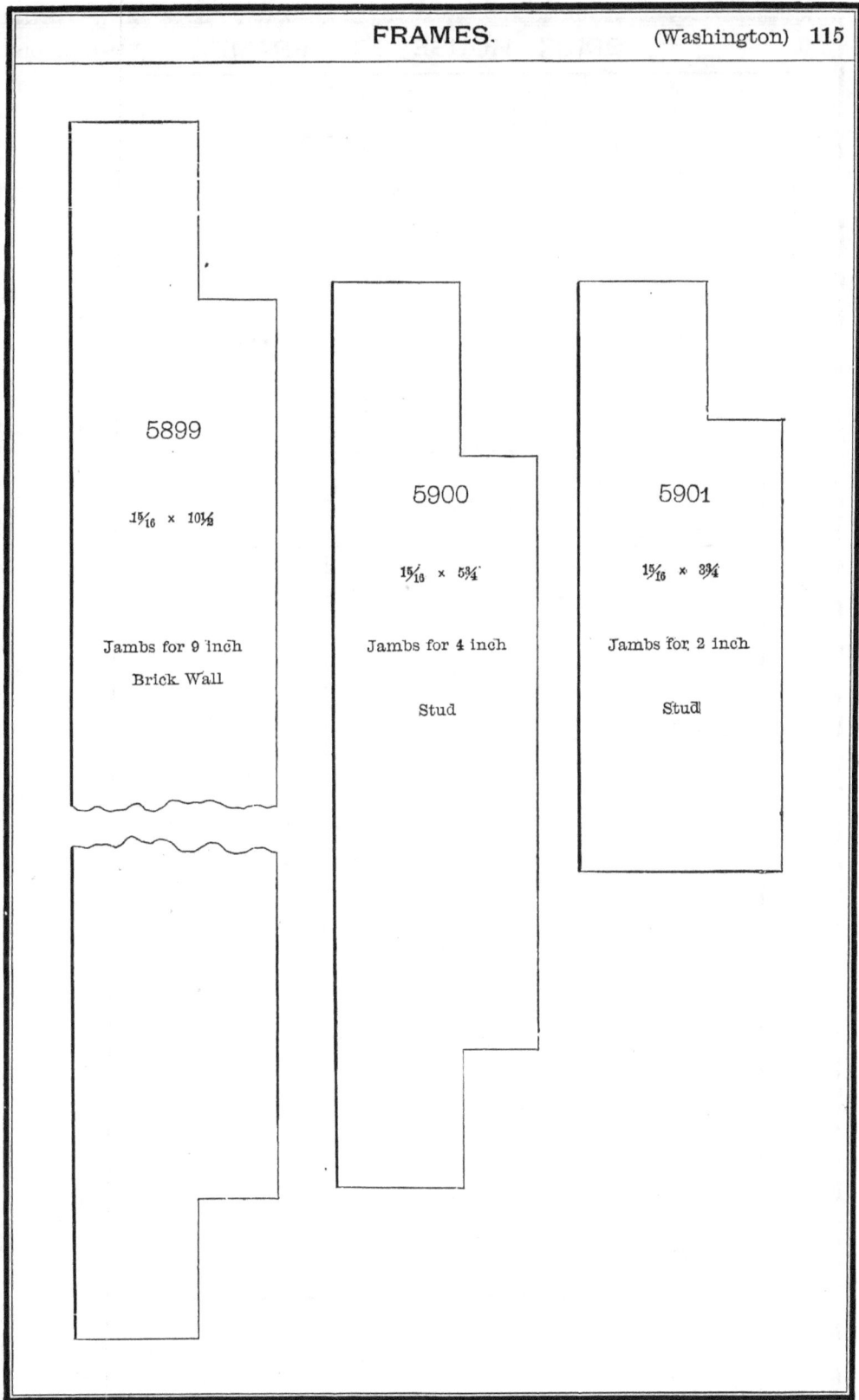

# BRICK HOUSE BOX FRAME. (Washington)

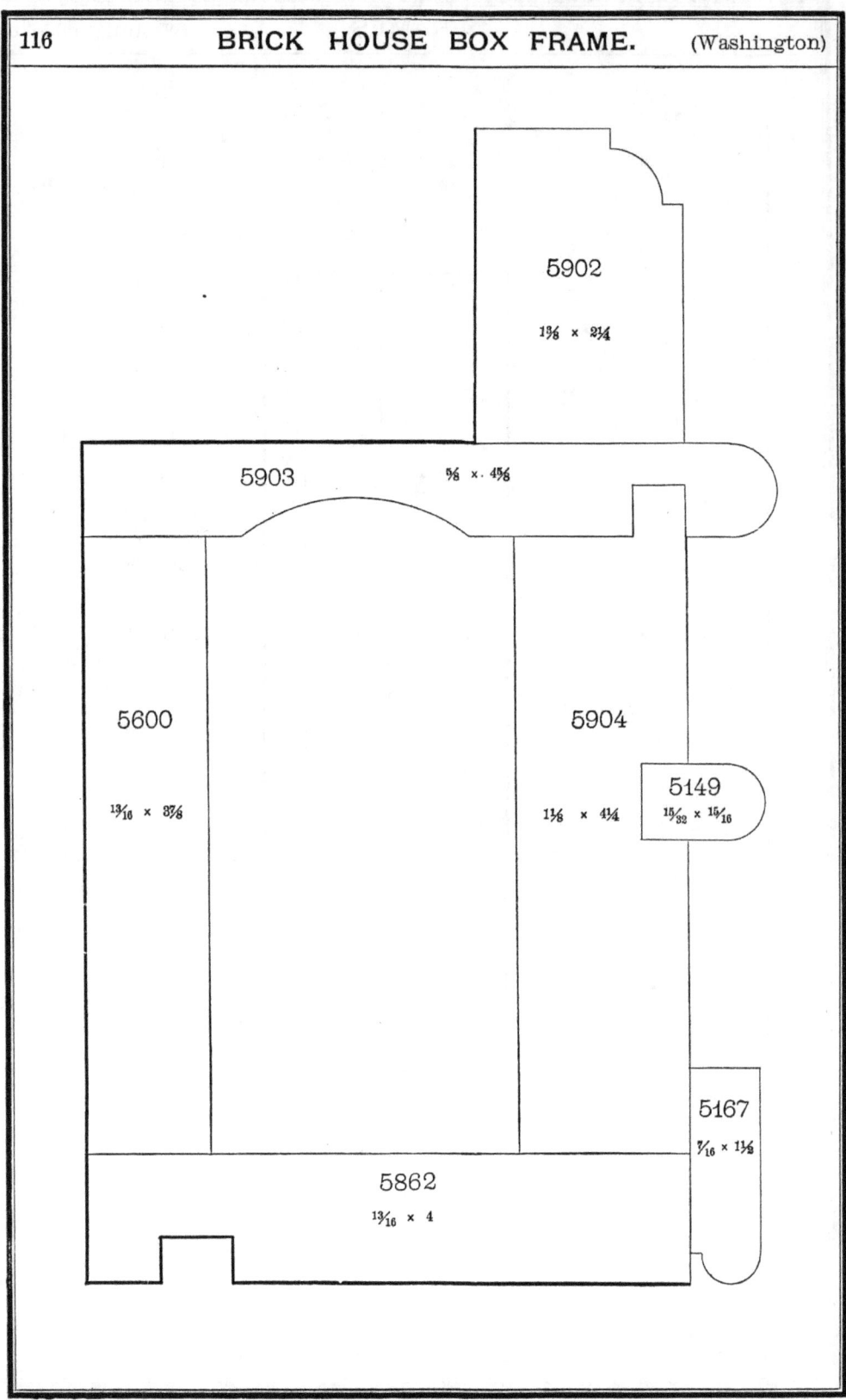

# BRICK HOUSE BOX FRAME. (Washington) 117

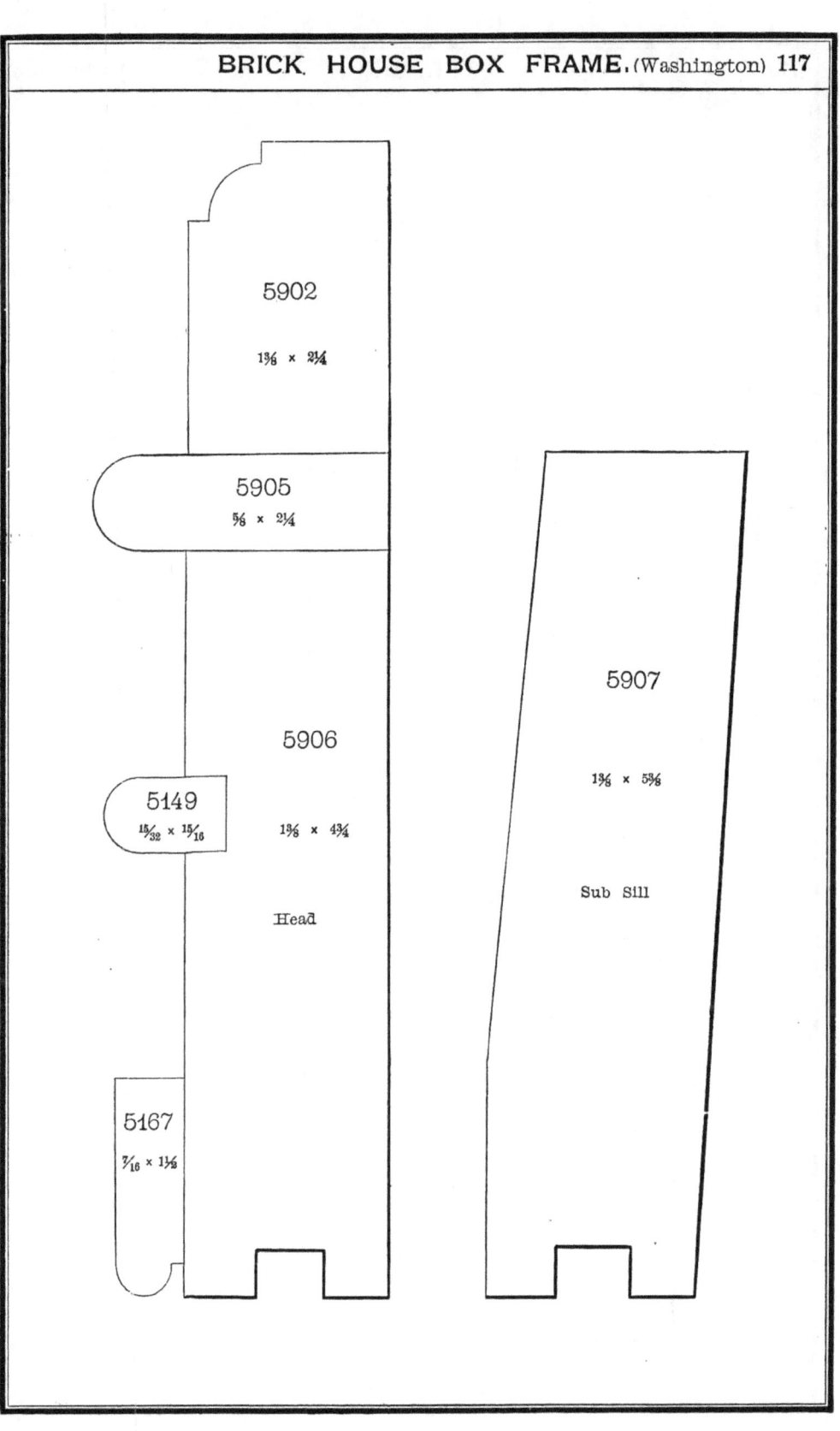

## FRAMES. (Washington)

| 5908 | 5909 | 5910 |
|---|---|---|
| 1⅜ × 5¾ | 1⅜ × 6¼ | 1⅜ × 7½ |
| Frame House Door Frame | Frame House Door Frame | Brick House Door Frame |

# FRAMES. (Washington) 119

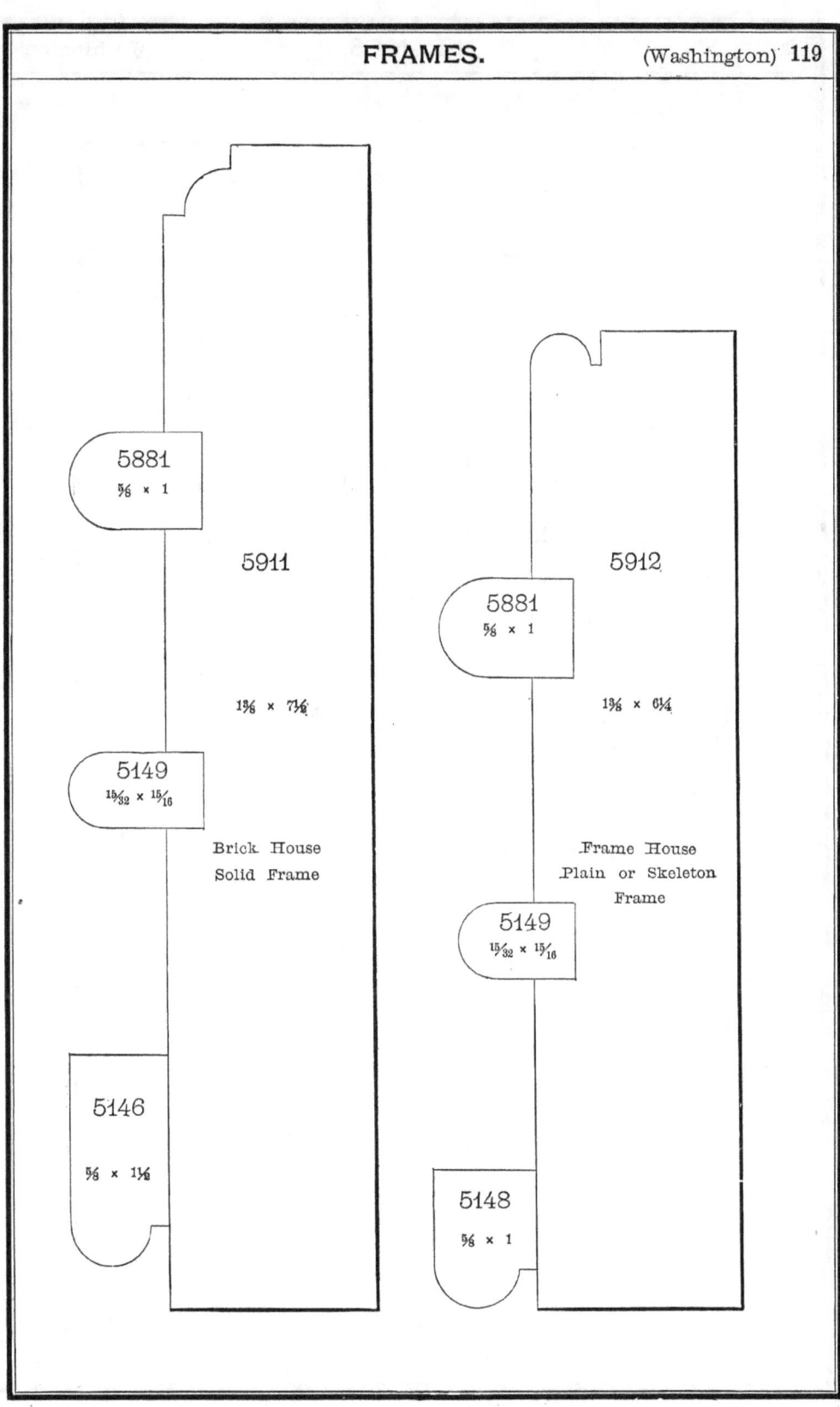

120        **FRAMES.**        (Washington)

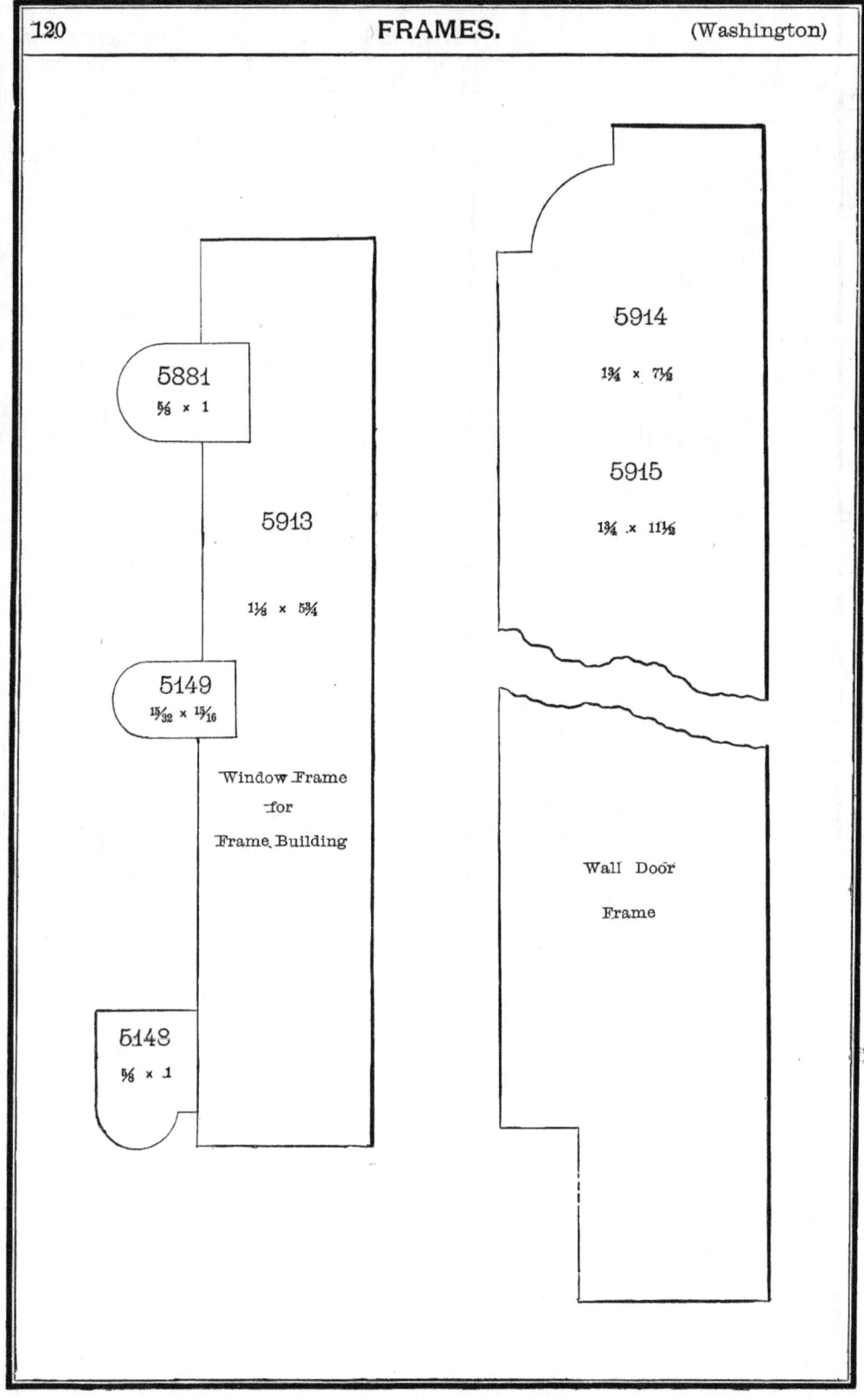

# ELECTRICAL MOULDINGS.

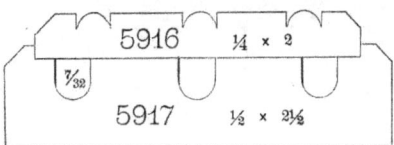
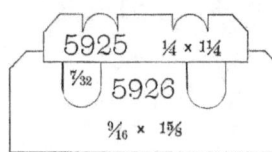
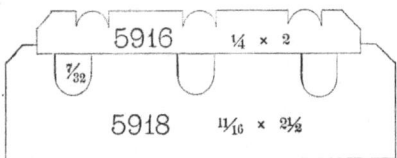
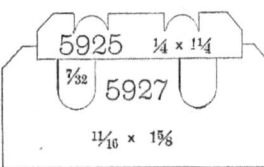
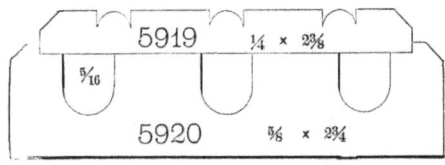
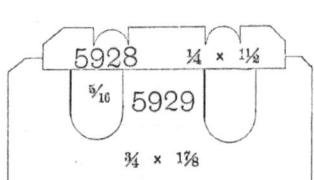
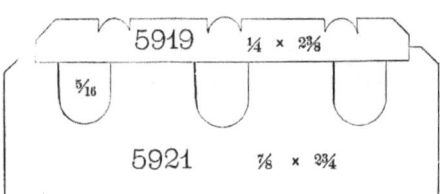
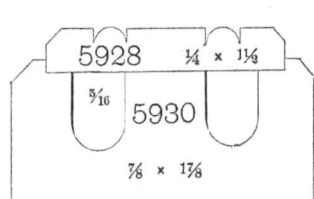
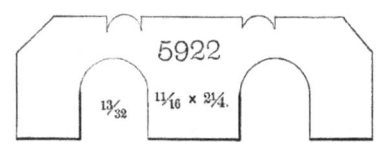
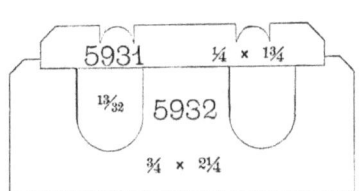
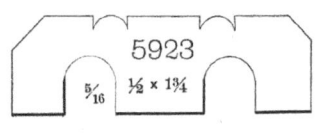
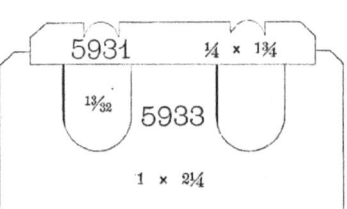
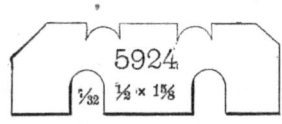

## ELECTRICAL MOULDINGS.

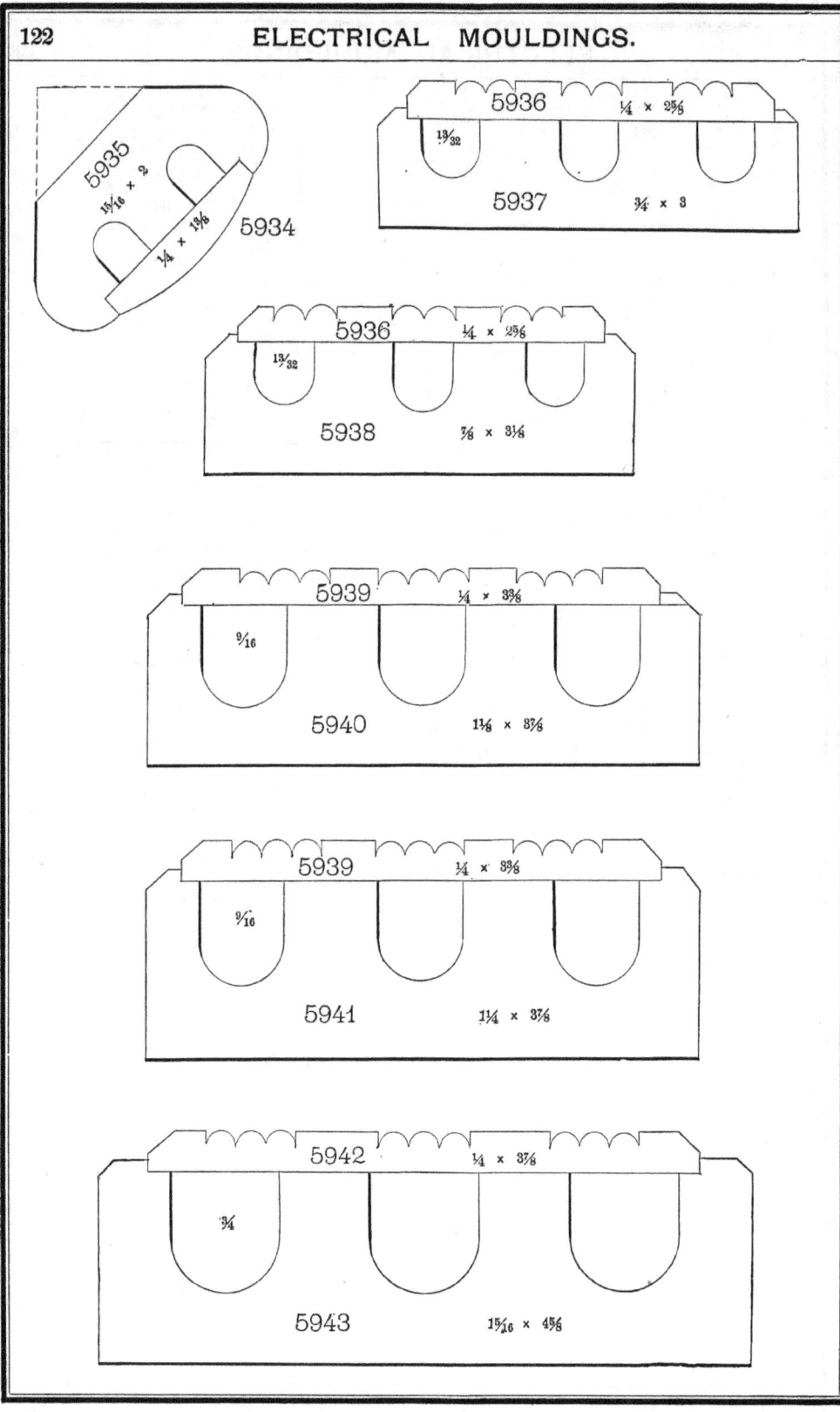

# ELECTRICAL MOULDINGS.

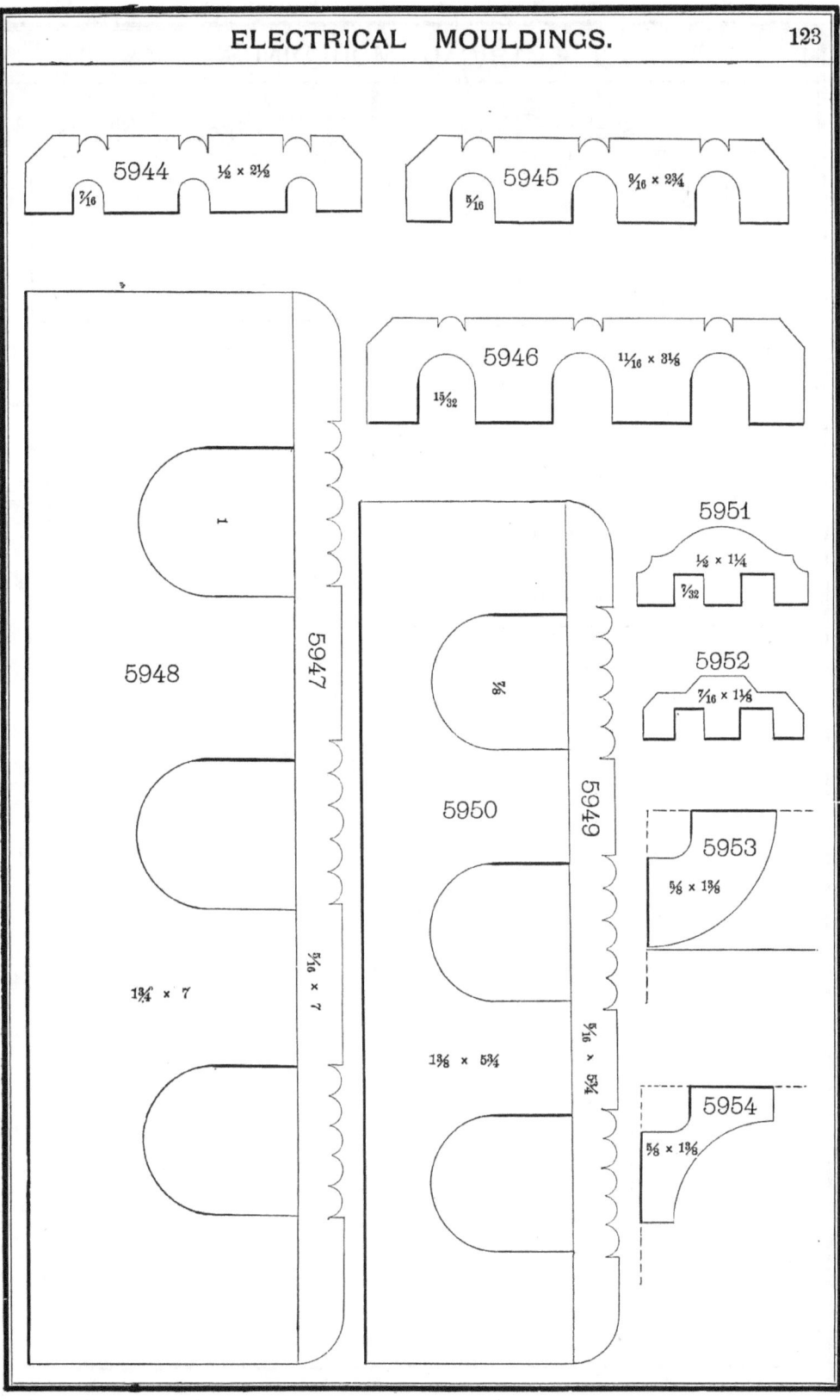

## ELECTRICAL MOULDINGS.

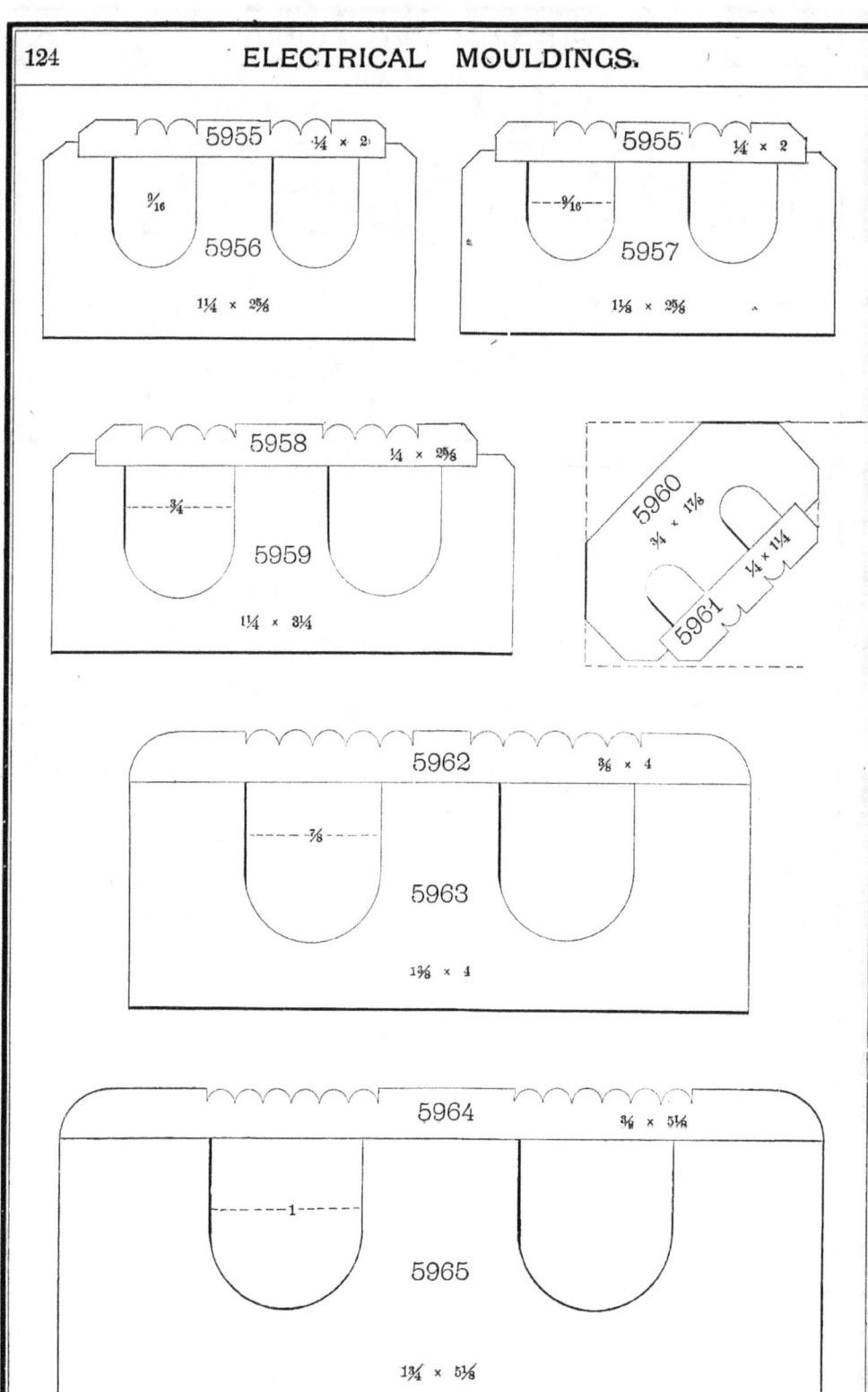

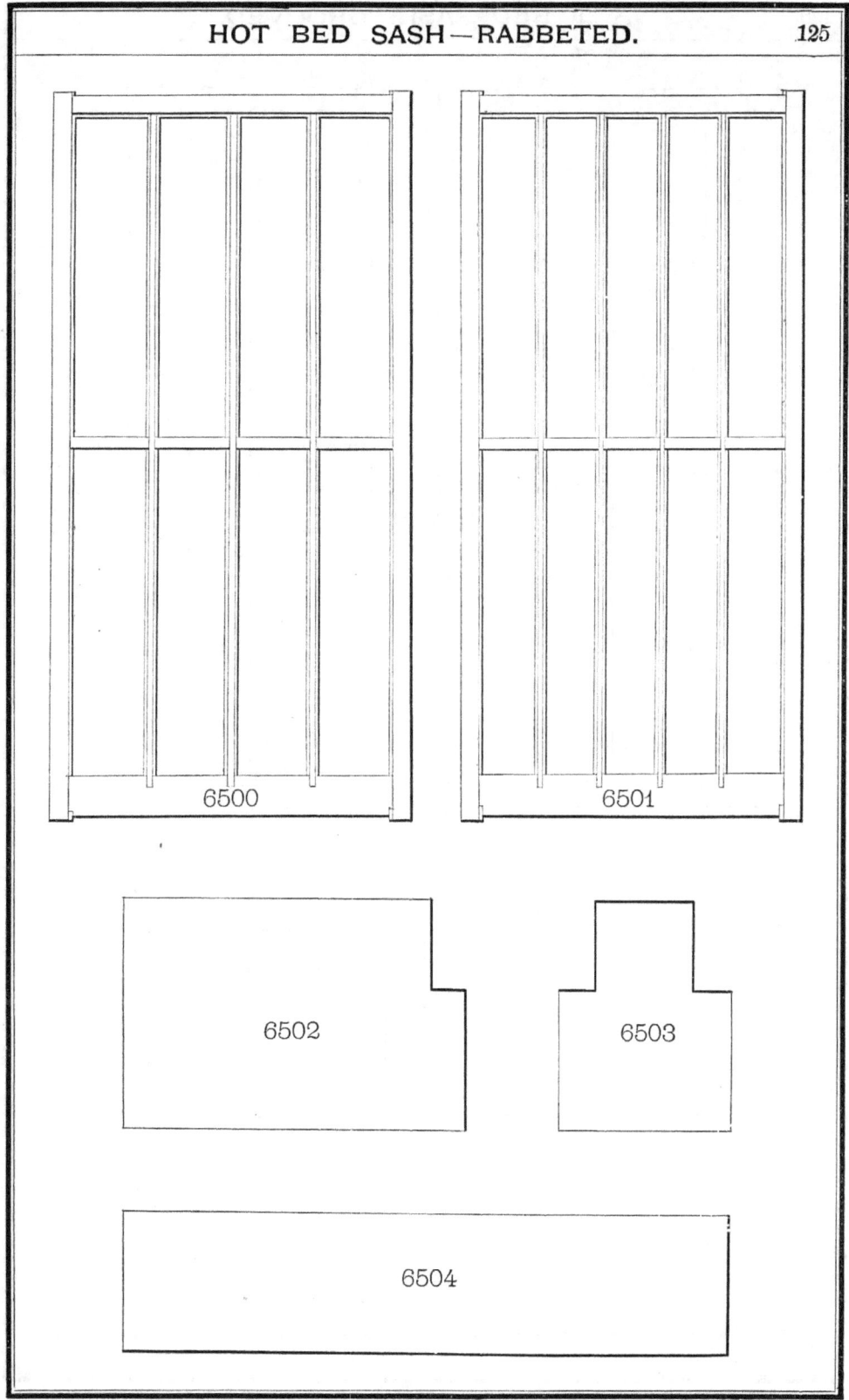

## HOT BED SASH—GROOVED.

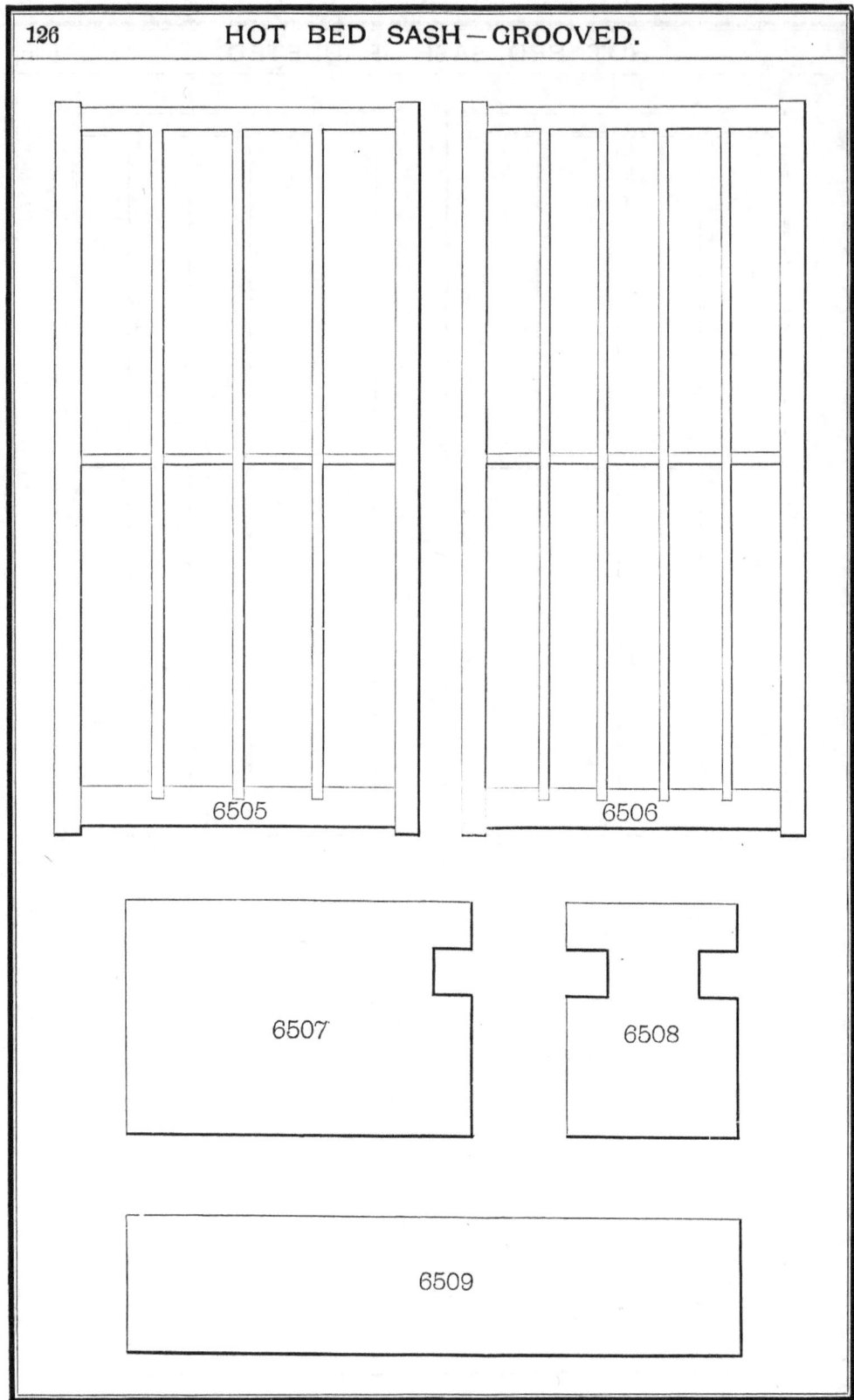

# HOT HOUSE FIXTURES. 127

## HOT HOUSE FIXTURES.

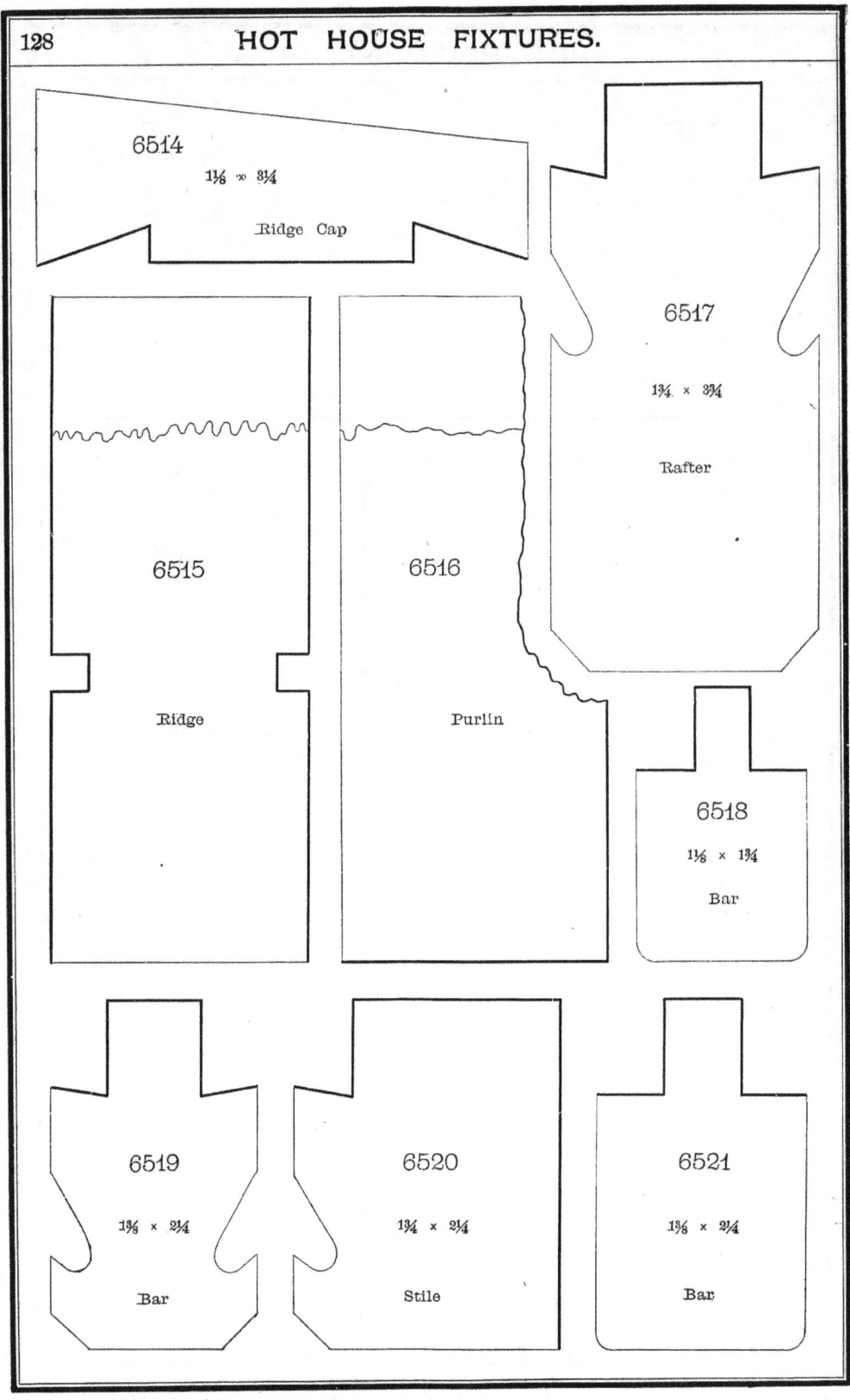

# STAIR RAILS.

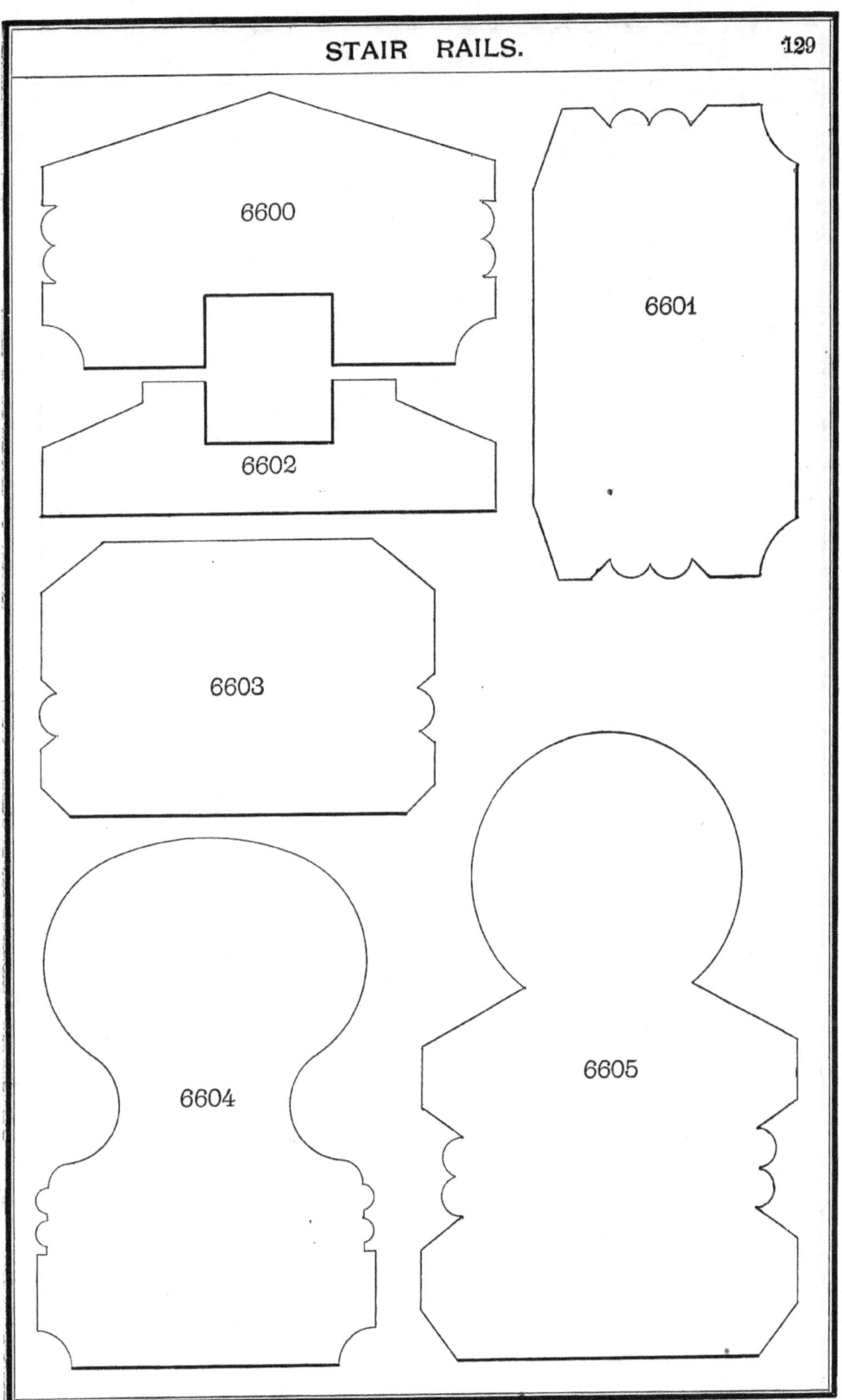

## STAIR RAILS.

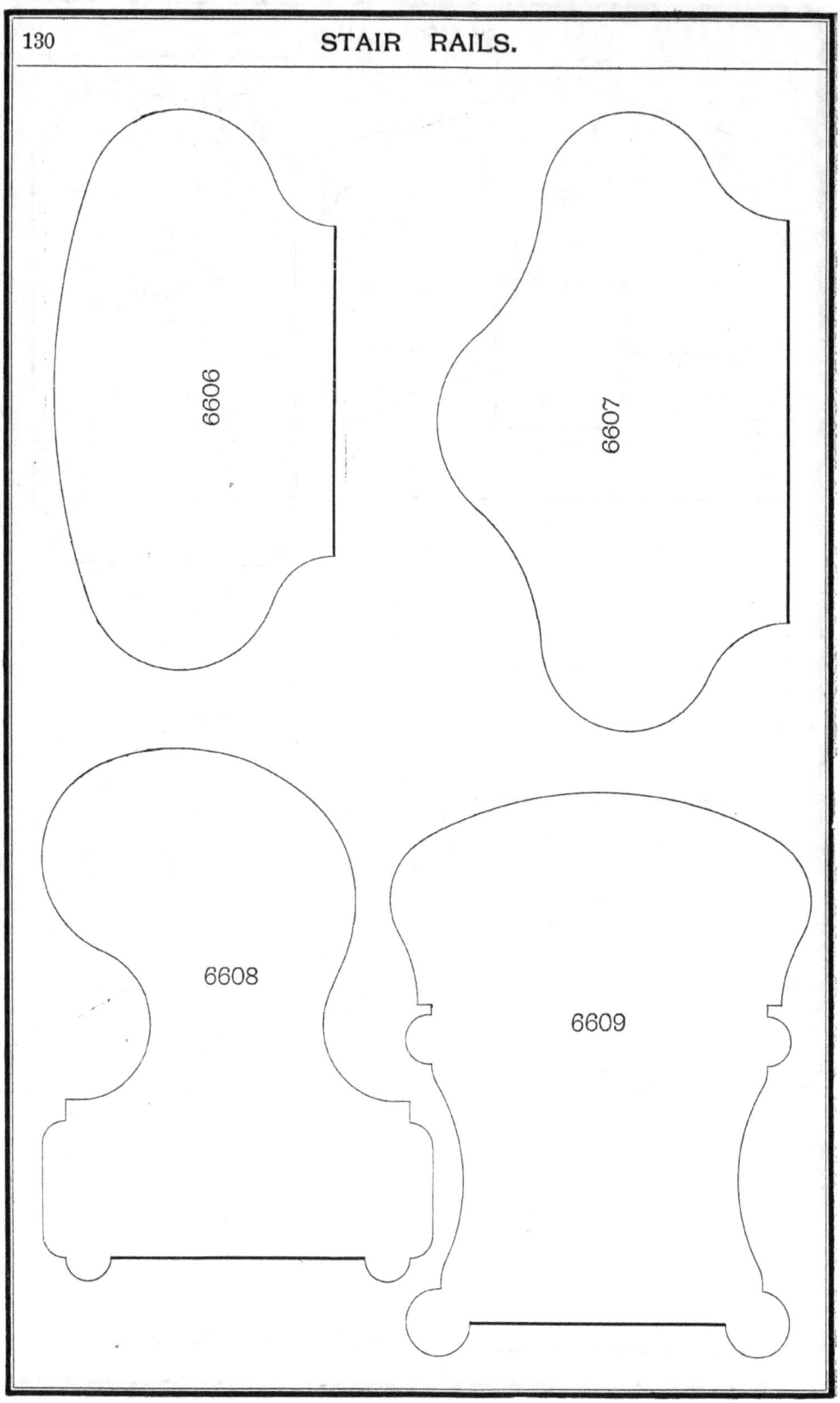

## STAIR RAILS.

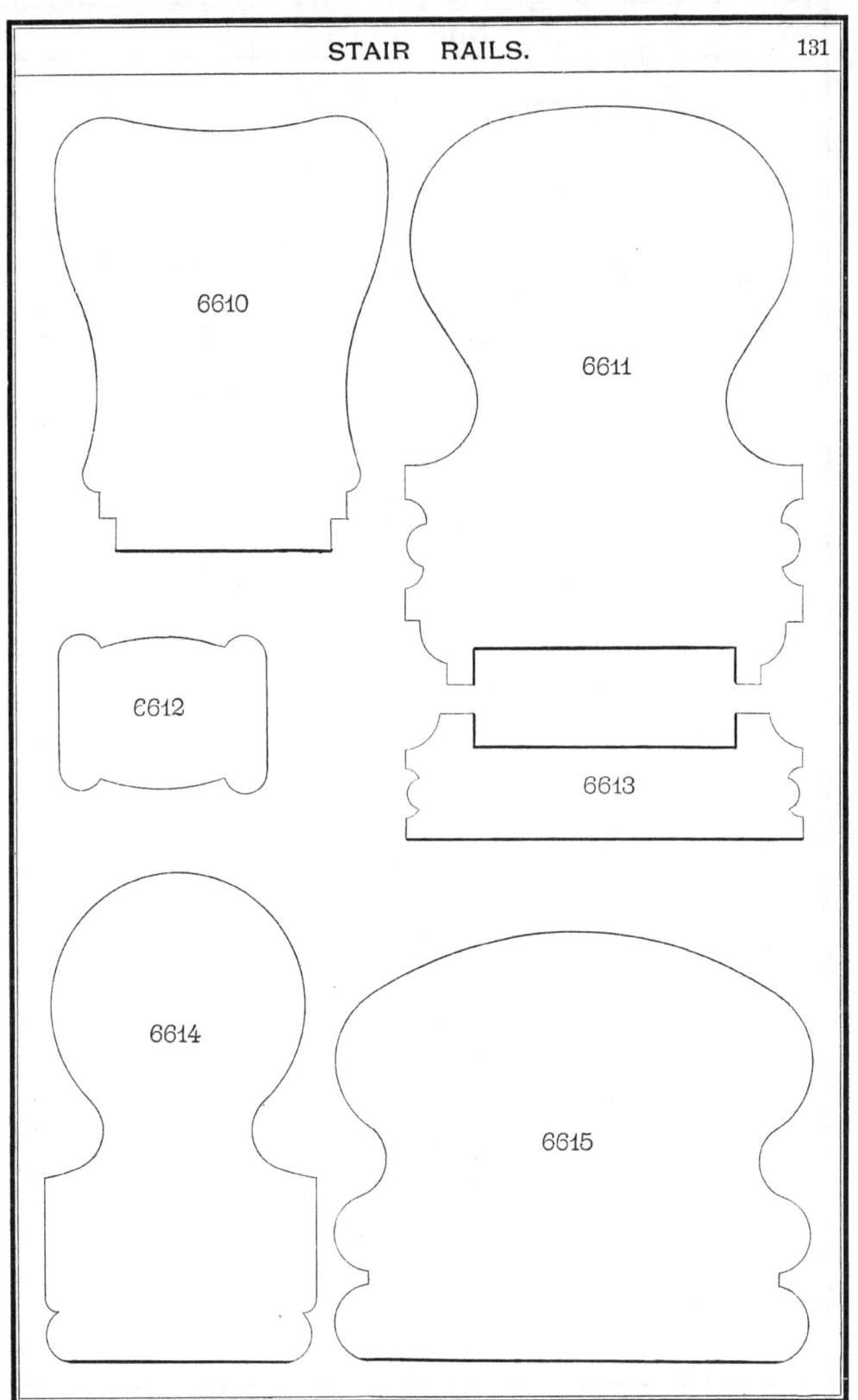

## STAIR RAILS.

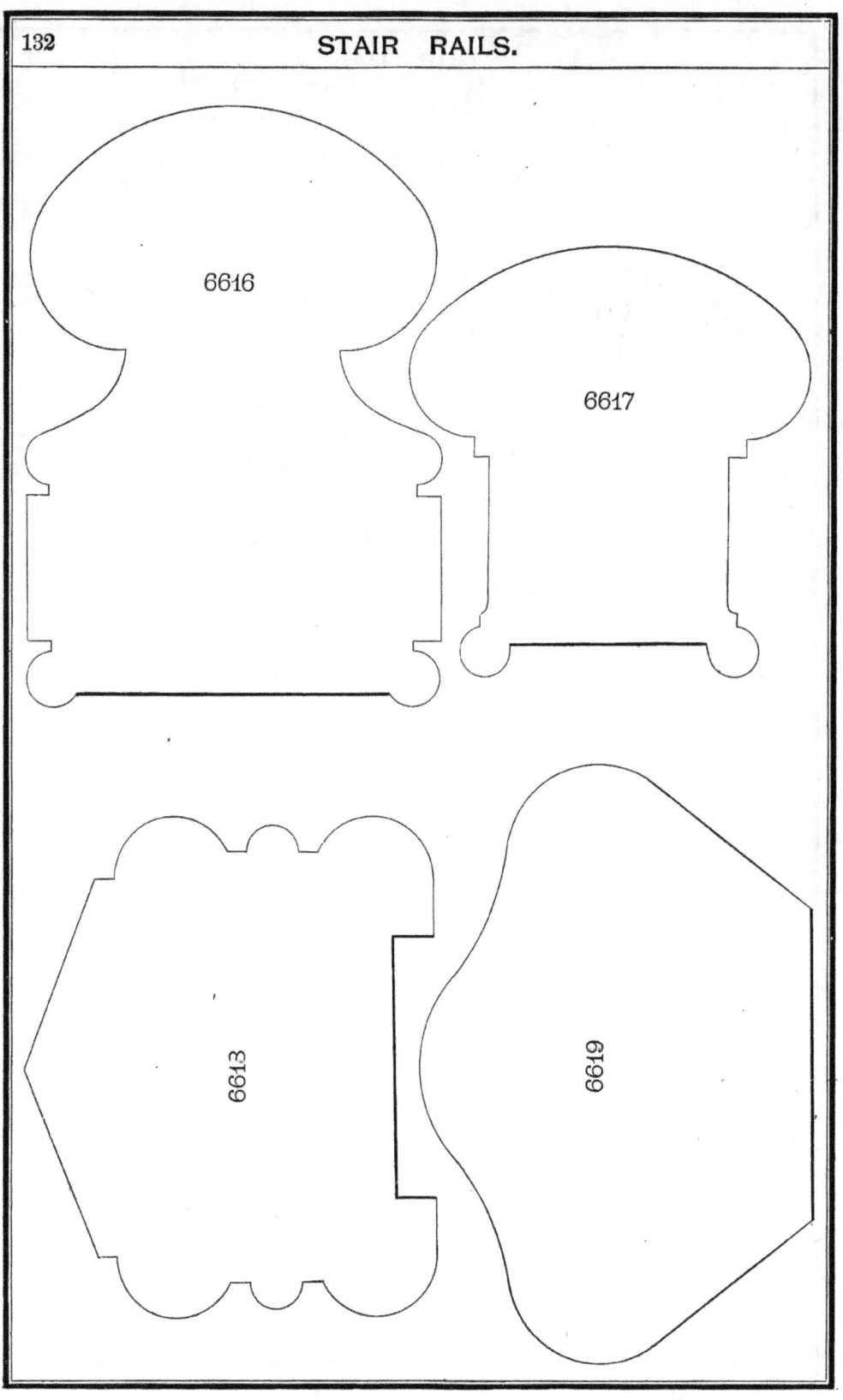

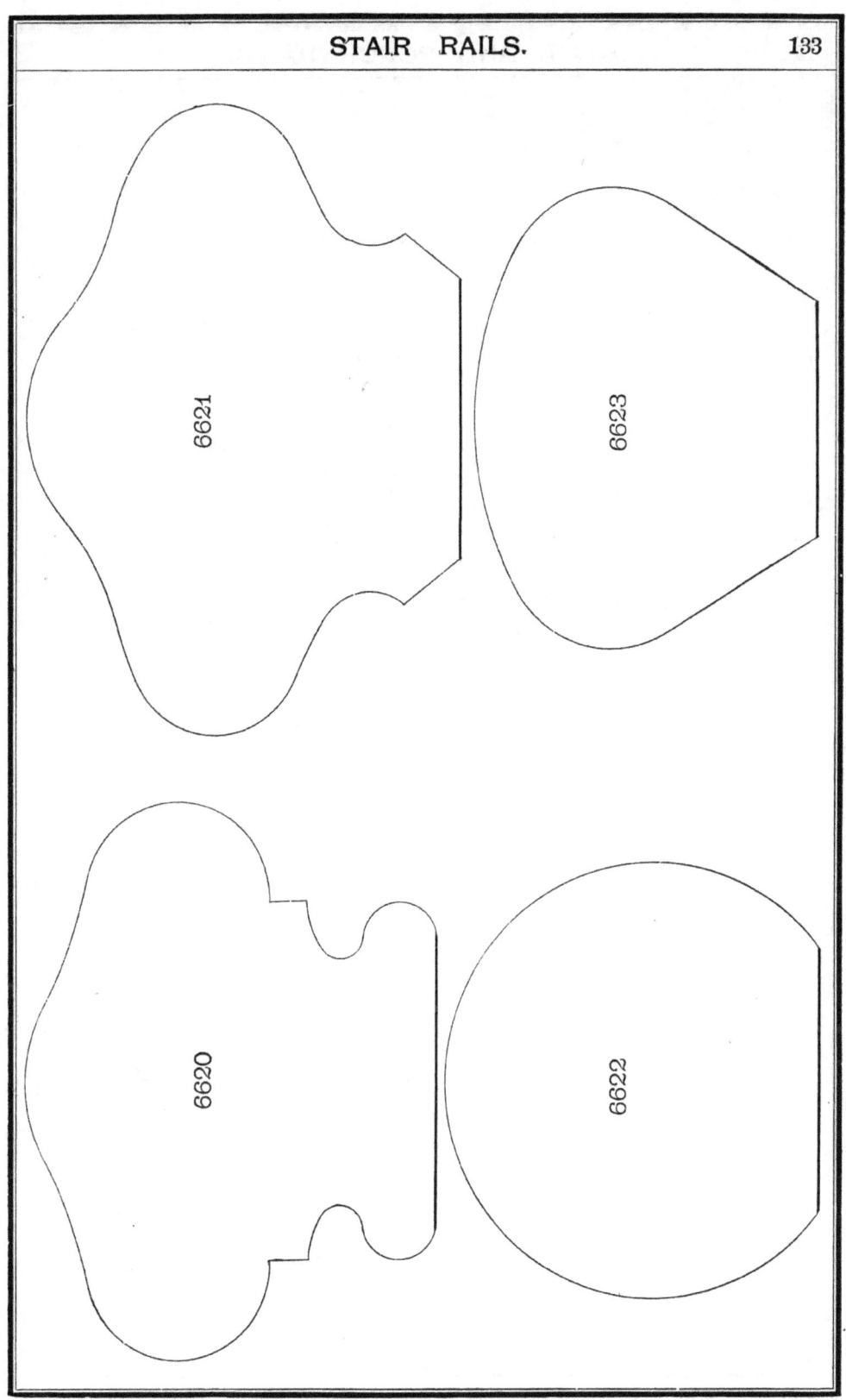

## STAIR AND PORCH RAILS.

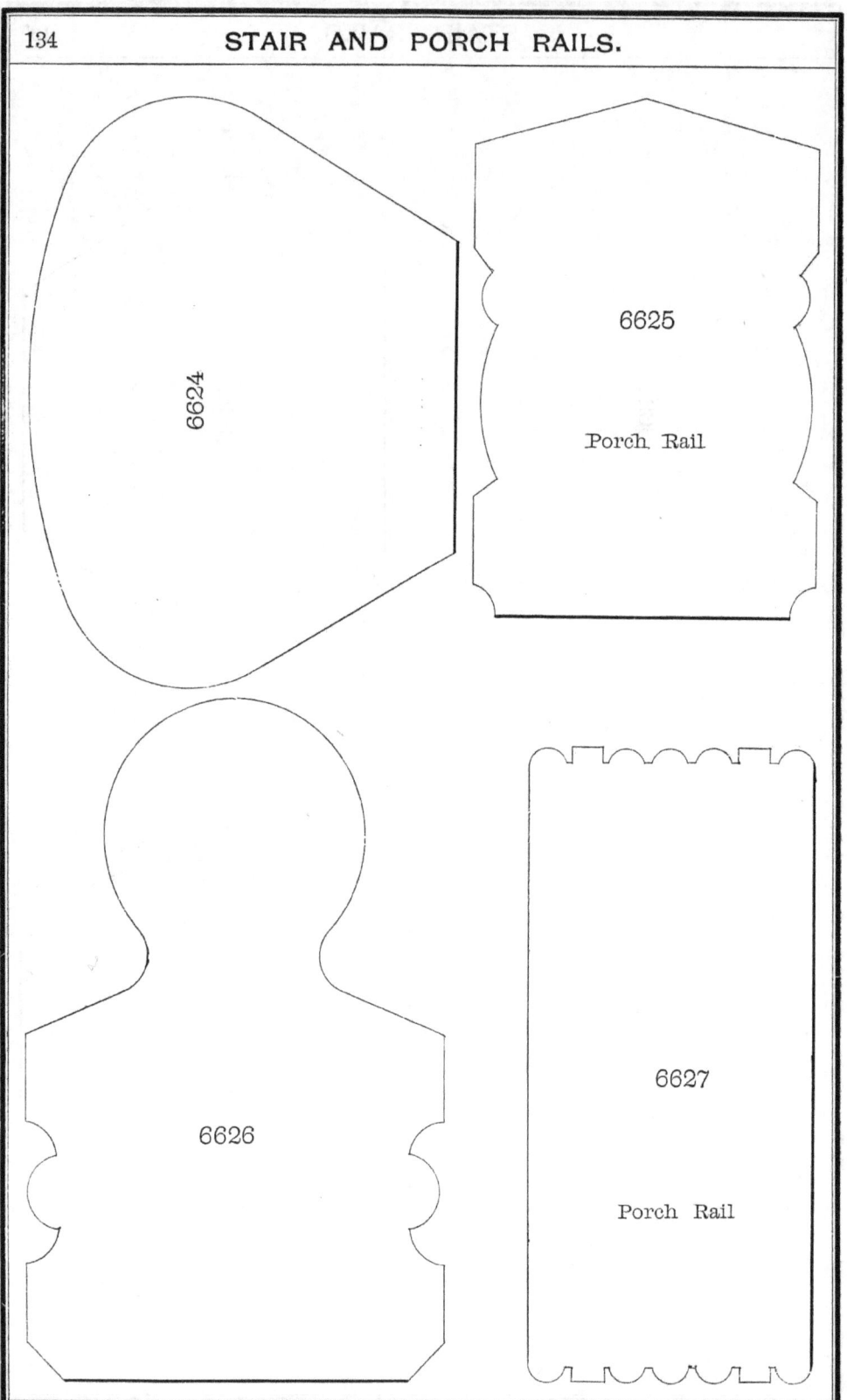

6624

6625
Porch Rail

6626

6627
Porch Rail

## PORCH RAILS AND BALUSTERS.

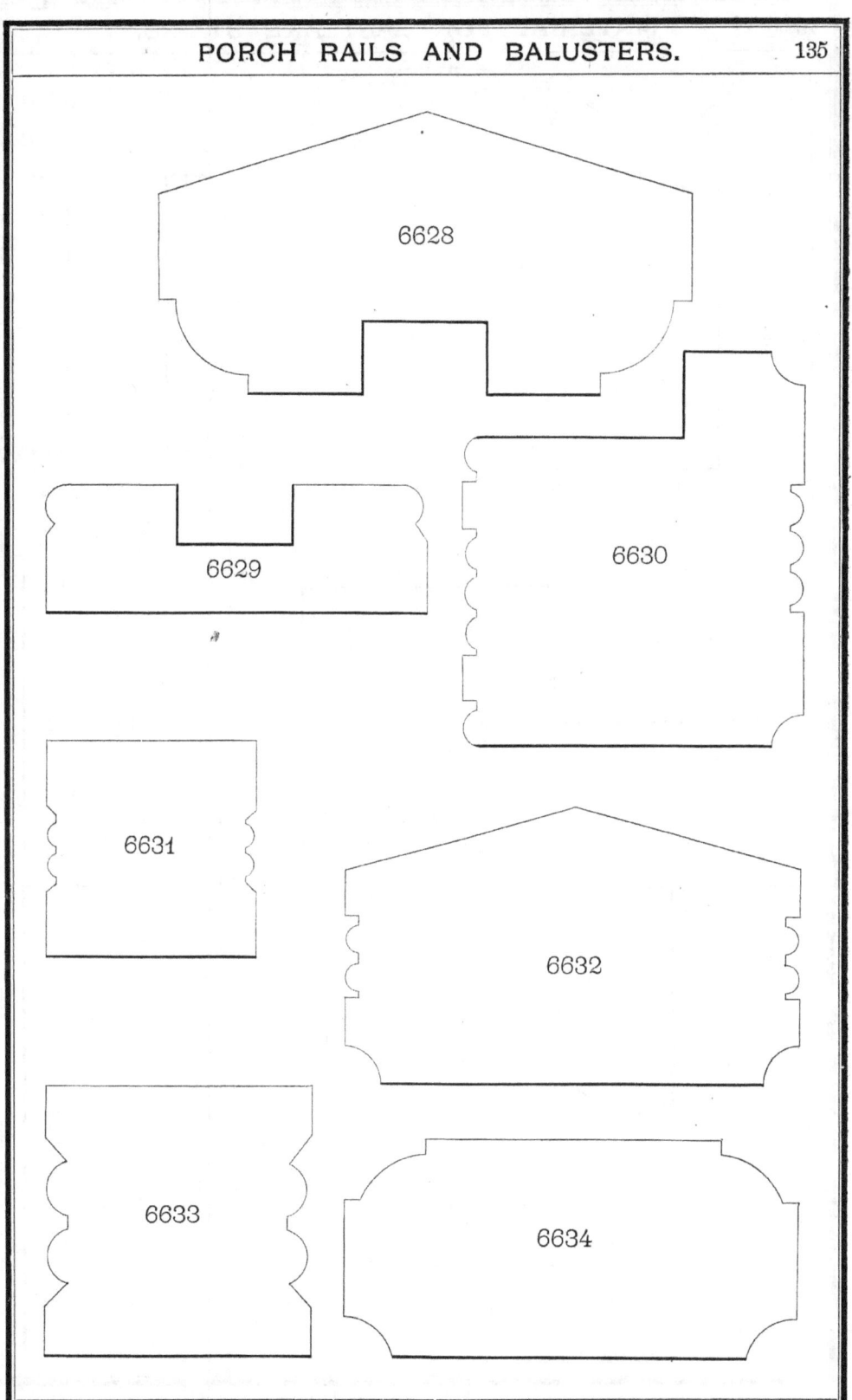

## MATERIAL FOR EASTLAKE STAIRS.

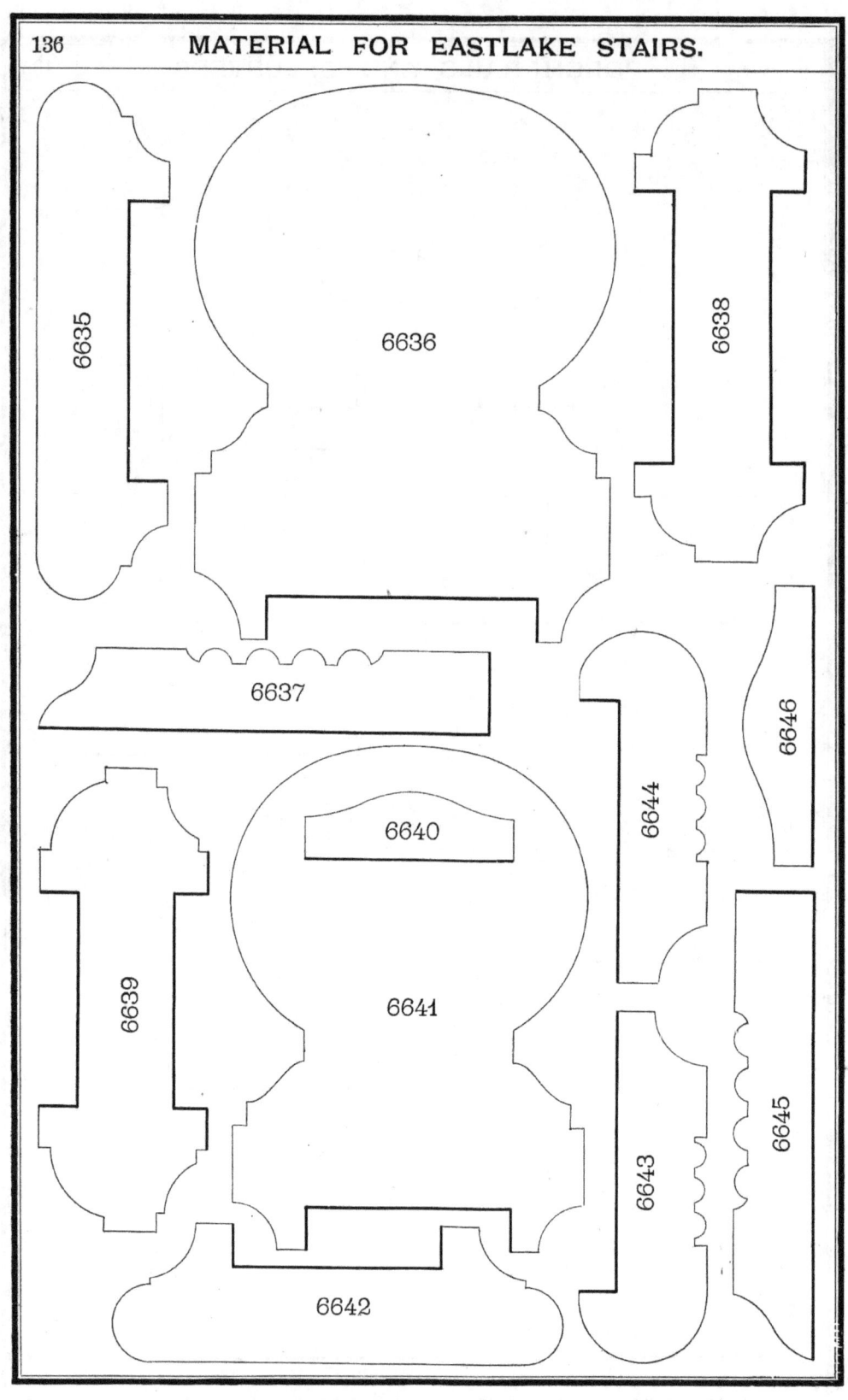

# PRICE OF MOULDINGS.

ADOPTED APRIL 15, 1896, BY

**The Wholesale Sash, Door & Blind Manufacturers' Association of the Northwest,
And by the Eastern Sash, Door & Blind Manufacturers' Association.**

| No. | Price. | No. | Price. | No. | Price. | No. | Price. | No. | Price. | No. | Price. |
|---|---|---|---|---|---|---|---|---|---|---|---|
| 5000 | $3.50 | 5064 | $1.00 | 5128 | $1.60 | 5192 | $1.15 | 5256 | $1.75 | 5320 | $2.00 |
| 5001 | 6.00 | 5065 | 3.00 | 5129 | 1.80 | 5193 | 1.40 | 5257 | 2.25 | 5321 | 2.50 |
| 5002 | 7.00 | 5066 | 3.50 | 5130 | 2.05 | 5194 | 1.00 | 5258 | 1.75 | 5322 | 2.50 |
| 5003 | 3.00 | 5067 | 2.50 | 5131 | 2.25 | 5195 | 2.25 | 5259 | 2.75 | 5323 | 2.65 |
| 5004 | 5.50 | 5068 | 1.00 | 5132 | 1.35 | 5196 | 1.75 | 5260 | 2.25 | 5324 | 2.65 |
| 5005 | 5.00 | 5069 | 2.00 | 5133 | 1.80 | 5197 | 4.15 | 5261 | 1.50 | 5325 | 2.50 |
| 5006 | 4.50 | 5070 | 2.65 | 5134 | 2.25 | 5198 | 2.25 | 5262 | 1.40 | 5326 | 3.60 |
| 5007 | 2.00 | 5071 | 1.50 | 5135 | 1.60 | 5199 | 2.25 | 5263 | 2.00 | 5327 | 3.30 |
| 5008 | 2.50 | 5072 | 1.25 | 5136 | 1.35 | 5200 | ---- | 5264 | 1.75 | 5328 | 4.00 |
| 5009 | 4.00 | 5073 | 1.00 | 5137 | 1.00 | 5201 | ---- | 5265 | 2.75 | 5329 | 4.00 |
| 5010 | 2.50 | 5074 | 2.25 | 5138 | 1.60 | 5202 | ---- | 5266 | 2.25 | 5330 | 4.50 |
| 5011 | 4.50 | 5075 | 5.00 | 5139 | 1.25 | 5203 | ---- | 5267 | 2.50 | 5331 | 4.25 |
| 5012 | 3.00 | 5076 | 1.00 | 5140 | 1.00 | 5204 | ---- | 5268 | 3.00 | 5332 | 3.75 |
| 5013 | 8.25 | 5077 | 3.15 | 5141 | 3.60 | 5205 | ---- | 5269 | 1.75 | 5333 | 1.00 |
| 5014 | 5.00 | 5078 | 5.65 | 5142 | .80 | 5206 | 1.00 | 5270 | 3.50 | 5334 | 1.25 |
| 5015 | 3.50 | 5079 | 6.25 | 5143 | 1.80 | 5207 | 1.15 | 5271 | 2.10 | 5335 | 1.15 |
| 5016 | 12.60 | 5080 | 4.30 | 5144 | 1.00 | 5208 | 1.40 | 5272 | 2.20 | 5336 | 3.50 |
| 5017 | 6.00 | 5081 | 3.00 | 5145 | 1.80 | 5209 | 1.00 | 5273 | 3.00 | 5337 | 2.00 |
| 5018 | 5.00 | 5082 | 2.00 | 5146 | 1.35 | 5210 | 1.75 | 5274 | 2.75 | 5338 | 2.75 |
| 5019 | 4.00 | 5083 | 7.50 | 5147 | 1.25 | 5211 | 5.95 | 5275 | 3.30 | 5339 | 3.00 |
| 5020 | 3.00 | 5084 | 3.60 | 5148 | .90 | 5212 | 1.40 | 5276 | 1.80 | 5340 | 3.15 |
| 5021 | 4.50 | 5085 | 1.25 | 5149 | .80 | 5213 | 1.75 | 5277 | 3.00 | 5341 | 3.00 |
| 5022 | 5.00 | 5086 | 1.15 | 5150 | 2.70 | 5214 | 3.00 | 5278 | 2.50 | 5342 | ---- |
| 5023 | 6.00 | 5087 | 4.40 | 5151 | 1.25 | 5215 | 6.55 | 5279 | 3.20 | 5343 | 1.00 |
| 5024 | 7.00 | 5088 | 5.00 | 5152 | 2.25 | 5216 | 4.50 | 5280 | 5.40 | 5344 | 1.65 |
| 5025 | 5.50 | 5089 | 1.00 | 5153 | 1.80 | 5217 | 5.95 | 5281 | 2.00 | 5345 | 1.00 |
| 5026 | 4.50 | 5090 | 2.50 | 5154 | .80 | 5218 | 3.00 | 5282 | 2.00 | 5346 | 4.00 |
| 5027 | 4.00 | 5091 | 1.70 | 5155 | 1.80 | 5219 | 1.15 | 5283 | 3.00 | 5347 | 3.50 |
| 5028 | 3.50 | 5092 | 1.00 | 5156 | 1.25 | 5220 | 3.00 | 5284 | 2.50 | 5348 | 3.75 |
| 5029 | 3.50 | 5093 | 2.25 | 5157 | 1.25 | 5221 | 1.00 | 5285 | 2.50 | 5349 | 1.00 |
| 5030 | 4.50 | 5094 | 4.40 | 5158 | 2.25 | 5222 | 3.00 | 5286 | 3.00 | 5350 | 2.25 |
| 5031 | 5.50 | 5095 | 4.40 | 5159 | 1.80 | 5223 | 1.50 | 5287 | 4.75 | 5351 | 1.00 |
| 5032 | 5.00 | 5096 | 1.15 | 5160 | 1.15 | 5224 | 1.25 | 5288 | 5.45 | 5352 | 1.00 |
| 5033 | 6.00 | 5097 | 1.00 | 5161 | 1.35 | 5225 | 1.75 | 5289 | 1.40 | 5353 | 1.00 |
| 5034 | 7.00 | 5098 | 1.00 | 5162 | 1.60 | 5226 | 1.50 | 5290 | 2.50 | 5354 | 4.50 |
| 5035 | 4.00 | 5099 | 1.00 | 5163 | 1.80 | 5227 | 1.50 | 5291 | 1.90 | 5355 | 2.65 |
| 5036 | 5.00 | 5100 | 1.00 | 5164 | 2.05 | 5228 | 1.25 | 5292 | 2.45 | 5356 | 3.60 |
| 5037 | 7.00 | 5101 | 1.00 | 5165 | 2.25 | 5229 | 1.25 | 5293 | 4.55 | 5357 | 4.50 |
| 5038 | 4.50 | 5102 | 1.00 | 5166 | 1.15 | 5230 | 1.65 | 5294 | 2.75 | 5358 | 2.50 |
| 5039 | 4.00 | 5103 | 1.50 | 5167 | 1.35 | 5231 | 2.00 | 5295 | 2.45 | 5359 | 3.75 |
| 5040 | 5.50 | 5104 | 1.25 | 5168 | 1.60 | 5232 | 1.00 | 5296 | 2.20 | 5360 | 4.50 |
| 5041 | 3.50 | 5105 | 2.00 | 5169 | 1.80 | 5233 | 2.15 | 5297 | 3.30 | 5361 | 1.15 |
| 5042 | 6.00 | 5106 | 2.50 | 5170 | 2.05 | 5234 | 2.00 | 5298 | 2.20 | 5362 | 1.00 |
| 5043 | 4.00 | 5107 | 3.00 | 5171 | 2.25 | 5235 | 1.15 | 5299 | 2.90 | 5363 | 1.25 |
| 5044 | 3.65 | 5108 | 1.40 | 5172 | 5.30 | 5236 | 2.00 | 5300 | 2.45 | 5364 | 1.50 |
| 5045 | 2.25 | 5109 | 1.75 | 5173 | 7.90 | 5237 | 2.25 | 5301 | 3.30 | 5365 | 2.00 |
| 5046 | 2.75 | 5110 | 1.15 | 5174 | 4.50 | 5238 | 1.75 | 5302 | 2.75 | 5366 | 1.15 |
| 5047 | 2.50 | 5111 | 1.00 | 5175 | 5.20 | 5239 | 2.75 | 5303 | 2.45 | 5367 | 1.00 |
| 5048 | 4.50 | 5112 | 1.00 | 5176 | 6.55 | 5240 | 2.00 | 5304 | 1.65 | 5368 | 1.25 |
| 5049 | 3.50 | 5113 | 1.00 | 5177 | 1.75 | 5241 | 1.40 | 5305 | 1.90 | 5369 | 1.50 |
| 5050 | 4.00 | 5114 | 2.70 | 5178 | 1.00 | 5242 | 1.75 | 5306 | 3.75 | 5370 | 3.00 |
| 5051 | 3.00 | 5115 | 1.15 | 5179 | 1.25 | 5243 | 2.00 | 5307 | 4.25 | 5371 | 2.00 |
| 5052 | 5.00 | 5116 | 2.25 | 5180 | 7.80 | 5244 | 1.75 | 5308 | 1.25 | 5372 | 3.00 |
| 5053 | 2.00 | 5117 | 1.00 | 5181 | 6.90 | 5245 | 1.40 | 5309 | 3.30 | 5373 | 1.00 |
| 5054 | 4.50 | 5118 | 1.20 | 5182 | 1.50 | 5246 | 2.00 | 5310 | 2.20 | 5374 | 2.50 |
| 5055 | 3.00 | 5119 | 1.40 | 5183 | 1.25 | 5247 | 2.00 | 5311 | 1.90 | 5375 | 1.00 |
| 5056 | 2.50 | 5120 | 1.60 | 5184 | 1.00 | 5248 | 2.25 | 5312 | 2.45 | 5376 | 1.40 |
| 5057 | 4.00 | 5121 | 1.80 | 5185 | 1.15 | 5249 | 1.15 | 5313 | 1.90 | 5377 | 6.00 |
| 5058 | 3.50 | 5122 | 2.00 | 5186 | 1.40 | 5250 | 1.40 | 5314 | 2.20 | 5378 | 1.00 |
| 5059 | 1.00 | 5123 | 1.15 | 5187 | 1.00 | 5251 | 1.75 | 5315 | 2.45 | 5379 | 1.50 |
| 5060 | 2.00 | 5124 | 1.60 | 5188 | 3.75 | 5252 | 2.25 | 5316 | 2.90 | 5380 | 2.00 |
| 5061 | 6.30 | 5125 | 2.05 | 5189 | 2.25 | 5253 | 1.40 | 5317 | 1.55 | 5381 | 2.00 |
| 5062 | 2.50 | 5126 | 1.15 | 5190 | 3.40 | 5254 | 1.65 | 5318 | 2.45 | 5382 | 1.65 |
| 5063 | 2.50 | 5127 | 1.35 | 5191 | 1.00 | 5255 | 2.00 | 5319 | 2.20 | 5383 | 2.65 |

When Mouldings are sold by the inch, they must be figured at the ripping width, that is, ¼ of an inch wider than the finished Moulding.

## PRICE OF MOULDINGS—Continued.

| No. | Price. | No. | Price. | No. | Price. | No. | Price. | No. | Price. | No. | Price. |
|---|---|---|---|---|---|---|---|---|---|---|---|
| 5384 | $ 2.25 | 5453 | $ 8.25 | 5522 | $ 5.00 | 5591 | $ 5.50 | 5660 | $ 4.00 | 5729 | $ 2.50 |
| 5385 | 1.65 | 5454 | 3.50 | 5523 | 5.50 | 5592 | 4.00 | 5661 | 4.50 | 5730 | 4.00 |
| 5386 | 1.65 | 5455 | .... | 5524 | 4.00 | 5593 | 4.50 | 5662 | 5.00 | 5731 | 4.75 |
| 5387 | 2.00 | 5456 | .... | 5525 | 4.50 | 5594 | 5.00 | 5663 | 5.50 | 5732 | 1.00 |
| 5388 | 1.50 | 5457 | .... | 5526 | 5.00 | 5595 | 5.50 | 5664 | 4.00 | 5733 | 2.25 |
| 5389 | .... | 5458 | .... | 5527 | 5.50 | 5596 | 4.00 | 5665 | 4.50 | 5734 | 3.00 |
| 5390 | .... | 5459 | .... | 5528 | 4.00 | 5597 | 4.50 | 5666 | 5.00 | 5735 | 7.00 |
| 5391 | .... | 5460 | .... | 5529 | 4.50 | 5598 | 5.00 | 5667 | 3.50 | 5736 | 7.25 |
| 5392 | 3.25 | 5461 | 3.25 | 5530 | 5.00 | 5599 | 5.50 | 5668 | 5.00 | 5737 | 1.15 |
| 5393 | 6.75 | 5462 | 2.50 | 5531 | 5.50 | 5600 | 4.00 | 5669 | 3.50 | 5738 | 7.50 |
| 5394 | 6.75 | 5463 | 2.50 | 5532 | 4.00 | 5601 | 4.50 | 5670 | 4.50 | 5739 | 2.75 |
| 5395 | 6.00 | 5464 | 2.00 | 5533 | 4.50 | 5602 | 5.00 | 5671 | 4.00 | 5740 | 7.50 |
| 5396 | 6.75 | 5465 | 2.00 | 5534 | 5.00 | 5603 | 5.50 | 5672 | 4.50 | 5741 | 1.00 |
| 5397 | 6.75 | 5466 | 2.00 | 5535 | 5.50 | 5604 | 4.00 | 5673 | 5.00 | 5742 | 3.60 |
| 5398 | 5.25 | 5467 | 2.00 | 5536 | 4.00 | 5605 | 4.50 | 5674 | 2.50 | 5743 | 7.00 |
| 5399 | 6.00 | 5468 | 2.75 | 5537 | 4.50 | 5606 | 5.00 | 5675 | 3.00 | 5744 | 1.00 |
| 5400 | .... | 5469 | 2.50 | 5538 | 5.00 | 5607 | 5.50 | 5676 | 4.00 | 5745 | 7.50 |
| 5401 | 9.75 | 5470 | 2.75 | 5539 | 5.50 | 5608 | 4.00 | 5677 | 4.50 | 5746 | 1.00 |
| 5402 | 11.25 | 5471 | 1.75 | 5540 | 4.00 | 5609 | 4.50 | 5678 | 5.00 | 5747 | 7.50 |
| 5403 | 5.25 | 5472 | 2.00 | 5541 | 4.50 | 5610 | 5.00 | 5679 | 4.00 | 5748 | .... |
| 5404 | 1.00 | 5473 | .... | 5542 | 5.00 | 5611 | 5.50 | 5680 | 2.50 | 5749 | .... |
| 5405 | 3.50 | 5474 | .... | 5543 | 5.50 | 5612 | 4.00 | 5681 | 3.00 | 5750 | .... |
| 5406 | 5.25 | 5475 | 8.00 | 5544 | 4.00 | 5613 | 4.50 | 5682 | 3.00 | 5751 | .... |
| 5407 | .... | 5476 | 2.00 | 5545 | 4.50 | 5614 | 5.00 | 5683 | 3.50 | 5752 | .... |
| 5408 | 2.00 | 5477 | 2.25 | 5546 | 5.00 | 5615 | 5.50 | 5684 | 4.00 | 5753 | .... |
| 5409 | 3.90 | 5478 | 2.25 | 5547 | 5.50 | 5616 | 4.00 | 5685 | 4.50 | 5754 | .... |
| 5410 | .... | 5479 | .... | 5548 | 4.00 | 5617 | 4.50 | 5686 | 5.00 | 5755 | .... |
| 5411 | 4.75 | 5480 | 4.00 | 5549 | 4.50 | 5618 | 5.00 | 5687 | 5.00 | 5756 | .... |
| 5412 | 3.60 | 5481 | 4.50 | 5550 | 5.00 | 5619 | 5.50 | 5688 | 5.50 | 5757 | .... |
| 5413 | .... | 5482 | 5.00 | 5551 | 5.50 | 5620 | 4.00 | 5689 | 6.50 | 5758 | .... |
| 5414 | 5.65 | 5483 | 5.50 | 5552 | 4.00 | 5621 | 4.50 | 5690 | 7.50 | 5759 | .... |
| 5415 | 5.30 | 5484 | 4.00 | 5553 | 4.50 | 5622 | 5.00 | 5691 | 1.25 | 5760 | .... |
| 5416 | 3.60 | 5485 | 4.50 | 5554 | 5.00 | 5623 | 5.50 | 5692 | 4.00 | 5761 | .... |
| 5417 | 3.60 | 5486 | 5.00 | 5555 | 5.50 | 5624 | 4.00 | 5693 | 1.50 | 5762 | .... |
| 5418 | .... | 5487 | 5.50 | 5556 | 4.00 | 5625 | 4.50 | 5694 | 3.60 | 5763 | .... |
| 5419 | .... | 5488 | 4.00 | 5557 | 4.50 | 5626 | 5.00 | 5695 | 4.00 | 5764 | .... |
| 5420 | 4.90 | 5489 | 4.50 | 5558 | 5.00 | 5627 | 5.50 | 5696 | 2.75 | 5765 | .... |
| 5421 | 2.65 | 5490 | 5.00 | 5559 | 5.50 | 5628 | 4.00 | 5697 | 5.50 | 5766 | .... |
| 5422 | 4.15 | 5491 | 5.50 | 5560 | 4.00 | 5629 | 4.50 | 5698 | 2.45 | 5767 | .... |
| 5423 | 3.40 | 5492 | 4.00 | 5561 | 4.50 | 5630 | 5.00 | 5699 | 2.00 | 5768 | .... |
| 5424 | 5.25 | 5493 | 4.50 | 5562 | 5.00 | 5631 | 5.50 | 5700 | 6.50 | 5769 | .... |
| 5425 | 5.65 | 5494 | 5.00 | 5563 | 5.50 | 5632 | 4.00 | 5701 | 3.40 | 5770 | .... |
| 5426 | 4.50 | 5495 | 5.50 | 5564 | 4.00 | 5633 | 4.50 | 5702 | 2.75 | 5771 | .... |
| 5427 | 8.05 | 5496 | 4.00 | 5565 | 4.50 | 5634 | 5.00 | 5703 | 3.00 | 5772 | .... |
| 5428 | 2.50 | 5497 | 4.50 | 5566 | 5.00 | 5635 | 5.50 | 5704 | 3.60 | 5773 | .... |
| 5429 | 3.75 | 5498 | 5.00 | 5567 | 5.50 | 5636 | 4.00 | 5705 | 4.50 | 5774 | .... |
| 5430 | 4.00 | 5499 | 5.50 | 5568 | 4.00 | 5637 | 4.50 | 5706 | 5.00 | 5775 | .... |
| 5431 | 4.00 | 5500 | 4.00 | 5569 | 4.50 | 5638 | 5.00 | 5707 | 2.95 | 5776 | .... |
| 5432 | 4.00 | 5501 | 4.50 | 5570 | 5.00 | 5639 | 5.50 | 5708 | 5.00 | 5777 | .... |
| 5433 | 4.75 | 5502 | 5.00 | 5571 | 5.50 | 5640 | 4.00 | 5709 | 2.25 | 5778 | .... |
| 5434 | 4.05 | 5503 | 5.50 | 5572 | 4.00 | 5641 | 4.50 | 5710 | 5.00 | 5779 | .... |
| 5435 | 3.00 | 5504 | 4.00 | 5573 | 4.50 | 5642 | 5.00 | 5711 | 2.25 | 5780 | .... |
| 5436 | 3.00 | 5505 | 4.50 | 5574 | 5.00 | 5643 | 5.50 | 5712 | 2.25 | 5781 | .... |
| 5437 | 3.60 | 5506 | 5.00 | 5575 | 5.50 | 5644 | 3.00 | 5713 | 5.00 | 5782 | .... |
| 5438 | 3.00 | 5507 | 5.50 | 5576 | 4.00 | 5645 | 3.50 | 5714 | 2.70 | 5783 | .... |
| 5439 | 3.00 | 5508 | 4.00 | 5577 | 4.50 | 5646 | 4.00 | 5715 | 4.00 | 5784 | .... |
| 5440 | 3.60 | 5509 | 4.50 | 5578 | 5.00 | 5647 | 4.50 | 5716 | .... | 5785 | .... |
| 5441 | 3.00 | 5510 | 5.00 | 5579 | 5.50 | 5648 | 4.00 | 5717 | 1.00 | 5786 | 5.25 |
| 5442 | 12.50 | 5511 | 5.50 | 5580 | 4.00 | 5649 | 4.50 | 5718 | 7.65 | 5787 | 7.90 |
| 5443 | 7.50 | 5512 | 4.00 | 5581 | 4.50 | 5650 | 5.00 | 5719 | 2.90 | 5788 | 2.75 |
| 5444 | 2.00 | 5513 | 4.50 | 5582 | 5.00 | 5651 | 5.50 | 5720 | 2.70 | 5789 | 3.40 |
| 5445 | 3.75 | 5514 | 5.00 | 5583 | 5.50 | 5652 | 4.00 | 5721 | 4.50 | 5790 | 1.25 |
| 5446 | 2.00 | 5515 | 5.50 | 5584 | 4.00 | 5653 | 4.50 | 5722 | 2.15 | 5791 | 7.30 |
| 5447 | 6.25 | 5516 | 4.00 | 5585 | 4.50 | 5654 | 5.00 | 5723 | 2.95 | 5792 | 1.15 |
| 5448 | 7.85 | 5517 | 4.50 | 5586 | 5.00 | 5655 | 5.50 | 5724 | 2.25 | 5793 | 2.75 |
| 5449 | 2.00 | 5518 | 5.00 | 5587 | 5.50 | 5656 | 4.00 | 5725 | 2.70 | 5794 | .... |
| 5450 | 8.65 | 5519 | 5.50 | 5588 | 4.00 | 5657 | 4.50 | 5726 | 7.00 | 5795 | 10.15 |
| 5451 | 3.00 | 5520 | 4.00 | 5589 | 4.50 | 5658 | 5.00 | 5727 | 2.25 | 5796 | 3.25 |
| 5452 | 3.75 | 5521 | 4.50 | 5590 | 5.00 | 5659 | 5.50 | 5728 | 5.00 | 5797 | 3.40 |

When Mouldings are sold by the inch, they must be figured at the ripping width, that is, ¼ of an inch wider than the finished Moulding.

## PRICE OF MOULDINGS—Continued.

| No. | Price. | No. | Price. | No. | Price. | No. | Price. | No. | Price. | No. | Price. |
|---|---|---|---|---|---|---|---|---|---|---|---|
| 5798 | $11.80 | 5827 | ---- | 5856 | $3.40 | 5884 | ---- | 5912 | ---- | 5940 | $5.80 |
| 5799 | ---- | 5828 | ---- | 5857 | ---- | 5885 | ---- | 5913 | ---- | 5941 | 7.00 |
| 5800 | ---- | 5829 | $1.00 | 5858 | ---- | 5886 | ---- | 5914 | ---- | 5942 | 2.35 |
| 5801 | ---- | 5830 | ---- | 5859 | ---- | 5887 | ---- | 5915 | ---- | 5943 | 8.35 |
| 5802 | 3.00 | 5831 | ---- | 5860 | 2.75 | 5888 | ---- | 5916 | $1.20 | 5944 | 2.50 |
| 5803 | ---- | 5832 | ---- | 5861 | ---- | 5889 | ---- | 5917 | 2.50 | 5945 | 2.75 |
| 5804 | ---- | 5833 | ---- | 5862 | ---- | 5890 | ---- | 5918 | 2.50 | 5946 | 3.15 |
| 5805 | ---- | 5834 | ---- | 5863 | ---- | 5891 | ---- | 5919 | 1.45 | 5947 | 4.20 |
| 5806 | ---- | 5835 | ---- | 5864 | ---- | 5892 | $1.75 | 5920 | 2.75 | 5948 | 17.50 |
| 5807 | ---- | 5836 | ---- | 5865 | ---- | 5893 | 2.70 | 5921 | 2.75 | 5949 | 3.45 |
| 5808 | ---- | 5837 | ---- | 5866 | ---- | 5894 | ---- | 5922 | 2.25 | 5950 | 10.35 |
| 5809 | ---- | 5838 | ---- | 5867 | 3.00 | 5895 | ---- | 5923 | 1.75 | 5951 | 1.25 |
| 5810 | ---- | 5839 | ---- | 5868 | ---- | 5896 | ---- | 5924 | 1.65 | 5952 | 1.15 |
| 5811 | 1.65 | 5840 | ---- | 5869 | ---- | 5897 | 4.05 | 5925 | .75 | 5953 | 1.40 |
| 5812 | ---- | 5841 | ---- | 5870 | ---- | 5898 | ---- | 5926 | 1.65 | 5954 | 1.40 |
| 5813 | 2.00 | 5842 | ---- | 5871 | ---- | 5899 | ---- | 5927 | 1.65 | 5955 | 1.20 |
| 5814 | ---- | 5843 | ---- | 5872 | ---- | 5900 | ---- | 5928 | .90 | 5956 | 4.75 |
| 5815 | ---- | 5844 | 2.50 | 5873 | ---- | 5901 | ---- | 5929 | 1.90 | 5957 | 3.95 |
| 5816 | 1.70 | 5845 | ---- | 5874 | ---- | 5902 | 4.05 | 5930 | 1.90 | 5958 | 1.60 |
| 5817 | ---- | 5846 | 1.50 | 5875 | ---- | 5903 | ---- | 5931 | 1.05 | 5959 | 5.85 |
| 5818 | ---- | 5847 | ---- | 5876 | ---- | 5904 | ---- | 5932 | 2.25 | 5960 | 2.00 |
| 5819 | ---- | 5848 | ---- | 5877 | ---- | 5905 | 2.25 | 5933 | 2.25 | 5961 | .75 |
| 5820 | ---- | 5849 | ---- | 5878 | 2.00 | 5906 | ---- | 5934 | .85 | 5962 | 2.40 |
| 5821 | ---- | 5850 | ---- | 5879 | ---- | 5907 | ---- | 5935 | 2.00 | 5963 | 7.20 |
| 5822 | ---- | 5851 | 1.00 | 5880 | ---- | 5908 | ---- | 5936 | 1.60 | 5964 | 3.10 |
| 5823 | ---- | 5852 | ---- | 5881 | 1.00 | 5909 | ---- | 5937 | 3.00 | 5965 | 12.80 |
| 5824 | ---- | 5853 | ---- | 5882 | ---- | 5910 | ---- | 5938 | 3.15 | 5966 | ---- |
| 5825 | ---- | 5854 | 2.25 | 5883 | ---- | 5911 | ---- | 5939 | 2.05 | 5967 | ---- |
| 5826 | 3.40 | 5855 | ---- | | | | | | | | |

When Mouldings are sold by the inch, they must be figured at the ripping width, that is, 1/4 of an inch wider than the finished Moulding.

www.ingramcontent.com/pod-product-compliance
Lightning Source LLC
Chambersburg PA
CBHW060423010526
44118CB00017B/2339